A Man Walks On To a Pitch

A Man Walks On To a Pitch

STORIES FROM A LIFE IN FOOTBALL

HARRY REDKNAPP

EBURY
PRESS

3 5 7 9 10 8 6 4 2

Ebury Press, an imprint of Ebury Publishing
20 Vauxhall Bridge Road
London SW1V 2SA

Ebury Press is part of the Penguin Random House group of companies
whose addresses can be found at global.penguinrandomhouse.com

Penguin
Random House
UK

This edition published in 2015
First published by Ebury Press in 2014

www.eburypublishing.co.uk

A CIP catalogue record for this book is available from the British Library

ISBN 9780091955533

Designed and set by seagulls.net

Printed and bound by CPI Group (UK) Ltd, Croydon, CR0 4YY

For everyone I have ever worked with, played with or enjoyed watching in my life in football

PROLOGUE

I was sitting in the changing-room at Wembley after our play-off final. The wild celebrations were going on all around – champagne, cheering, singing, bouncing, the usual. Queens Park Rangers were going up. We hadn't deserved it, I knew that. Derby County had been the better side, but we had won the game, in the last minute and with 10 men. That's what happens sometimes. My telephone rang. It was Harry Gregg, the old Manchester United legend – one of the Busby Babes. He had been watching the game. He knew the mixed emotions I would have been feeling. 'Harry, I want you to hear a quick story,' he said. And he told me about the time Northern Ireland beat England 3–2 at Wembley in 1957. Harry was in goal that day, against an England team that included his Manchester United team-mates Duncan Edwards, Tommy Taylor and Roger Byrne, plus Billy Wright as captain and Johnny Haynes at inside-forward. Some great players there. After the game, Walter Winterbottom, England's manager, said he thought Northern Ireland had been lucky. This was put to their captain, Danny Blanchflower. 'Ah yes,' he said, with a smile, 'but sometimes it's better to be lucky than good.' And I believe that. I can hear Danny, a clever man, saying it now. Every manager will know what he means. We have all had good days that have not been lucky, and lucky days when we've not been good – and I know what days I prefer. It was a good story to hear just then.

I don't know why I was feeling so ambivalent about the way we'd won against Derby. Maybe, in my head, when Gary O'Neil got sent off I was mentally preparing myself for my last game in football. I would have retired had we lost, I'm pretty sure of that. I don't even know if the owners would have wanted me to stay on; it's quite likely they would have desired a change, too, and I understand that. Yet in my heart I knew I couldn't go another season in the Championship with the limitations to our squad. I knew the calibre of players we could buy would drop considerably and there was enough dead wood around as it was. I had done my best in my first full season there and it hadn't been good enough. It would have been time to let someone else have a go, to see if a fresh eye on the place could bring it back to life. I'm not saying this was going through my mind as I stood on the Wembley touchline – I was completely focused and absorbed by the game – but it was something I had considered in previous weeks. I knew the likely consequence of failure would be that I was managing my last match in professional football.

When we went down to 10 men, I couldn't really see any way out of it, to be honest. I'd be a liar if I said I still thought we could win in open play. My hope was that we would survive and get to penalties. And even that was going to be difficult. We played with two strikers, which, looking back, was a mistake. There wasn't a lot in the game but they had more possession and that comes from having an extra man in midfield. Once O'Neil went off it was just backs to the wall. I thought we might struggle through 90 minutes, but I wasn't confident about the additional 30 minutes' extra time, with everyone exhausted. We weren't a young team and a few looked like they were running on empty already. I had my best striker Charlie Austin playing on the left wing, where he looked as if he didn't have a clue, but my only option was to play two banks of four with Bobby Zamora up on his own. I couldn't have asked Bobby to do Charlie's defensive shift. It was a mess.

And then, suddenly, it was a miracle. With seconds on the clock, the ball dropped to Bobby, and he stuck it right in the corner. It was too late for Derby to do anything about it. They knew they were done.

It was a strange feeling after the game, really. Sandra had come up with our grandchildren, so she had to go home to the South coast, Jamie was away at the Champions League final and I felt too emotionally drained to do much celebrating. I knew they would all be back at Loftus Road getting drunk, but I didn't fancy that at all. I had to stay in London because we had a parade at the ground the following morning, so I planned a quiet night. I showed my face at the party, then sneaked out the back door and went back to the Grosvenor House hotel for a late dinner and the Champions League final. Club sandwich, plate of chips, cup of tea, lovely. And then, watching the football, I got a phone call from Don Shanks, the old Rangers player. He's a good lad, Don, and I'd got him a ticket for the game. He was with a friend of his and they were about to arrive at Aspinall's club in Curzon Street for a glass of wine. So I watched extra time and joined them. I'm not sure I was great company. The reality of it all was beginning to dawn on me.

I woke up in the hotel the following morning still feeling a bit guilty about our win. I felt for Steve McClaren, Derby's manager, I felt for their players and the people at the club. I was still uncomfortable about the way we had made it back to the Premier League. But then another thought hit me. Two years ago I had flown to Munich to watch Chelsea play in the Champions League final. I was manager of Tottenham Hotspur and we had finished fourth, qualifying for the Champions League. Chelsea had come sixth. And like the sixth best team in the Premier League, they got completely outplayed by Bayern Munich on the night, just as they were by Barcelona in the semi-final. Yet somehow they won. Bayern smashed them to pieces, Chelsea equalised with two minutes to go; Bayern missed a penalty in extra time, Chelsea won the shoot-out. And because they did, they took our Champions League place. Twenty-five days later, I was sacked by Tottenham. Had we reached the Champions League that wouldn't have happened. And at that moment I thought – and pardon the language – fuck it. What am I beating myself up for? It's football. Stuff happens. So we didn't deserve to win? What about the times when we merited victory and didn't get it? What about me getting the sack because Chelsea by some miracle ended up with our Champions League place? I walked down to breakfast, feeling better at last, and who should be standing there but Roberto Di Matteo, the Chelsea manager in Munich. He looked happy enough. Why was I agonising over a football match we had won? Yes, it was rough on Derby – but there are a lot of good people at Rangers, too. Let them be happy for a change, I thought. And I never looked back.

Yet looking back is what this book is about. It's a look back on my 60 or so years in and around the British game, from the earliest memories of going to Millwall and Arsenal with my dad, to my thoughts on thankfully not having to face up to Luis Suárez again as a Premier League manager this season. For each decade, I've picked a best XI, too, and told as many stories as I can remember about the characters involved. I hope you enjoy it. And, don't forget: if you can't be good, be lucky.

CHAPTER ONE

THE FIFTIES

We used to go to Arsenal a lot, me and my dad, but football wasn't as tribal then as it is now, so Highbury wasn't our only destination. Millwall's ground, The Den, was another haunt, and coming from East London we would wait at the entrance of the Rotherhithe Tunnel for a lift across the river. A lot of Millwall punters did the same. Eventually a car would stop and in we'd jump. It didn't take too long. I bet you would wait there for hours now, but in those days people were friendlier and more trusting. They were going to football, we were going to football, so we all went together. My dad might give them two bob for the petrol and we'd set off.

It was all part of the tradition of watching Millwall. They were the dockers' club really, and a lot of the men on our estate worked on the docks. I would have been about seven when I first started going there – it was certainly before I went to Arsenal – with my dad and his brother George. Arsenal was my dad's club, but football was cheaper then and fans didn't think twice about going to watch another team play. Millwall were in the

Third Division (South) but it was always a tasty atmosphere. On Saturdays they used to come out of the docks, go into the pub, and out of the pub and into The Den. Football hooliganism was unheard of, but once I began travelling around, even as a kid I knew Millwall felt different. Then there was the time my dad got his jaw broken.

I don't know what happened exactly, I wasn't there, but he went over to Millwall with his mate Johnny Wood, who was a bit of a rogue and spent most of his life in prison. Johnny lived in Poplar when he wasn't inside and was known for being a bit cheeky. My mum blamed him every time there was trouble. Well, he must have picked on the wrong bloke that day, because someone took offence and my old man ended up getting a clump. It was just before Christmas and he ended up with his jaw wired all over the holiday; he couldn't even eat his turkey dinner.

He didn't have much luck with Christmas dinner, my dad. Another year, he knocked off on Christmas Eve and went straight to the pub, as the dockers always did. He had one job that day – to pick up the capon chicken for tomorrow's dinner from Coppins butchers. Unfortunately, he got a bit side-tracked. By night time, with all the shops closed, he still hadn't come home. I was sitting indoors with my mum and I could tell that she'd gone a bit quiet. Suddenly, she sprung out of her chair. 'Right,' she said, 'we're going out to find your father.' And off we went, around every pub in Poplar looking for him. Mum was lifting me up at the windows and I was looking in. At the Earl of Ellesmere pub in Ellesmere Road, we found him. The Far Famed Cake Company was in Rifle Street nearby, and all the girls from the factory were having a Christmas knees-up, too. Dad was there, with Johnny Wood and a crowd of his mates, all dancing with the girls and having a right laugh. 'There he is, Mum,' I said. 'I can see him.' 'Right,' she said, 'call him out, get him out here.' So I went to the door and got his attention. 'Hello, Harry,' he said, all merry from the party. 'Here's my Harry boy. What do you want, Ha –' and, bosh, she'd got him. Claimed hold of his collar and kicked his backside all the way home to our flats. Every 10 paces she'd kick him again. 'Where's our chicken?' Wallop. 'What do you mean you ain't got no chicken?' Boot. 'How can you forget the chicken?' Bash. Crack of dawn the next morning Dad and I were down Petticoat Lane, around the old Jewish stallholders, who were the only ones that traded on Christmas Day, trying to buy a chicken. My dad didn't even know what he was looking for, really. He didn't have a clue what was good or bad. He came home with a boiling chicken, not the lovely big roaster that mum had ordered from Coppins. It was the chicken they use to make stews and soups. So he got hit round the head with that and all. It ate like string. Tough as anything.

He didn't have a clue about the niceties, my dad. All he cared about was football. Most of my earliest memories of watching games in the fifties involve my dad. On the odd occasion I'd go with a mate. I had a friend called Johnnie Jennings whose dad was a big West Ham fan and occasionally I'd go over to Upton Park with them – but even though we lived in the East End it wasn't all Hammers fans on our estate.

By the time I was 11, I was being scouted by professional clubs, so we used to get offered a lot of tickets. Then we could take our pick of matches: Arsenal, Tottenham Hotspur, West Ham United, even Chelsea, which was a bit far afield for us on public transport. We would go if one of our favourites was playing, though. My dad had a few players he really liked, but top of the pile was probably Tom Finney. If Finney was in town with Preston North End he would always want to go. I remember one night at Arsenal when Tommy Docherty played centre-half and Finney was the striker. You could tell The Doc was in awe of Finney because he barely kicked him. Usually he took no prisoners as a defender, but on this day he let Finney walk all over him. Preston won 3–0.

It was a real thrill seeing the big players in those days, it was something you looked forward to and talked about at school all week long. The only match that was on television was the FA Cup final, and that was so special the streets would be deserted when the game was on. Everybody would find somebody they knew with a television and watch the game – and then afterwards all the doors would be flung open and the kids would come roaring out to play football and pretend to be their heroes.

Few people wore colours in those days. I remember my mum knitted me a red and white scarf for when I went to Arsenal, but there were no replica shirts or club merchandise. We had a wooden rattle, like everybody else, but that was about it. These days the police would confiscate it at the turnstile, they would think you were going to club somebody over the head with it – but crowds then were not even segregated. You see old film of the fans in their caps sharing cups of tea – my dad even used to put a collar and tie on to go to some games. That was just the way people dressed.

Everyone went by bus, including the players. Peter Sillett was the captain of Chelsea – Stanley Matthews rated him as his most difficult opponent at full-back – and he used to tell a story about going out to the bus stop to get home after one game. Chelsea had lost and there were still a few fans hanging about. Players weren't recognisable figures in those days – we didn't see them being interviewed on television every week – so they didn't know that they had a Chelsea player standing beside them. The fans were going through the team, slaughtering them all one by one, and finally it was Peter's turn. As they tore him to shreds, Peter says he sunk deeper and deeper into his overcoat in case they spotted him. 'Finally,' he said, 'just to be on the safe side, I joined in.'

I was lucky growing up in London because there was so much good football on my doorstep. We could afford to be picky. There was always a game a bus ride away – we rarely needed to get the train. Fulham, too far. Wembley, too far. We didn't go to the England games. The only ground I can remember visiting by train was Tottenham, once they were interested in signing me. They would send two tickets to every home game for us, and they had some great players in that era, like Danny Blanchflower, who were worth the trip. That meant a 106 bus to Stoke Newington, a train to Seven Sisters, and then a bloody long walk.

The most memorable games of the time involved foreign teams – clubs from Moscow coming over to play Arsenal, or Honved of Hungary against Wolverhampton Wanderers. Even the programmes felt different for those games, glossier and thicker as if to say: this is important. We didn't see foreign teams or foreign footballers in those days: with one exception. I'm going to start my team of the 1950s with this individual, because his story really is quite remarkable.

BERT TRAUTMANN
(MANCHESTER CITY)

Bert was the first foreign star in English football, and a really strange one because he came here as a German prisoner of war, and stayed. I'm not sure that could happen now, with all the media attention and the way supporters are. I think it would be too horrible for him. Trautmann was a typical German. As kids, he was what we all imagined Germans to be – blond hair, blue eyes, tall, imposing. He'd been a member of the Hitler youth, a Luftwaffe paratrooper, and had fought on the Eastern front in Russia. It seems amazing to me even now just thinking about it. He was captured and sent to a prisoner-of-war camp in Lancashire, and when the war was over he ended up playing for St Helens Town, who were an amateur team in the Lancashire Combination league. Frank Swift, who was Manchester City's goalkeeper, contracted TB and they went in for Trautmann. There were huge protests at first, particularly among the Jewish community, but the chief rabbi of Manchester came out in his defence and it calmed down.

Back then you went to matches just to watch certain individuals, and Trautmann definitely came into that category. He was exotic, he was different. The media wasn't as sensationalist back then, but we all knew his background, all knew whose side he was on in the war. I suppose it is testament to what he was like as a player and a person that he won the crowds over. He would smile and applaud them if they were nice to him and, in the end, he became one of us. Incredible, really, when you think what people had gone through with the bombing and losing loved ones – for him to be accepted like that, it shows how good we can be as a country when we put our minds to it.

Back then, people just got on with life. They loved their football, they loved their team, but they didn't have the hatred you see now. It sounds sentimental and nostalgic but I won't make apologies for that; fans were different towards each other, and it was better without that nastiness towards the opposition at games. A player who went back to his old club would be applauded. Nowadays they spit at him in the street. It would be the same for Trautmann. Now, he would be targeted, slagged off the whole game. Back then, it didn't happen. We saw him for what he was: a goalkeeper who had endured a unique set of circumstances. There was no question of verbal abuse the times I saw him. Fans weren't segregated then, anyway. Over at Arsenal, you could find yourself next to some Manchester City fans and you'd end up having a cup of tea together. So you couldn't then start calling their goalkeeper every name under the sun. It must still have been very, very difficult for Trautmann, though, because of his background, and that's why he makes my team ahead of, say, Ted Ditchburn at Tottenham Hotspur or Sam Bartram of Charlton Athletic. I just look at where he came from and think, 'If we all ended up liking a bloke who had fought for the Nazis, he must have been good.' And in 1956 he was the first foreign player to win the Footballer of the Year Award – it was the year he also won the FA Cup, playing with a broken neck.

I remember watching that game, too. Manchester City beat Birmingham City 3–1 and Don Revie was brilliant playing as a deep centre-forward, quite a radical position for the time. He was the man of the match, but what everyone remembers now is that Trautmann broke his neck and played on, although we didn't have a clue he was so badly injured at the time. There were about 15 minutes to go and Peter Murphy was chasing the ball into the penalty area. Trautmann came out, as brave as anything, and dived head first at his feet. Murphy's knee hit his neck and broke it, although that only showed up in the X-ray later. I can guarantee one thing: the trainer wouldn't have had any idea. In my imagination, I can hear him now. 'Come on, Bert, give it a twist, lad, you'll be all right.' Drop of water down his jumper with a sponge and off he'd go again – there were no substitutes then, so all the trainer was interested in was keeping 11 on the field. 'That's better, Bert. You'll be fine now, son.' It seemed every FA Cup final some poor soul broke something. There was no sports science in those days, no proper physiotherapy or qualified medical staff.

The money aside, in many ways it was a great time to be a footballer. Trautmann was a draw and very famous, but there was no media swirl around him as there would be now. I remember watching Mesut Ozil miss a penalty for Arsenal last season, and the next morning everyone was on at him for being German and missing a penalty. Germans don't miss penalties, you see. Now you think of the baggage that Trautmann had with him so soon after the war ended, but he was allowed to be what he was. If anything, it may even have worked in his favour, because to me as a kid he seemed more imposing, bigger and athletic because of his background.

The English goalkeepers? Bartram at Charlton was a local hero. He kept goal for the club either side of the war. London used to have thick smogs and one day he was playing for Charlton at Chelsea when the fog came in and the game was stopped. It cleared a little and the match restarted with Charlton now on top. Then the fog got worse than ever. Sam noticed the crowd had got quieter but thought it was because they couldn't see and Charlton were playing so well. Then a figure appeared out of the gloom before him. Sam got ready to dash out and make a save. It turned out to be a copper. 'What are you doing out here?' he said. 'They all went inside 10 minutes ago.' As I say, different days.

Sam went on to be a journalist for the *Sunday People*. He used to pay me for tips when I was a player at West Ham United, so when I went to Bournemouth I thought I'd have a bit of fun. The night before my debut in 1972, I phoned Mel Machin, one of the other players. I put on a Northern accent and said I was Sam Bartram and was looking for inside information on Bournemouth. I said I'd pay £50 upfront, with a £25 weekly retainer. Mel was right up for it. He said he was in the same card school as our manager, John Bond, so always heard the latest gossip. He said Bobby Kellard at Portsmouth was a current target. 'That's lovely, Mel,' I told him. 'The cheque's in the post and I'll call next week.'

The following day Mel rocked up in a new suit. He was sitting next to Ted MacDougall, telling him all about this great deal he had. I couldn't contain myself. I leaned into the conversation. 'Hello, Mel,' I said, in my best Sam Bartram voice. 'Er, hello, Harry,' Mel replied, a little unsure of what was going on. I carried it on for a little while. 'What are you talking like that for?' he said. 'I'm Sam,' I told him, 'Sam Bartram.' Mel went spare, but John Bond loved it. 'Harry's going to run rings around you lot,' he predicted. Then in the afternoon we lost 3–2 to Watford.

Later when he was going through all the players individually he turned on me. 'And if you think you can come down here taking the piss out of everybody …'

As a goalkeeper Sam was more the traditional type, whereas Trautmann seemed to have more flair; he was almost acrobatic, and we hadn't seen that before. He still had to look after himself, mind you, because every goalkeeper took a physical battering. That never seemed to bother him, though. I suppose when you've thought you were about to be taken off by the Russians and shot, it wouldn't.

ALF RAMSEY
(TOTTENHAM HOTSPUR)

We all know what Alf is remembered for, but at first he was the right-back in the great Tottenham Hotspur team of the 1950s, the 'push and run' team. It is hard to explain their significance to a younger generation, but I would compare them to the modern Barcelona, the way their game was all about short passing and movement. It wasn't quite as sophisticated, obviously, but when Tottenham started playing that way they won the Second Division title and the next season won the league by four points (the equivalent of six today). That 1950–51 team was special, with Arthur Rowe coaching and Eddie Baily pulling the strings at inside-forward. Eddie went on to be Bill Nicholson's assistant at Tottenham in the 1960s and a scout at Chelsea and West Ham. He was a brilliant footballer, a fantastic, intelligent quick passer, but as a scout nothing much impressed Eddie. 'Players? Fucking players?' he'd say. 'They get you the fucking sack.' He's not wrong, by the way.

What they called push and run back then is now known as the one-two and every team does it. But at the time it was revolutionary. A player would find his team-mate with a short pass and then carry on his run to receive another short pass in return. Newcastle United came fourth and won the FA Cup in 1950–51, but Tottenham beat them 7–0 playing push and run that season. And Ramsey was a master at it. He had come to prominence playing for his army division during the war, and went to Portsmouth and then Southampton, before Tottenham got him.

He wasn't fast, so there is no way he could play right-back now, but Alf excelled at the intricate passing that made Rowe's Tottenham tick. He was good on the ball, very cultured for the time, and an outstanding penalty taker. They used to call him 'The General' at Tottenham because he was always in charge, so it is no surprise that he went on to be such a successful manager.

Alf's use of the ball was always first class. And I think people forget how hard it was to play good football with the equipment they had in those days. Look at the boots with the big hard toe-caps. How could you have had any feel for a football with a set of those on? Clearing out the garage the other day, I found a pair of my dad's old boots. Forget push and run, it's a wonder they could run at all. Metal toecaps, studs banged in the bottom with the nails coming through the sole. And the ball was so heavy that when it got wet it as good as filled with water. Modern players really feel the ball; they have light boots and moulded soles. Even the ball is lightweight. Those boys didn't even have rubber studs – by late in the season when it had dried out, or in the middle of winter when it was frozen, the only thing harder than the studs was the pitch. Apart from August and September there were two kinds of surface, rock hard or mud heap. So it was unbelievable, really, to show the skill that the Tottenham team demonstrated in that gear. I'd love to organise a game one day, get 22 top players together, the stars of the Premier League, put them in the old equipment and see how they coped. Now that would be interesting.

I remember Bryan Robson telling me that when Juninho first came over to Middlesbrough in the 1995–6 season, he couldn't believe the quality of our pitches. In the FA Cup that year they played against Notts County, who were a third-tier team, and Juninho thought Bryan was lying to him about the division they were in. He looked at the neat little stadium and the nice pitch, and decided they were in a higher division than Bryan was saying. A team at that level in Brazil would have been playing on dirt, he said. Notts County were too posh. That is how far we have come, but in Alf's day they just had to overcome those disadvantages.

I never got to know Alf as a manager, which was a shame. He came from that pre-war generation, very old school, very aloof. He was born in Dagenham in East London, but had elocution lessons, which was strange for the time. Maybe he thought it would help him keep his distance from the players. I know Terry Venables came from the same area and when he got called into the England team, his dad thought it might help him with the manager to mention some old names from the past. He knew this bloke that was friends with Ramsey, so he told Terry to say that Charlie – or whoever – sent his regards. After the first training sessions, Terry thought it would be the right moment. Catching up with him as they left the field he seized his chance. 'Mr Ramsey, my dad told me to say hello to you from Charlie, in Dagenham.' Ramsey looked at him very coldly. He had done everything to cover his old accent and now pronounced Argentina with an H. The last thing he wanted was to be reminded of his past. Finally, he spoke in the most cultured accent he could muster. 'Fuck off, son,' he said. I think Terry only played for him twice.

When you think how much Ramsey and Bobby Moore achieved together for England, it's surprising how seldom Alf's name comes up in conversation. I think he was a quiet man, not given to great shows of emotion. And in those days managers were still distant figures, who took their lead from the managers that they had worked with as players. Tommy Lawton played in the same era as Ramsey, certainly throughout the early 1950s, and I remember watching a fascinating interview with him about his time at Everton before the war. He went in to see the committee – Everton was run by a committee in those days – because his contract was up. Players only signed for a year back then. Tommy said he knocked on the door and walked in, and the head of the committee, Theo Kelly, looked up as he entered. 'Lawton,' he said, 'go outside the door, knock again and when I say enter, come in and stand over there by the door. When I say come over, you can come over to my desk and when I say sit down, you can sit down at my desk.' So Tommy said he went outside and did the whole thing exactly as Kelly said. He was the leading goalscorer in England that year, but by the time he left Kelly's office he felt he would be lucky to get a game at Tranmere Rovers. No surprise that it was Kelly who failed to persuade Lawton to stay at Everton after the war.

Yet that was the football culture that Alf Ramsey came from, so it is any wonder he stayed aloof from his players?

BILLY WRIGHT
(WOLVERHAMPTON WANDERERS)

Looking at the photographs of that great Wolves team, the first thing that strikes you about Billy Wright is his size. These days, the centre-halves are giants, but Billy actually looks slightly smaller than many of his team-mates. There really was nothing of him. '10 stones in weight, but 10 tons in the tackle' was one phrase I heard about him, and he was only 5 ft 8 in. The best central defenders of that time didn't have to be tall. Joe Shaw at Sheffield United was another one. He might have been even smaller than Billy.

If you look at what he achieved, it seems impossible. He played 70 consecutive games for England, captained them 90 times and won 105 caps – the first player to reach the century in world football. And this was a time when England did not have a huge amount of games, and Billy lost seven seasons to the Second World War. Imagine the records he could have set.

He got his break at Wolves because they were advertising for trialists in the local newspaper. With modern scouting networks, that would never happen now. Wolves thought he was too small at first, but Major Frank Buckley, the manager, relented and took him on as an apprentice for eight months. He was a centre-forward, then a wing-half and eventually a centre-half.

One of the things those of us who grew up in the fifties most remember about the game at that time was the first matches under lights against international opposition. Wolves installed floodlights at Molineux in 1953 and played a succession of matches against foreign teams: Racing Club of Buenos Aires, Moscow Dynamo, Spartak Moscow, and in 1954 they played Honved, the Champions of Hungary. It was a year after Hungary had beaten England 6–3 at Wembley, and then 7–1 in Budapest, and Wright was the captain of that humiliated England team. I cannot emphasise enough what an effect those matches had on us, because these players were our heroes and to see them taken apart like that – well, we couldn't believe it.

Billy Wright, in particular, was as much a celebrity as a footballer. He didn't live life like David Beckham, or George Best, and I don't think he had that personal charisma, but he was good looking with really blond hair, and had married one of the Beverley Sisters. Everyone knew him, as kids we all looked up to him, and suddenly we were seeing him getting pulled all over the Wembley pitch by Ferenc Puskás. Destroyed, really. So why is he still in this team? He was the best of his generation in Britain. There was no shame in getting beaten by the Hungarians. They were the best of their generation in Europe.

Hungary were the first to play a deep-lying centre-forward, and their wingers would withdraw to midfield to help with defence. Puskás called them the first total-football team, because everybody attacked and everybody fell back. I suppose the formation would be 2–3–3–2, although that is hard to picture for anyone brought up on the modern game. Wright ended up following Puskás as he dropped nearer to midfield and was left completely exposed when Hungary broke. It wasn't his fault. We had never seen anything like it. There were 105,000 at Wembley for the first game and

Hungary were a goal up in a minute and 4–1 up after 27 minutes. We thought we would get revenge in Budapest, but they put seven past us, which was just stunning.

Hungary should have won the 1954 World Cup but suffered a series of brutal matches on the way to the final, meaning they lost to West Germany, although they'd beaten them 8–3 in the group stage. That was one of only two games they lost between 1949 and the Hungarian Uprising in 1956, and in that time they revolutionised football. The system and ideas of their coach Gusztáv Sebes, evolved into 3–2–3–2, then 4–2–4 with high wingers and eventually the 4–4–2 pressing game. He started the policy of picking a team, rather than just the best players, thinking that if he selected from a handful of clubs rather than just a wide collection of individuals, there would be more unity. Finally, his idea that any player should be capable of playing anywhere pre-dated Holland and total football.

So this was the background when Honved came to Wolves in 1954, with Billy up against five of the Hungarian players that had won 7–1. It was more than a friendly. It really felt as if the future of English football was at stake. The game was so big that it was shown on television, with Wolves wearing special old-gold shirts made out of satin, and when Honved went 2–0 up after 14 minutes we all feared the worst. Yet Wolves fought back to win 3–2 and Billy was fantastic in the rest of that game. Wolves were a great team at the time and Billy was a real footballing centre-half, so much more than a tackler. Even at 2–0 down, and with all that had happened before, he was a great competitor, and you can see why he was England's captain for so long. You would have to be a special player to get through that, and he did.

ROGER BYRNE
(MANCHESTER UNITED)

A few years back I watched a television drama called *United* about the Busby Babes and the Munich air disaster. According to the programme, the team's captain was Mark Jones, the big centre-half. I was horrified and still cannot understand why nobody corrected that mistake when the script was being looked over. Left-back Roger Byrne was the captain of the Babes. He wasn't the greatest footballer in that team by any means, but he was a magnificent leader and one of the finest full-backs of his time, a huge part of Manchester United history.

Byrne broke into the United team in 1951 and was captain by 1953, through to his death at Munich less than five years later. In that time he also made 33 England appearances and once he got into the team was never out of it, an achievement that remains a record. He wasn't the greatest tackler, nor the best header of the ball, and he had no left foot despite playing on the left, but Byrne played full-back like a sweeper with tremendous intelligence and reading of the game. And when he had the chance he went on great forward runs, which was unusual in fifties football, when the full-back positions were often given to the least athletic members of the team. He was ahead of his time, and those who saw him regularly tell me that, among the wingers, only Peter Harris at Portsmouth was faster.

When you look back on those days, with two full-backs and one centre-half, I always wonder what would have happened if teams had started playing two up, because every club set up the same way at the back. The full-backs could not have covered because they had the wingers to deal with – but tactics weren't as big a part of the game. Byrne was ahead of his time the way he played, because of his attacking instincts. The special qualities of the lesser known members of the Babes are lost now because we tend to focus on Duncan Edwards and some of the other individuals. Players like Byrne get forgotten – but they were an extraordinary team, a magical team, and going to see them always felt like an event.

Byrne was 28 when he died, so he was more experienced than many of the boys around him, and it is a tribute to his ability, his tenacity and the way he could inspire by example that Sir Matt Busby trusted him with the leadership of the group. He was their father figure, a player with a lot of class and charisma that outweighed his technical shortcomings. I suppose only in retrospect, with the knowledge that this was one of the greatest club teams in history, do we realise how good Byrne was. At the time, of course, people weren't going to see Manchester United for the performance of the solid left-back. They wanted to watch Duncan. It seems a shame Byrne is still getting pushed into the background even now. He really deserves more credit.

DUNCAN EDWARDS
(MANCHESTER UNITED)

People always ask whether Duncan Edwards was as good as everybody says. Absolutely, he was. Bobby Charlton was a fantastic player, but he said watching Duncan made him feel inadequate. The day he died the *Daily Mirror* headline read, 'A boy who played like a man', and I think that's right. He was so young, but you would never have known it because he was the driving force of that great Manchester United team. He had it all: left foot, right foot, phenomenal balance and poise; he could dribble, he could tackle; there was 14 stone of him, strong as an ox. When he got on a run he couldn't be stopped.

He had a saying before games, apparently: 'We haven't come here for nothing.' Bobby said to me that if United were ever in trouble, the players would be thinking, 'Come on, Duncan, get us out of this.' And he'd go up and smash one in from 30 yards, straight in the corner. We'll never know what he might have achieved had he lived; he could have been England's captain in 1966, instead of Bobby Moore. He would only have been 29 then, and it is hard to see him not being in that England team.

I saw the last game the Busby Babes played in this country, a 5–4 win at Arsenal on 1 February 1958, and that would have stuck in my mind even without Munich. It was a fantastic game, such incredible quality, and the next I heard was a radio bulletin saying Manchester United's plane had crashed on the way back from Belgrade. It wasn't like today with 24-hour news stations; you had to wait until the morning paper or until it was time for the news on the radio to find out what was going on. I would have been a 10-year-old schoolboy, listening to the radio in our flat on the estate with my mum and dad. Mum always had the radio on: *The Billy Cotton Band Show*, *The Archers* and the news, and that's where I heard about Manchester United and Duncan Edwards. I remember going into school and we said prayers for them all. Everyone was very, very upset, even the teachers, and as kids it really affected us. I think we were in shock, particularly when he died, because for so long the bulletins had been positive.

Matt Busby and Duncan Edwards were recovering, they said. I kept a scrapbook and I'm sure there is a picture from a newspaper in it of Duncan sitting up in his hospital bed: he was going to be all right. Sadly, his condition worsened due to severe kidney damage, and he died. I was devastated. He was my idol.

Those early European games were an ordeal for English clubs. I have spoken to a number of players who were involved in them and they have said it could get really scary, particularly behind the Iron Curtain. The plane would be joined by MiG jets, which would escort them, often keeping them deliberately low so the flight would be skirting the top of the clouds and really bumpy. Obviously, that wasn't what caused the Munich disaster, but flying was a pretty unnerving experience in those days.

So what made Duncan special? In modern terms he was probably a defensive midfield player, but he had so much more his game. His shot was tremendous, so much power. I remember reading that in youth tournaments for United he was so exceptional, so much better than any player on the pitch, he'd start up front, get a couple of goals and then move back to centre-half and defend the lead. He was only 18 when he made his debut for England against Scotland, yet even with so many great players around him he didn't look out of place. England won 7–2 and the age of his team-mates shows how exceptional Edwards was. Stanley Matthews played at the age of 40, Bert Williams the goalkeeper was 35, Billy Wright the captain was 31, Nat Lofthouse was 29. And there was Duncan Edwards – 18 years, 183 days, and probably better than any of them.

And it was all natural ability. Not coaching. Natural ability. Like all the best players of that time in England, Edwards worked off his instincts. There wasn't teaching as we know it now. Maybe you would get some advice from your dad or you'd go to watch your favourite players and see how they did it, but we all learnt our football the same way, on the streets, and Duncan Edwards would have been no different. There was nothing else to do but play outside, nothing for kids on TV even if you had one, so we lived our whole life playing football, and that was where you developed your skills. It was better than sitting indoors watching the potter's wheel or test card, waiting for the next programme to come on.

There was no special gear, no special boots. The young Duncan would have got home and put his slippers on – plimsolls, like you wore for gym – and gone out and played until it was time for dinner, or bed. I would say until it got dark, but even that didn't matter some days. In the winter we just ran around in the dark for as long as we could. So there was no one to tell you to play on the half-turn or how to kill a ball in mid-air. You just worked it out. My Sunday football team was taken by a couple of lovely old dockers. They wouldn't have thought to coach us or known how, really. We just played.

Even when you went to a professional club it was no different. At West Ham we trained on the forecourt, where the main entrance was. Tuesday and Thursday nights, with a few old floodlights. You never saw a pitch. If we couldn't get outside we'd go into the little gym they had under the main stand. There was just enough room to do some short passing or have a small game. And every player would be wearing slippers, just the same. It was not greatly different at Tottenham, except they had a proper big gymnasium, so had a tiny advantage over the other clubs. But the most sophisticated training we did was playing three against four; there still wasn't room for much else. Seven or eight of you would have a little game, then make way for the next group. That was it. No proper technical work. Nobody taught you how to play a position or where to run. What Duncan Edwards did would have been all his own instinct or reasoning.

Take dribbling. Running with the ball was a big part of Edwards's game, but he would have had to learn that control without coaching. No different to George Best in the 1960s, no different to all the other wingers, including me. You learnt on the streets. There might be 14 on each team, so you didn't see much of the ball. When it arrived you wanted a few touches, so you tried to keep it as long as you could by learning to run with it and beat people. Scotland had a great tradition of producing players like that – Jimmy Johnstone and Willie Henderson had a famous rivalry in the 1960s with Celtic and Rangers – and I still think nothing beats seeing a winger going on a run, just surging past people. There is a Scottish phrase – the tanner-ball player – and people now think it was a compliment, but that isn't true. The Scots used to refer to tanner-ball players because rubber balls cost a tanner and there were thousands of kids who could do anything with them. When it came to the big pitch, and a big game, with a real ball and the need for tackling, heading and intelligent positional play, they couldn't convert those skills. That's all they were – tanner-ball players. Johnstone and Henderson were a lot more than that. But every kid knew how to dribble. These days it is all passing – that's what makes players like Lionel Messi and Cristiano Ronaldo stand out – but great dribblers were 10 a penny in Duncan

Edwards's day. The ones who made it had something more. They were clever, like Duncan.

The greatest players have all got that innate, natural feel for the game. Even Messi. Yes, he came through the academy at Barcelona, but when they brought him over he was already a fantastic little dribbler who had learnt in street football in Argentina. They took one look at him, and offered him a contract written on a napkin because they had no paper to hand; but he wouldn't have been able to get a trial had he not been extra special, and that initial talent was all natural. Diego Maradona was the same. See some of the early video footage and the pitches he's playing on are horrendous, but then this little figure comes into view, playing with the ball, juggling the ball – he's tiny but the stuff he is doing is incredible. The player that I remember as a manager was Joe Cole. At the age of 11 he was like that too. He could do everything with the ball. His dad, George, had no interest, never kicked a ball in his life, never played football. So that was all Joe.

In the fifties, though, all the clubs did was assess those kids. They would organise a few sessions, a bit of passing, back and forward, side-foot, nothing too difficult, then put on a game to see who was best. Duncan Edwards took his skills to Manchester United, really – he gave them more than they gave him. I'm not saying Sir Matt Busby did not coach, but Duncan wouldn't have anywhere near the work going into him that went into Messi at La Masia. Imagine a young Edwards at Barcelona today. His talent would have been amazing. In those days, even the professional clubs had very unsophisticated regimes. A few times around the cinder track, or up and down the steps of the terraces for fitness.

I remember jogging down the Epping New Road with the West Ham team along a path with no pavement and giant lorries thundering past. If you slipped, you were dead. You'd have great players like Eddie Baily advertising cigarettes. I saw an old copy of *Charlie Buchan's Football Monthly* that said Leyton Orient had introduced a great new fitness regime involving cross-country running, and first prize for coming top at the end of the week was a set of golf balls. I've known players who would give up a £20,000 fine to get out of a hard running session.

What we know now and what we knew then, it's like two different worlds. Imagine the players now if they were sent running through the forest. Muddy and wet, slipping down hills, tripping over the roots of trees. How people didn't injure themselves, I don't know. But we all just ploughed on. Now, in a typical week you might play on Sunday because of a television commitment, so on Monday the players have a little stretch and a rub down, and the fitness coach advises you to keep it light on Tuesday because you are still getting over the game. Wednesday is a day off, so you train properly on Thursday and do fuck all again on Friday, because it's the day before you play again on Saturday. So that's one day training all week. The boys from Duncan Edwards's era wouldn't believe it. They used to play on Saturday, day off Sunday, and the manager would run the bollocks off them on Monday because he would know half of them had been out on the beer all weekend. They ran those boys like there was no tomorrow. You couldn't do that now. Players ask: 'Why are we running? What good is this going to do?' They think they are such perfect specimens. Yet none of them could live with Duncan Edwards.

DANNY BLANCHFLOWER
(TOTTENHAM HOTSPUR)

Intelligence – that's what stands out about Danny. He wasn't just a phenomenal footballer, he was a phenomenal brain. A great reader of the game, a great leader, he was the mind behind the best teams Tottenham have produced, as well as being such a clever midfield player and passer. Danny's Tottenham team did the double at the start of the 1960s, but it was being built throughout the 1950s, when he was the supreme wing-half of his generation, following the tragic demise of Duncan Edwards. Danny's brother Jackie was among the Manchester United players involved in the Munich air crash, and was so badly injured he could not resume his career.

Danny went to Tottenham from Aston Villa in 1954 and was at the peak of his powers from about 1957 onwards. He was more wiry than powerful, but could dictate the tempo of a game and was clever at finding space. He'd burst into unguarded areas and set up the centre-forward with a perfect pass, all in an instant. The best teams strike fast, and Blanchflower's speed of thought made Tottenham the fastest counter-attacking team of all. He arrived under Arthur Rowe, who retired in 1955 due to ill health, and it wasn't until Bill Nicholson came that he began to thrive. At first, they clashed and Danny was dropped; but Nicholson was an astute man and when Danny came back into the side he did so as captain and the club never looked back.

He must have been infuriating to manage at times – rearranging tactics on the field without consultation if he thought they were not working, which he did in the 1956 FA Cup semi-final, only for Tottenham to then lose 1–0 to Manchester City – but I don't think British football has ever produced a better thinker. For example, he invented the wall. You know, the wall that every team in the world now puts in front of a free-kick taker to block his shot? Danny Blanchflower thought of it first.

It was a World Cup qualifier, Northern Ireland against Italy in Rome, on 24 April 1957. Italy had a brilliant free-kick and penalty taker called Sergio Cervato, who played for Fiorentina. In those days, players just marked up from free-kicks, but Danny knew that was pointless because this guy always took a direct shot. So before the game he suggested to the manager that they put a line of players, a wall, between Cervato and the goal. The manager, Peter Doherty, didn't know what he was talking about. He thought Danny was mad. But the players listened, and did it. Italy got a free-kick after three minutes and the players all lined up in a wall. Danny told me that Italy seemed perplexed by the tactic, and so was the referee. So when Cervato picked up the ball, moved it five yards wide of the wall, turned round and shot it into the net, he gave a goal. Italy won 1–0, but Northern Ireland ended up winning the group and went to the 1958 World Cup. Danny got Footballer of the Year that season – he could have got it for that idea alone.

I was lucky enough to play against Danny for West Ham when I was a teenager. I would have been about 16, playing in the A team against Tottenham at our training ground in Chadwell Heath, and he was coming back from injury. He seemed a lovely guy, not at all aloof like the managers of the day, very approachable and down to earth. I remembered him from my time as a schoolboy, training with Tottenham in the summer and watching all the first-team players doing their tricks and showing off for us during the lunch break. We were all in awe of him. We'd go to watch the midweek European games as well, and Danny was always the star. I remember him exactly as he was against West Ham's A team that day, spraying the ball about with long passes, keeping it tight with intricate short passes; his team knew if they fed him the ball he wouldn't give it away. He had that control – the game revolved around him. His finger was on the pulse; he knew when to slow it down, when to launch a quick attack. He was just a tremendous brain; a true football intellectual.

Jimmy Greaves told me that there were occasions when Tottenham were losing and Danny would just take over at half-time. Bill Nicholson was a great manager, but he was a quiet man, whereas Danny was so confident, whatever the situation. If Bill was stuck, he would let him speak. As a manager, there are times when it just feels right to let a senior player have his say. If he's a good guy, and you know he has good ideas, there is no harm in it at all. Not every time, and not so it becomes a free-for-all; but I imagine Bill trusted Danny, and trusted him to make a positive impact. Jimmy said Blanchflower dictated the culture of the dressing-room at Tottenham and it was never vicious or negative.

Danny is responsible for one of the greatest quotes about football. 'The great fallacy is that the game is first and last about winning,' he said. 'It's nothing of the kind. The game is about glory. It is about doing things in style, with a flourish, about going out and beating the other lot, not waiting for them to die of boredom.' But there is another of his that should be equally famous. 'Winning isn't everything,' he said. 'Wanting to win is.' Nothing in the modern game makes either of those sayings less true.

We miss people like Danny because in recent years the teams have become a lot quieter. I don't believe players think about the game today the way they once did; they are not as interested in the tactics or the philosophy. That is what makes some of the pundits they have on Sky so special, the guys who work alongside my son Jamie, like Gary Neville and Jamie Carragher. They want to talk about every element of football, which so few players do – and that is why they stand out. Very few players have an awful lot to say now. I think in Danny's day a lot of the lads had more to say, a bit of personality. When I hear about the strength of character in Danny's Tottenham team, I am slightly jealous because my Tottenham team certainly wasn't like that. The dressing-room became very quiet if we were losing and no one had much to say at all. I'd never stop players making a contribution, so I don't think it was a lack of encouragement from the management – they just weren't interested.

There are exceptions in the modern game, obviously; Tony Adams, John Terry. I watched the game last season in which Chelsea won at Manchester City, and during the warm-up Terry must have held court with the rest of the players for about 10 minutes. They were going through their stretches in a big circle and he was pointing at this one and that one, really laying down the law. You could see straight away why, no matter how many times Chelsea have changed managers, he has been the captain. I imagine Adams would have been the same. And when Chelsea came out that night, they absolutely bossed City and you could see Terry's influence all over the field, in the way they went about their work. Yet there is a world of difference between carrying that message as a player and inspiring players to think about the game, or through the sheer intelligence of your words – which is what Blanchflower did. When he stopped playing he carried that conviction into his newspaper column. It isn't easy being that guy when you haven't got the ball at your feet, but Danny never stopped thinking, never stopped stating his case, even after he had retired.

BOBBY COLLINS
(EVERTON)

Right, I'm going to cheat here a little bit. Bobby Collins spans two decades as an inside-forward. He made his debut for Celtic in 1949, joined Everton in 1958 and moved to Leeds United in 1962, where he is credited with being the driving force behind the creation of Don Revie's great team. Yet that 1960s team is hard enough to pick as it is, so I'm going to find room for Bobby a decade earlier, not just for his great performances with Everton, but for what he was going to do later in his career – and also because my friend Joe Jordan would kill me if I didn't select him. Joe idolises Bobby. There was nothing of him, he was the smallest player on the pitch, but with the biggest heart and the fiercest tackle. Leeds had a production line of them under Revie – Billy Bremner and Johnny Giles were cast from the same mould. Yet Bobby was arguably the best of them all.

Most memories of Bobby focus on his fearsome physical approach. He could be brutal, and would take on players who were head and shoulders bigger than him, but there was more to his game than just a vicious streak. He played for close to a quarter of the century, only retiring in 1973, and no one can sustain that career on nothing more than brute force. Yes, he was a terror, but he was also a master of passing, shooting and ball control, the full midfielder's repertoire. He could curl a ball from distance as well as anyone in the game, and he was another thinker, a fine tactician and motivator, with limitless energy and desire.

Roy Vernon, a team-mate with Everton, called Collins 'the complete inside-forward', and there were times when his approach seemed to teeter on the brink of madness, tearing around the pitch as if his life depended on it. Opponents never had time on the ball when Collins was around, yet once possession was won he could slow the game down and dictate the play from there. I think it sums up his ability that when Harry Catterick decided Bobby had run his course at Everton at the age of 31, two of the greatest managers of any era, Bill Shankly at Liverpool and Revie at Leeds, wanted him to sign. Revie won out and Bobby helped transform the club. Leeds were known as a team that could look after themselves, and it was Bobby who started that.

Jack Charlton told me that the day before the FA Cup final against Liverpool in 1965, Leeds were playing a little five-a-side game just to warm up and Norman Hunter hit a ball which smacked Collins in the face, making his nose bleed. It was a complete accident, but when the game restarted, Collins flew at Norman, caught him two-footed halfway up his leg, knocked him over and then knelt over him throwing punches, and Jack had to drag him off. 'Come on, Bobby,' he was shouting, 'we've got the Cup Final tomorrow.' But that's how he was. The Leeds players all said he could go off like a madman in an instant, yet they respected him completely. Maybe he did rule by fear but, by God, it was effective. Few players have changed a club around the way Bobby did Leeds.

I know Sir Alex Ferguson thinks Eric Cantona was a transforming influence on Manchester United because of his standards and attitude, and I feel that about Paolo Di Canio at West Ham. One player can make a difference. Even at Bournemouth, we were never the same after Luther Blissett arrived – he had been to Italy and just introduced a new level of professionalism. That is what Collins did at Elland Road. Jack says Bobby would kill his own mum for a win – and that rubbed off on the rest of the players. Joe says he was a massive influence on all the players, particularly the young ones who became that next generation. He was just the governor. He would teach all the kids how to look after themselves on the football field, how to sort an opponent out if he was getting too cocky. Maybe that is what comes from being brought up on those Old Firm derbies. I know Bobby was a friend of Tommy Docherty, but the first time they played each other, The Doc put him in the stand. He said he knew from that moment how he would have to play to survive – and that is the knowledge he passed on. He wasn't dirty – he just taught them both sides of the game.

JOHNNY HAYNES
(FULHAM)

Johnny Haynes was the golden boy of his generation. The great inside-forward. He had this marvellous reverse pass – he'd look one way and switch the ball in the other direction, across field, out to the opposite wing. Tommy Trinder, the Fulham chairman, said he was so good he'd pay him £100 a week if he could. The maximum wage was £20 at that time. Then they got rid of it, so Johnny asked for his hundred quid. He got it, too. He was the highest paid footballer in the land – deservedly – although he could have made that twice over with AC Milan.

I would have been a baby when Johnny became a television star, playing for England Schoolboys against Scotland at the age of 15. Few people had televisions in those days, so they watched whatever was on and saw this kid in an England shirt dominating the game from the inside-left position with a range of extraordinary passing. Johnny's name was made that day. He was born in Tottenham territory, Edmonton, and supported Arsenal – but he was persuaded to join Fulham and played for them from 1952 to 1970.

It was different then and players tended to stay with the team they joined as a boy, unless the club got rid of them or took a transfer fee. You didn't think about leaving unless the manager wanted you out. Nobody thought, 'I'll sign a contract here, and then move on in three years.' There were no agents or people taking their cut to sell you. It just wasn't part of the game. I don't think many players even left to better themselves – not between clubs in the same division, anyway. It was preferable, really – because a club like Fulham could have the best inside-forward in Britain, and keep him for close to 20 years. Imagine if Wayne Rooney had come through at Fulham 10 years ago – how long would he have lasted? They couldn't even keep him at Everton. Yet, in the 1950s, Preston North End had Tom Finney, Fulham had Haynes – it made the game more interesting. I suppose the one exception in the modern era was Matt Le Tissier at Southampton. He could have left the club on a number of occasions, but had no real ambition. He just wanted to be a great footballer and play for his club. He could have gone to Tottenham, many times, and Matthew Harding, the wealthy director at Chelsea who died in a helicopter crash, used to keep a picture of him in his wallet. Signing Matt was his dream. Yet he wasn't interested. He's a bright lad and he knew exactly what he wanted; he was happy where he was.

So loyal club men were more common in Johnny's day, but Fulham knew they had to pay top wages to keep Johnny. Every club in the country would have taken him in his prime – sometimes offering promotion too, with Fulham often outside Division One – and it was just a pity that he suffered a terrible knee injury in a car crash in Blackpool in 1962 or he would surely have made Sir Alf Ramsey's World Cup-winning team in 1966. He fought his way back to play another eight seasons in the league, but never got back into the England set-up after that accident. I don't think Alf ever picked him.

Johnny wasn't one for dribbling past opponents. He beat them the modern way – with his passing. He scored plenty, too, but the goals he created were the best – for Jimmy Hill at club level and Jimmy Greaves with England. Jimmy Greaves said he was his favourite team-mate, putting him even above Sir Bobby Charlton. I know Jimmy thought Johnny was the more ambitious passer – he would pick out eye-of-the-needle through passes all the time, and goalscorers love those because it sets them up one on one against the goalkeeper – whereas Bobby would sometimes switch the play too much. Jimmy would make his run, get into the kind of position where Johnny might have tried to find him, only to see the ball from Bobby sailing over to the opposite flank. So he'd have to check his run, go out and come in again – and Jimmy didn't like running at the best of times. So he loved Johnny, always splitting the defence, finding the gap and the clever angle. Johnny could hit those long balls, too – but he was at his best finding the spaces that others didn't see, often making his best passes blind, as if telepathic. In the 1960–61 season, Johnny orchestrated a run of six England victories that accrued 40 goals. They didn't keep lists of assists in those days – but I'd guarantee his name would have been on the majority of them.

Bobby Collins was my other inside-forward and I think they would be a good blend: chalk and cheese. Bobby was a good player, but he'd sort a few out as well. Johnny wasn't like that. He didn't go around kicking people; he was just class. I've seen very few midfield players with his awareness; he seemed to know where everybody was before the ball had even arrived. He was like a quarter-back in American football. It was as if the whole game was unfolding in front of him and he was just looking to put that ball on a sixpence; except it all seemed to happen in an instant around Johnny. If you look at how a player like Toni Kroos operates for Bayern Munich, that was Johnny. He would have fitted straight into any team run by Pep Guardiola. He was like a Barcelona player, really; he would have loved tiki-taka. Nobody could get it off him when he was on his game; he would turn, play the right pass, keep it simple, get it back, go on – and then hit the killer pass that opened up the team.

People often have the debate about whether players from Haynes's era could have survived modern football, but I've no doubt about it. Johnny Haynes could have lived with anyone, in any era. I'm not so sure about the modern players surviving in his time, though. I see a lot of good athletes about today, but not so many with great ability, natural ability. Technically, I'm not sure they would have been able to deliver.

I met Johnny later on in his career, through Bobby Moore, who was a mutual friend. He used to come and have a drink with us at the Baker's Arms and was a normal fella, just one of the chaps. My dad was always excited when I said I'd been with Johnny because he absolutely loved him as a player. I played in a couple of charity games with him and saw, first-hand, how perfectly he passed the ball. He really was a different class. The clubs don't allow it now, but we seemed to play quite a lot of games for charity in those days and they could get quite competitive.

I remember one down at Margate in the sixties, and I think Johnny might have been there. We played the Lord Mayor's XI versus the Jimmy Tarbuck XI and about seven of us went down, just from West Ham. It was the day after the season ended but, even so, can you imagine that now, the manager letting seven of his team risk injury to play in some poxy charity game? It was at Hartsdown Park, where Margate play, and it was a sell-out. The Lord Mayor had all the local stars, good non-league players from Margate and Ramsgate, around that area, Jimmy had himself, a few celebrities and us. It was a fairly even game, sensible, not too competitive, but the professionals just see it as a bit of fun anyway. Even the non-league players know the score. They're up for it, but not in a silly way. Nobody was going to get injured. It's the celebrities you have to watch, though. They're always the first ones to lose it.

Sure enough, with five minutes to go, we got a penalty when Tommy Steele, the musical actor, was brought down. He picked the ball up and prepared to take it. With that, Tarbuck took the ball off him, put it on the spot and got ready to shoot. Then they started having a furious row. Tommy thought he should take the penalty because he earned it, but Jimmy got the last word. 'Tom, have a look at the programme,' he said, deadly serious. 'It says Jimmy Tarbuck XI – that's me.' And he took the ball and scored. At the end of the match, Tommy stormed into the dressing-room, snatched his clothes off the peg and took off with the raging hump. 'Don't ever ask me to play again,' he said as he left. I'm told he didn't speak to Tarbuck for ages. They fell out like you wouldn't believe. All over a silly penalty in a charity match. Mind you, it could have been worse. Driving back from Margate after a good night out, Bobby Moore's car ended up on the top of a roundabout. He missed the junction completely. I must have still had my wits about me, though. I knew something was wrong when one minute I was following his rear lights, and the next his headlights were facing me.

STANLEY MATTHEWS
(BLACKPOOL)

When Matthews came to town, you'd want to go. Simple as that. He could fill a stadium, almost on his own, even at the age of 50. To play at that age is incredible, particularly on the wing, but I think it says most about the way the game has changed. Ryan Giggs has played for Manchester United into his forties, which is an amazing achievement, but he has had to move into central midfield. The game was so much easier for wingers then because the tactics and athleticism were not so advanced. If you watch the old footage, the ball comes out to Stan on the wing and he would start taking it forward, almost jogging with it, as if there was an obstacle in the distance ahead. Suddenly, after about five seconds, into the picture comes the left-back to meet him. Now he'd jockey, just jockey, concede ground, go backwards and Stan would run the ball up to him. Now the left-back has to take a gamble, he'd lunge at the ball with a slide tackle and Stan would just flick it over his foot and go past him. And that was him gone, out of the game, while Stan was on his way to the byline to pick out a cross – it was always the same. And don't get me wrong, he was brilliant at it. If Stan had to adapt to modern football, I'm sure he would – yet these days he'd be confronted with a left-back who is faster than any winger and as soon as the wide player came near him – bosh! In the 1950s, full-backs played like sweepers and had to cover a swing of 50 yards. So Matthews, Finney and the rest had all the time in the world. Full-backs could even be slow. It's incredible to think of it now, but if you didn't have a lot of pace, they would stick you at full-back. That is probably the biggest change in modern football. The pace at the back.

I think Matthews in the modern era would have had to change his game. Wingers cannot simply stay wide these days because every coach has worked that one out. A player as important as Stan would be confronted with specific defensive tactics. He'd be marked. Not by the full-back, by an extra player. As soon as he got the ball, that player would have been on him. I saw it happen to Gareth Bale at Tottenham; when clubs see an individual is so important, they double up. That is why we had to move him inside or switch flanks. I'm sure it was happening to Stan by the end. He played with Stoke City until 1965, so I am certain by then he was not being allowed to carry the ball into space without pressure. He was 50, too, and I think they used to water the pitches quite heavily at the Victoria Ground to slow the game down for him. As a winger of the time, I might be biased, but I think that period in the sixties was the hardest for the wide men. The game was changing, with quicker full-backs, but you got little protection from the fiercest tackles. So Liverpool had Tommy Smith, who was fast, but was also allowed to kick you without the referee being greatly interested. I would have lost a lot of money to a friend of mine who said Smith only got sent off once in his career. I put it at eight or nine, but when we looked it up he was right: just the once. The tactics had changed, although they weren't particularly complicated. See that quick bastard with the ball – as he goes past, kick him. If they had thought of it sooner, maybe Stan wouldn't still have been turning out so late in life.

Yet, despite the limitations of defensive play in that era, the bottom line remains: if Stan came to your town, you would pay to see him play. Always. My team was Arsenal and I reckon Stanley Matthews in a Blackpool shirt used to put 10,000 on the gate at Highbury – he often drew the biggest crowd of the season. We're spoiled now. We see the best players every week, on television. In those days, to coin a phrase used by American sports writers – if you don't go, you don't know. It's one of those feelings of excitement that football has lost in the all-seater era. Now, you have your ticket, row P seat 47, and if you haven't booked it weeks in advance for a big match you'll be lucky to get one. Back then, you might play for the school team on Saturday morning and then you and a few lads would get together and decide which game to go to. You didn't need an advance ticket, there wasn't segregation. If Matthews was playing at Tottenham, or Tom Finney at Arsenal, that made your mind up.

I was too young to remember the 1953 FA Cup final – the Matthews final as it was called – but I think we had just got a television set in our flat. It had a tiny 9-inch screen with a magnifying glass hooked on with a couple of big army belt straps to make it into a 12-inch. We'd sit there looking at nothing most days, and there was about 30 minutes between each programme, but the FA Cup final was always the highlight. One match a year wasn't much to keep you entertained, though, so if you wanted to see Stan it had to be at the game, in the flesh.

And everyone wanted to see Stan. He was such a big star he even had his own brand of football boots – made by the Co-op in a factory in Heckmondwike, West Yorkshire. Very few players did endorsements in those days – one was Johnny Haynes, who was the frontman for Brylcreem – but to advertise kit was something unique. The Co-op made one million pairs of Stanley Matthews boots between 1948 and 1964. Sportswear wasn't really a commodity in the fifties. There were no replica shirts and when they did come out in the late sixties, it was only a plain shirt that you sewed a badge on, so Nottingham Forest, Liverpool and Manchester United all had one shirt and the difference was the club emblem, which came separately. Even the players bought their boots and shin pads from local sports shops – in West Ham's case it was A. E. Sedgwick's in Forest

Road, Walthamstow. The club had an account and the players used that. You had one pair of boots, which came with a packet of studs – maybe two pairs once rubber and moulded studs came in – and if you didn't like the boots the club provided you had to pay the difference. It didn't matter who you were. If Bobby Moore's boots amounted to a quid more than the allowance, it came out of his pocket. If you lost your boots, you had to buy a new pair, and no excuses. You couldn't just go in and say your kit had been stolen – you still got the cost deducted from your salary at the end of that week. And nobody swapped shirts. They'd have killed you. Your kit was your kit and you would try to hang on to it, tie-ups and all.

I don't think players now realise what it was like in those days. It didn't matter who you were – even Stanley Matthews would have had to pitch in and help with the skip containing the team's kit. When West Ham played away, we'd all dump our stuff in the skip and get on a minibus from Upton Park, driven to one of the big stations by Stan, the assistant manager. It was an old vehicle, not some long, luxurious air-conditioned coach, and often there would be two basket skips – one for boots, one for kit. Now, there is container after container full of gear wherever you go because every player travels with five pairs of boots. It's like moving an army – quite incredible. In those days all the players would be squeezed around the two skips in the bus, and whenever Stan stopped sharp the bloody things would fall on your head or your foot. At the station all the players helped with the skips, pushing them along the platform, and then you'd have to give a hand loading it on and off the train. Some clubs would leave the shifting to the reserves – particularly in the days before substitutes. You travelled with extra players in case of unforeseen injuries, meaning the directors had to pay any win bonus to everybody in the 13-man squad. They didn't like that, so for your two quid – the win bonus, which you might not get – you were given the job of carrying the skip. Even if Stanley Matthews was coming back from injury and wasn't in the team that day it would have been no different. In the days of maximum wages, nobody would have complained. That extra money would come in handy – even for a player who could put 10,000 on the gate.

TOM FINNEY
(PRESTON NORTH END)

Every era throws up its greats, from Lionel Messi and Cristiano Ronaldo to Tom Finney and Stanley Matthews. I'll lean on my old man here, and say Finney for me. Dad was Finney mad. If he was in town he went to see him play and I was lucky enough to see him at his peak playing centre-forward for Preston against Arsenal one night. What a player. I think it was his versatility that shades it over Stan. Matthews was a right-sided winger, and one of the best, but his left foot was weak and his heading ordinary – Finney could do the lot. He could play wide on either flank or through the middle. Tommy Docherty still says he's the best he's ever seen, and Bill Shankly said he would have been great, even playing in an overcoat. I know some who watched football in that era compare him to Messi, and that's good enough for me. These days players are defined by what they win – they have to be with a Champions League team, have to have a cupboard full of medals, yet Finney never won a single trophy with Preston and is still regarded as an all-time great. We set different standards for success then. He played in a team that couldn't win anything, but that never counted against him. He was still the best – and everybody acknowledged that. He was in the England team, he was revered – we seem to have lost touch with such qualities as a measure of success. Now it's all medals, medals, medals. Adam Lallana and Luke Shaw have a good year for Southampton and suddenly people are saying, 'When are they going to leave for a proper club?' – just as they used to about Matt Le Tissier. As if no club is proper unless it's up the top. Preston had one of the finest, most versatile, footballers in the world – but that couldn't happen today.

Finney learnt to play by dribbling around lamp-posts while doing his newspaper round. He used to go to Preston's ground as a schoolboy for coaching and free milk. His hero was Alex James, a Scottish inside-forward who spent four years with Preston before leaving for Arsenal. I think kids now try to imitate something they see Ronaldo or Messi do, but it was different for us because everything happened in real time. We didn't have TV and slow-motion replays; we couldn't watch every detail of a drag-back or a trick. You were there, Finney got the ball and he was away – you'd have to have great eyes and fantastic memory to see how he pulled it off. The exception was the FA Cup final, but even then you wouldn't imitate the players – just the teams. As soon as the game ended, all the kids would be out and we'd be pretending to be Manchester United, say, or Aston Villa. That day was the highlight of the year – but Finney only got to one FA Cup final, in 1954, and

Preston lost 3–2 to West Bromwich Albion. I was only seven so I can't really say I remember it, but I know that Finney didn't play well. He spent the night before the game receiving the award for Footballer of the Year in London before travelling back to Preston's base in Weybridge, so maybe that explains it. That ceremony is more sensibly held on the Thursday before the FA Cup final now – and these days if the winner is playing on the Sunday, his manager will make sure he collects his prize and goes home. Players were not protected the same way in those days. On the back of a week of interviews and photographic sessions – and no doubt a few hundred calls from old friends wanting tickets – the last thing Finney would have needed is a late night and more glad-handing. No wonder he played as if exhausted; being Preston's most famous son would have weighed heavily on him that week.

Finney was another that could add numbers to the gate, but when you were walking to the ground you had no idea where he was going to be playing, so there was always extra excitement. I think the most incredible thing about that time was that England lost to the United States in the 1950 World Cup. When you look at the players in the team that day: Finney, Stan Mortensen, Billy Wright, Jimmy Dickinson, Wilf Mannion … it is quite incredible. They left Matthews out, and he couldn't get on because there were no substitutes. Can you imagine the outcry about that result now? They would be saying that England should never pick those players again.

Yet Finney remained loved. What made him special? I think, basically, he had such elegance, such poise and grace – and his personality reflected the way he played the game. It wasn't just that he never got booked – nobody did in those days; you had to almost kill someone for the referee to take your name. What set Finney apart is that few can remember him even being spoken to by a referee. He was never in trouble, always the gentleman. Amazingly, he didn't even begin his professional career until he was 24 because the Second World War intervened, but the impact he made kept Preston as a First Division club through much of his career. They were relegated after he retired and have never played in the top division without him.

Even Matthews idolised Finney. In his autobiography he placed him beside four others: Pelé, Diego Maradona, George Best and Alfredo Di Stefano. In one game he played for England, the Portuguese captain Alvaro Cardaso walked off the field and demanded to be replaced because he was so tired of being given the runaround by Tom. England won 10–0. Not only could he play wide or up front, Finney also converted to the deep lying centre-forward position in some games, once England had seen the Hungarians playing it. He was voted Footballer of the Year for his performances there in 1957 – the first person to win the award twice. He scored 27 goals from that position in one season, and 26 the following year. And he was brave. Bill Shankly described him as a player that would go through a mountain; and for all the reports of his fanciness on the wing, his opponents say he tackled as hard as any defender. It says everything that the moment he retired, Preston began falling through the league, never to return. It would be no insult to call him a one-man team – and he would have been that at a lot of clubs bigger than Preston, too.

JOHN CHARLES
(LEEDS UNITED)

King John, they called him. I've got him ahead of Stan Mortensen in my team. Mortensen was a wonderful striker, still the only player to score a hat-trick in an FA Cup final, for Blackpool against Bolton Wanderers in 1953. Yet John's versatility sets him apart. He could play centre-forward, he could play centre-half. He was a hero in the English game, then he became a legend in Italy with Juventus. Mortensen was one of the great goalscorers in the English game – but Charles was that, and more. He may have been the best all-round footballer to have come out of Britain.

What people most remember about John is his strength in the air. He was a classic gentle giant – that was what they called him in Italy, '*Il Buon Gigante*' – a lovely man away from the football pitch, but a monster on it, fearless and strong, a real powerhouse. He was always the best in the penalty area, and at either end. There wasn't a better player in the team to defend a corner, and not a better player to attack one either. Yet he went to Italy, where the game was more technical and tactical, and fitted straight in; he had a very high level of skill for a player his size. He started off in defence at Leeds United, but they moved him to the front line in the 1952–3 season. They spotted there was more to his game than just heading and physicality. He had a lovely first touch that was wasted playing at the back in those days. So they changed him and he scored 26 goals in his first season as a striker. The next year he was the Football League's top scorer.

He was a prolific goalscorer for Leeds, but it was after seeing him play for Wales against Northern Ireland in 1957 that Umberto Agnelli, the president of Juventus, took him to Italy. Players didn't have agents in those days, but Kenneth Wolstenholme, the commentator for the 1966 World Cup, acted on John's behalf in the deal. He got a £10,000 signing-on fee – when the limit in England was £10. Italy felt like another world in those days, let alone another country. By then, Italian coaches had discovered *catenaccio* – man-for-man marking – and it was very hard to score over there. Yet John played 155 games for Juventus and scored 93 goals, an incredible achievement. The most amazing aspect of it is that he often spent half the game in defence. If John gave Juventus the lead, they would often then move him to centre-half to shore up the game. Manchester United would do that with Duncan Edwards, too, but in youth matches, not Serie A, arguably the strongest league in the world at the time. For this reason, John was considered by many the best player in the world. His transfer was a world record fee and, even recently, I saw he was still voted the best foreign player at Juventus – ahead of Michel Platini and Zinedine Zidane.

How good was he? Well, Nat Lofthouse said he was the best defender he played against, and Billy Wright said he was the best striker he ever faced. He managed to be incredibly delicate on the ball, and devastating in a shoulder charge a minute later. Jack Charlton called him a one-man team, the most effective player he ever saw. There were others from that era who might have been more skilful, but none who could do a job for the team like Charles. I know Jack also said John didn't close his eyes when he headed the ball. That usually happens automatically, but his stayed open. He was 6 ft 2 in anyway, but had such a leap that his chest was often resting on the shoulders of the defender when he scored.

And a gentleman? How about this? An Italian friend of mine says that John is alone in being as admired by supporters of Torino as Juventus. In his first Turin derby game, he bustled past a Torino defender but accidentally caught the player with a trailing arm and laid him out. No foul was given, but John saw what had happened and kicked the ball out of play for him to be treated, even though he was clean through on goal. The rival fans have never forgotten that gesture. My friend says that 20 years after John had left Italy they were still using one of his goals in the introduction of Italy's equivalent of *Match of the Day*.

Despite playing at centre-half John never got a booking throughout his career. It was a brutal game back then, particularly in Italy. John thought a lot of the tackling powder puff compared to England, but there were some real nasty sorts. He played with a little Argentinian forward called Omar Sívori, who was a great player, the nearest thing to Diego Maradona in those days, and in one game a centre-half did John with his elbow. So the next time the ball was loose, Sívori went over the top and broke the guy's leg. As he hit him, the other centre-half came in and snapped Sívori in two. So both players are on the floor, screaming, with King John in the middle of it, completely bemused. He could look after himself on the pitch – everyone had to in those days – but he was never dirty or gratuitous. Giampiero Boniperti was his other forward partner, and did a lot of his dirty work. If John got kicked he would turn to his team-mate. 'You do something to them – I can't,' he would say.

I think the one thing all of the players in my Fifties XI have in common is that they were also great fellas. Down to earth, all of them, and not flash, despite their incredible ability. I know the media coverage was different and the money, too, but they were connected with the people, they mixed with the fans – they weren't up the West End spending £300 on bottles of champagne. I can remember meeting John Charles at a party in, of all places, a block of flats in Canning Town. He was mates with Ken Brown and John Bond and had come up from the West Country with them – and there he was, the colossus of Italian football, one of the greatest players in the world, just having a beer at a house party in East London. My friend Frank McDonald reminded me of it the other day. Another time, I was down at Swansea City with Bournemouth for a youth game, and he was there. It was a miserable night, teeming down with rain, but he came over and had a cup of tea and a chat. Footballers belonged to the people then. Better, wasn't it?

THE FIFTIES: THE TEAM

BERT TRAUTMANN

Manchester City

ALF RAMSEY

Tottenham Hotspur

BILLY WRIGHT

Wolverhampton Wanderers

DUNCAN EDWARDS

Manchester United

ROGER BYRNE

Manchester United

DANNY BLANCHFLOWER

Tottenham Hotspur

BOBBY COLLINS

Everton

JOHNNY HAYNES

Fulham

STANLEY MATTHEWS

Blackpool

TOM FINNEY

Preston North End

JOHN CHARLES

Leeds United

CHAPTER TWO

THE SIXTIES

I was fortunate to spend the sixties working for one of the greatest football minds this country has ever produced: Ron Greenwood. It is no exaggeration to say that Ron changed the game in England, and his influence went right through it, from the day-to-day training at clubs to that magnificent afternoon in 1966 when England won the World Cup. I remember watching that game, and all of England's matches through that tournament in fact, and was able to pinpoint the moves and tactics that were straight from the Chadwell Heath training ground of my club, West Ham United. This is taking nothing away from Sir Alf Ramsey, but there were three West Ham players on the pitch that day in July, including the captain Bobby Moore, and it showed. West Ham fans like to boast, only half tongue-in-cheek, that their club won the World Cup – but in a way we did. The passes that Bobby played into Geoff Hurst, Martin Peters's near-post runs, the way the full-backs overlapped – those ideas came straight from West Ham's famous academy. People talk about master coaches in football and I'll be frank and say I haven't seen too many; but Ron was among the few. I signed for West Ham straight out of school when I was 15, and I knew right away it was a special club with different ideas because of Ron.

We had just left an era when the technical side of the game was almost disparaged by many managers. There were some great players, of course, but it was as if they were left alone to sort out their problems. Some managers had a terrible attitude. Don't give them the ball – they'll want it more on Saturday. They thought coaching was running a team around a cinder track or up and down the steps of the terraces, and no sooner had I joined West Ham when the apprentices were packed off to Lilleshall in Shropshire, which was the Football Association's national training centre. About 13 of us went from West Ham, plus hundreds of other good kids from clubs all around the country. I was put in a group run by Johnny Hart, who had been a top-quality inside-forward with Manchester City, and whose son Paul went on to be a very good footballer and manager, too. We would train and then have practice matches against the other groups. The first time we played, I got the ball from one of our midfield players and then motioned to him to come round me on the overlap. I did it with the full-backs as well. 'Come past me,' I said, 'and we'll go two on one against them.' Jack Mansell, who played as a defender for Brighton and Hove Albion, Cardiff City and Portsmouth, was in charge of this session. He blew the whistle and stopped it. 'What are you doing, son?' he asked. 'What are you doing there?'

I'd been at West Ham for five weeks, pre-season. I don't know where Ron had got it from, whether he came up with the idea himself or had seen an innovation abroad, but he had arrived back that summer, 1963, with a whole new approach to wide play. Before, when the winger had the ball, he was on his own and it was up to him to get past his man and cross. It was one versus one, you against him – and if the opponent was better or quicker than you, the move broke down. Ron didn't like those odds. We spent the entire month pre-season working on overlapping play; the midfield player coming round the winger, the full-back bolting upfield to receive the pass on the inside. The plan was to double up on the opposition's wide defender. As he went towards the winger, the ball would be played to the overlapping full-back or midfielder – he couldn't keep an eye on both of them, and his team-mates would not know what was about to happen so would not offer sufficient support. All of West Ham's wide players – John Sissons and Trevor Dawkins, too – were being schooled that way. But I didn't realise what we were doing was so different, until I went to Lilleshall. Alf Ramsey had come nearest to changing the full-back role at Ipswich Town, but Ron was taking wing play in a new and radical direction. Everything we were doing at West Ham was designed to create two versus one. That night at Lilleshall the coaches had a meeting. The following day, every one of their coaching sessions worked on overlapping wide play. It was if the penny had dropped – they had seen the future. That was Ron Greenwood's doing.

Danny Blanchflower invented the wall at free-kicks, Dick Fosbury invented the Fosbury Flop that revolutionised the high-jump technique by flipping over backwards, and Ron Greenwood laid the ground for the wonderful overlapping full-backs we see today. He changed the game, committed defenders in ways others had not imagined. He was always thinking, always one step ahead. The way England got Hurst and Peters to get across defenders at the near post – I would credit Ron for that. The goals that England scored in 1966 were no accident. I used to watch Ron work for hours with the pair of them – when to pull away, how to time the return run. The old way was to wait behind the defender and try to out-jump him. It was Ron who wanted them getting across the face of the marker into that near-post area. And then you see Bobby Moore put the ball down, Hurst come across and – bam. Maybe Ron was too easy with the lads and that was why West Ham did not experience the success they deserved in that time – but he was always forward thinking, a true football brain and a fantastic coach.

I don't want to be disrespectful to modern coaches – after all, I've been one – but having worked with Greenwood and seen how clever he was and how much impact his ideas had, I get a bit sceptical when I hear that this one or that one is so great. I have thought that way ever since I left West Ham – after my very first move as a player, down to Bournemouth with John Bond. John had a fantastic reputation as a coach at the height of his career, but anyone from West Ham who saw him work first-hand would have known straight away that most of what he did was taken from Ron. Every ex-West Ham player was influenced by him, including me. Ron was a visionary. In that era, much of the coaching was ordinary. Clubs all did the same stuff, with a sprinkling of the manager's personality on top. It is a bit like that now. One coach plays 4–2–3–1, then the whole world plays 4–2–3–1. Ron wasn't like that. These were original ideas, innovative and insightful. A lot of what Ron did stands up today: how to make a yard, the areas to target with the ball, the movement in the box. John Bond took Ron's ideas, but added a bit of discipline. You couldn't get away with stuff under John as you could with Ron. But the rest of it, the technical side, the nuts and bolts – nothing changed. I'm not ashamed to admit that I still use lessons from Ron Greenwood today.

Alf Ramsey made the bold decision to pick Geoff Hurst for the World Cup final ahead of Jimmy Greaves, but it was Ron Greenwood who turned Geoff from an average midfield player into a fantastic striker. Ron taught him his movement, so that as soon as Bobby Moore put the ball down his first thought was, 'Where's Geoff? Is he switched on? Is he ready?' We all know what used to happen next. The same with Martin Peters. He was famously described as being 10 years ahead of his time, but it was Ron, as much as Martin, who was a decade in front.

Looking ahead for a moment, one of the sensations of English football in the seventies was Ted MacDougall at Bournemouth, who ended up signing for Manchester United. He still holds the record for individual scoring in the FA Cup – nine goals in a tie for Bournemouth against Margate in 1971 – and in season 1970–71 he had 16 league goals by October. The goal that might have clinched his move to the top division was a spectacular diving header away to Aston Villa. They were a Third Division team at the time, but there were still 48,000 at Villa Park and the game was shown on *Match of the Day*. Everyone was talking about it, but it was a textbook Ron Greenwood/West Ham goal from years earlier. MacDougall played the ball out to Tony Scott and then got across his defender for a magnificent diving header from Scott's right-sided cross. I immediately knew where I had seen that move before. In fact, when I went down to play for

Bournemouth in 1972, it was like stepping back in time. John Bond would be there with Ted, 'Pull away, pull away, pull away, take them away with you. You are pulling away and now they are backing off you. Now you can get in front of them.' I thought Ron Greenwood had followed me down. John was like his echo.

Football was much more open in the sixties; and less predictable. I can remember when I was still an apprentice professional West Ham had back-to-back matches against Blackburn Rovers. They played at home on 26 December 1963 and away at Ewood Park two days later, 28 December. The Boxing Day game ended West Ham 2, Blackburn 8; two days on, the score was Blackburn 1, West Ham 3. Work that out. The only change Ron made between the games was that he brought Eddie Bovington in for Martin Peters and used him as a man marker. That was unheard of, too, in those times. The Italians had invented *catenaccio*, but nobody in English football used it.

People remember the sixties as an era of brutality in football, but it never felt that way playing in it. We knew no different. A player brought up in today's game would be appalled, but that was just how the game was played as far as we were concerned. Looking back, the sheer physicality of it does surprise me now, particularly when you consider the consequences of injury. A broken leg could end a career, yet people still took that risk every week, flying into tackles or in some cases trying to inflict serious harm. It is amazing there weren't more bad injuries, really – not least because the physiotherapists were usually unqualified ex-players. A bloke would come out, put a sponge on your leg and that was the extent of his knowledge done. No one complained. We didn't know any different, we just got on with it. There were no agents to stir up a fuss. Contract negotiation was non-existent. The manager called you into his office and gave you another £2 a week and you went home delighted. Nobody asked for a fiver, and it didn't matter who you were – at West Ham, even Bobby Moore got the same cold treatment as the rest of the team. You made your appointment to see the manager at the end of the season and were usually in and out in two minutes. It wasn't a negotiation as such. These days a player sits down to discuss his contract with the club and three months later they're still talking. Back then the deal got signed that minute, or forget it. You could count on the fingers of one hand the players who acted up. When a teenage Graeme Souness asked to leave Tottenham Hotspur, and told Bill Nicholson he was the best player at the club, it caused a real stir. Players just didn't talk like that to the manager in those days.

The game was harder then, but it certainly wasn't faster. There was more space about, too, with players dropping off. Now pressing has come into the game and everybody is on you at 100 mph. The balls are lighter, the boots are lighter, there is more speed in football; players run faster, jump higher. You see the difference in what players could get away with back then, though. Games would finish 10–10 on penalties these days, looking at some of the things the referees let go. I was watching the 1970 FA Cup final replay the other day between Chelsea and Leeds United, and how that was still 11-a-side by the end I'll never know. There is one moment when Peter Osgood comes in from behind on Jack Charlton, and Jack just turns around and kicks him as hard as he can. Nothing sly, no pretence – and not even a booking for either of them. There is another incident when Eddie McCreadie catches Billy Bremner in the throat – no exaggeration – with a tackle and the referee waves play on. It wasn't just the Leeds team that knew how to look after itself.

It was Bobby Collins that instilled that attitude in them – if somebody is going to get hurt it won't be us – and then Bremner and Johnny Giles carried it forward. Not every team had a nasty streak, but most had one or two players who could put it about, and no matter how high you went in, Leeds would always go higher. Even so, my favourite team from that era? Leeds, without a doubt. I think that hard edge has led to them being underestimated. Take that away and, as footballers, they were a perfect balance; from the full-backs, Paul Reaney and Terry Cooper, through the centre-halves, Jack Charlton and Norman Hunter, to the midfield with Giles and Bremner who were rock solid. Then there was Peter Lorimer with his rocket shot, Eddie Gray, a genius on the wing, and Mick Jones working non-stop for Alan Clarke up front. That team just had a lovely feel. And, yes, they were tough. I imagine they had to be – you wouldn't have survived training with that lot if you couldn't look after yourself. But once on the pitch they were as one, I've never seen a team so unified. Hurt one, and you had to deal with the whole mob.

Yet anyone who thinks they were one-dimensional, all aggression without the technique to match, didn't see them play. There is a famous game against Southampton that they won 7–0, and some of the football that day was quite magnificent. Little flicks, wonderful crossfield passes, glorious goals. And that was a useful Southampton side – Jimmy Gabriel, Denis Hollywood, John McGrath, Ron Davies; they had some hard men who wouldn't have taken kindly to being made to look like fools.

Denis Hollywood was a Scottish full-back and a real handful. I remember Jimmy Gabriel telling me he had a fancy-dress party around his house one Sunday afternoon and Denis came dressed as a schoolboy. He had a drink then for some reason decided he wanted to cycle to his home about seven miles away with his little school uniform and cap on. Halfway there some bloke cut him up. Denis pedalled like a maniac, caught him at the lights and dragged him out of his car into the street. Unbelievable. The bloke must have thought they had some tough schools in Southampton.

Yet that was the culture of football at the time. There were good players and good teams but also a pub mentality that didn't really leave English football until the influx of the foreign players. From the great Liverpool team to the World Cup-winning England team and the King's Road lot at Chelsea, just about every club liked a night out. Most of the teams were made up of local boys and they all got on great. At West Ham we mucked in together and roughed it when we had to. I remember the terrible winter in 1963, clearing the snow off the forecourt at Upton Park with the rest of the players so we could train. Job done, we would play on it for two hours in silly little plimsolls, sliding everywhere. These days, the medical staff would have conniptions about the damage you could do to your calf muscles – but nobody knew, or cared, about that side of the game then. Even Bobby Moore trained on the forecourt at Upton Park. I remember as a junior we had to wait for the main group to finish, sitting inside looking through the steamed-up windows because all the training pitches were under snow. It was a terrible winter; our first team played one game – away at Sheffield United – between December 29 and March 2. It was either the forecourt or up and down the steps in the stand just to keep our fitness up – until Ron found a little gymnasium in Harlow in Essex.

We drove out there, which seemed like miles, in the worst winter ever, snow all over, and we were slipping and falling over because the gym only had a little wooden floor. We'd play four-a-side – there was no room for anything else – then do some ball skills until it was time to let the next lot on. Eventually we found a place in Forest Gate that took eight-a-side – and we all thought that was luxury compared to the slog out to Harlow. These days, if a training pitch isn't like Wembley, the players complain. Modern players moan about everything. They'll walk into a room with £200,000 of equipment and find some fault to pick at – no bananas in the fruit bowl or the temperature isn't right. We used to spend a month running through forests, dodging cars on the Epping New Road. That was our pre-season. Get back on the coach with everybody cramping up. Nobody had heard of stretching exercises. We didn't even warm up. The first time we saw the pitch was when the bell went to signal two minutes before kick-off. We might take the odd shot against the goalkeeper if we were feeling adventurous. There was no such thing as a warm-up. We thought a warm-up was standing by the radiator in the dressing-room on a cold day.

That doesn't mean there weren't some wonderful players about in that time, though. Here's 11 of them.

GORDON BANKS
(LEICESTER CITY)

I know there has been a lot of revisionism of late about That Save. But for my money, it's still one of the most amazing things I have seen on a football field, and it sets Gordon Banks apart from his contemporaries. There were some great goalkeepers from that era – Peter Bonetti, Pat Jennings, the young Peter Shilton, who played his first game for Leicester City as Gordon's understudy in 1966 – but even without winning the World Cup for England, I'd say Gordon was the man. And That Save, from Pelé at the 1970 World Cup? Even now, I don't know how he does it.

Brazil versus England, 7 June 1970, Guadalajara. Carlos Alberto breaks down the right and feeds the ball to Jairzinho, who skins Terry Cooper, gets to the byline and crosses. Pelé jumps higher than anybody from about 10 yards out and heads the ball downwards into the bottom-left corner. Somehow, Banks scrambles across and, with his right hand, scoops the ball up and over the bar, even though it appears to be behind him. 'The save of the World Cup,' David Coleman calls it, immediately. I watched it again, recently, and none of the England players even make a fuss, though. And that is what is special about Gordon. That type of brilliance was almost expected of him. Pelé, I'm told, actually shouted, 'Goal!' Banks says that the only comment was from Bobby Moore, who told him he must be getting old. 'You used to hang on to those, Gordon,' he said.

The greatest save of all time, as some have called it. Who can say for certain? Double saves always look the most spectacular. Jim Montgomery for Sunderland against Leeds United in the

1973 FA Cup final, or Jerzy Dudek for Liverpool against AC Milan in that epic 2005 Champions League win. Colombian goalkeeper René Higuita's scorpion kick from a shot by my son Jamie against England at Wembley must take the prize for sheer panache, but what Gordon does stands out because it is so matter-of-fact, yet so remarkable. He tracks the ball all the way over from right to left, so is just in the perfect place when Pelé makes his header. The ball bounces in front of him, making it awkward, but Banks adjusts and uses the upward momentum to push it even higher to safety. Everything happens in a split second, and looks so instinctive, but there is incredible wisdom there, the sight of a man who has worked so hard to master his craft making the exceptional look easy. I've seen Peter Schmeichel make great saves with his star jumps learnt in handball games in Denmark, but there the ball strikes his arm. Gordon's save is no accident. He is completely aware of where he must be and what he must do, from beginning to end. Maybe other factors have helped it live in the memory, too: it was a wonderful game, in a brilliant World Cup against the best team, and player, there has ever been. It was the first World Cup in colour, too, and we were all watching. Yet even discounting this, there is one unarguable fact: Pelé wrote in his autobiography that it was the best save anyone had made from him. And he would know.

Gordon came from a generation that didn't have the support system of modern footballers. He was a coalman's mate and a bricklayer before being spotted by Chesterfield – and was once let go by an amateur club after letting in 15 goals in one game. He could only turn professional after doing two years' national service with the Royal Signals Regiment. Yet he stood out from the start and only had one full season at Chesterfield before Leicester City signed him for £7,000. One game in particular stands out, the 1963 FA Cup semi-final: Leicester City 1, Liverpool 0. I think the official figures are that Liverpool had 34 shots at goal to Leicester's one. Gordon says it was the best performance of his career. He made his debut for England that same year. He lost his first game against Scotland and I know he thought his second would be his last, because Sir Alf Ramsey gave him such a bollocking for conceding a 30-yard free-kick from Pelé. By the time 1966 came around he was the best in the world. Gordon didn't let in a goal from open play in that tournament until the final. Before that, he had only been beaten from the penalty spot, by Eusébio.

What happened after 1966 seems incredible, even by the crazy standards of football clubs. Within eight months of winning the World Cup, Leicester put Gordon on the transfer list. They had this young kid called Shilton and they fancied him more. These were the days when teams couldn't just use the loan system as they do now. If that situation occurred these days, Shilton would merely be loaned out to get experience. Back then, Leicester had a decision to make. They had arguably the best two English goalkeepers of all time – and they went with youth.

Ron Greenwood at my club, West Ham United, was in the market for a goalkeeper that year, too. He paid £65,000 for a lad called Bobby Ferguson from Kilmarnock when he could have got Banks for less. Ferguson became the world's most expensive goalkeeper at the time. Gordon went to Stoke City for £50,000. I'm told Ron didn't fancy his wages, which were £50 a week higher than Bobby's – but it seems a strange decision looking back. Bobby was a good young goalkeeper but he was no Gordon Banks. And he can't have been much bigger than 5 ft 10 in. Gordon went on to make more fantastic saves for Stoke – and he cost me a Wembley appearance in the 1972 League Cup final.

There were no penalty shoot-outs to decide cup ties in those days – we played until we dropped, replay after replay, and our tie with Stoke lasted four matches and a total of seven hours. We were hot favourites to go through. Tony Waddington had built a good Stoke team, but a lot of the players were experienced – a nice football term that is a polite way of saying old – and we won the first leg at their place 2–1. Bobby Moore was magnificent that night and Geoff Hurst scored our first goal from the penalty spot. Geoff only had one penalty style. Blast it towards the top corner out of the goalkeeper's reach. Gordon got his fingers to it, but could not keep it out. I made our second goal for Clyde Best from the left wing. We were halfway to Wembley. The second leg was played on 15 December 1971, and Stoke scored late in the second half to level the tie on aggregate. For the last minutes of the game we were all over them. I was getting round their full-back Mike Pejic and, sensing danger, Gordon came out and bundled me over. Penalty. Up stepped Geoff again. If he scored we would be 3–2 up with seconds remaining and on our way to Wembley. I don't think the penalty was as good as his first, but it would still have beaten 99 per cent of goalkeepers. Not Gordon. It wasn't quite where the last one had gone, but he adjusted in mid-air and got both hands to it. We couldn't believe it. Gordon told me that was the best penalty save of his career – it turns out that our £50 a week wasn't such a saving after all.

As a winger, your first priority was always to keep the ball away from Gordon. He was very athletic, very determined. He had a strong mind and he made it up early, so anything in his radius he could come and collect. That was always Ron Greenwood's instruction to me: corners, crosses, keep it away from Banks. He was brave too, quick off his line and not scared about getting hurt. Goalkeepers had more protection then than in the fifties, but it was still a physically hard job. Against Leeds United, Jack Charlton would stand on the goalkeeper and obstruct him – like Sam Allardyce's teams do now. Leeds were probably the first to have a plan like that.

So after Banks saved Geoff's penalty, we played extra time, then a 0–0 replay with extra time at Hillsborough. We had to toss a coin to decide the next venue. We wanted a game in London – so our fans didn't have to travel north again – Stoke were proposing Old Trafford. Ron Greenwood called, and lost. When we got out we discovered some nutcase had poured sand into the petrol tank of the team bus and we had to wait for another one to arrive and take us back to London. Ron wasn't best pleased, to say the least. We finally lost the fourth game 3–2 – and everyone remembers that match for Bobby Moore going in goal when Bobby Ferguson went off the field for treatment for about 20 minutes. He saved a penalty in that time, too – but couldn't do anything about Mike Bernard following up for the rebound.

It was only a few months later that Gordon had the car crash that cost the sight in one eye and forced his retirement from the game in England. That was such a terrible shame. He did play on for Fort Lauderdale Strikers in America, but I don't think he enjoyed it. He thought it was too much like showbusiness – Gordon is very down to earth. In one game, he and a few other players had to carry a coffin into the middle of the pitch. Out jumped their manager, dressed as Dracula. 'Tonight, The Strikers are coming back from the dead!' roared the stadium announcer. Gordon said they had only lost two games.

Recalling Gordon's performances over those League Cup ties, though, it seems astonishing that Leicester ever let him go. Certainly, there was never any doubt about him for England, and no doubt about his place in history either. He was the best there has been – even if he did stop me playing in a Wembley final.

PAUL REANEY
(LEEDS UNITED)

There can be no greater praise for Paul Reaney than George Best saying he regarded him as his most difficult opponent. George fancied himself against anybody, but Reaney had a way of putting the shackles on unlike any other full-back of the time. For a start, he was lightning fast. And as George put it, he liked to get stuck in. They all did at Leeds. Reaney was a London boy, but he fitted in with that team perfectly. He was a good technical footballer, an excellent athlete and could put it about. I know George rated him, and Manuel Sanchís at Real Madrid, very highly. They were similar players – quick, physical, uncompromising defenders. I think if you'd asked 99 per cent of the wingers from those days, they would have named Paul Reaney as their least favourite opponent. There was no messing with him. You were going to get a kicking all game, and you knew it.

George Cohen was the right-back for England at the 1966 World Cup, but Reaney came into his own in the late sixties. It shows the talent around at the time that he only played three games for England, but he also had terrible luck. Leeds were fighting for the treble in the 1969–70 season when Paul broke his leg in a match at West Ham. It was 2 April 1970. Leeds were halfway through a European Cup semi-final with Celtic, had beaten Manchester United to reach the FA Cup final and were trying to chase down Everton for the title. They were nine points adrift going into the match with West Ham, but had two games in hand. A young kid we had got from Walthamstow Avenue, Keith Miller, was making his full debut for us. He had come on a couple of times as a substitute, but had not started a game. Reaney was 25 and at the peak of his career, a certainty to be on the plane to Mexico with England. And then it was all gone. There was no malice in the challenge, it was a simple collision, but it broke Reaney's leg and he didn't play again until next season. One minute it was all there in front of him; the next, nothing. I felt almost as sorry for Keith really. He was just starting out and it was a completely fair challenge. We knew that it was no foul by the reaction of the Leeds players. Had Keith taken a liberty, let's just say we would all have known it. There would have been murders – I don't know a team that was more protective of one another than Don Revie's Leeds. Anything in it and they would have all been after Keith, and the rest of us. But it was an accident, and they knew that. It probably affected them, though, because they drew that match 2–2 and their season faded away. Everton won the league, Celtic knocked them out of the European Cup and Chelsea won the

FA Cup. Keith Miller never played for West Ham after that day. He was sold to John Bond at Bournemouth for £10,000, did very well and went on to captain the club. And Keith Newton played right-back for England in the 1970 World Cup finals.

So it feels a little bold, leaving out a man who won the World Cup, George Cohen, and Keith Newton who kept Reaney out of the England team for much of his career – but Reaney, for me, was the pick of them all. He was such a fantastic player, hard as nails and very aggressive. Joe Jordan has told me stories about the way he would target Best when Leeds played Manchester United. He would always get very tight, right up his arse, kicking him, kicking him, all game. That was how Reaney marked, never more than a yard away, a real hard nut. He was a very good tackler too, very clean in the way he took the ball. César Azpilicueta at Chelsea reminds me of him in that way. He is very difficult to play against, too – even though he is used on his opposite side. I was a winger, so full-backs were the enemy, but I could always appreciate the art of the best ones, the guys that were all over you like a rash. I never saw Reaney get a chasing, either. If George Best couldn't outwit him there weren't too many others who could have.

It would be very easy for me to just pick England's World Cup-winning team for my Sixties XI, but I always felt Reaney had the edge on Cohen. George was a different player. Attacking, quick, you wouldn't have seen anyone run him, but Reaney was better technically and the best on the ball.

Defensively, too, he played almost as a man-for-man marker. Against Best, he would be leathering him, whacking him with every tackle. George got treatment like that all the time. He could ride a tackle like no player I have ever seen. Exceptional.

Yet Reaney found a way of stopping George that eluded other players. His physical approach, obviously, was important – but his timing and positioning were faultless, too. I was quite lucky, really, because wingers in those days didn't tend to change sides, so I was up against Terry Cooper when we played Leeds, who could not have been more different to Reaney. What made Leeds special was that they were both great attacking players who would bomb forward at every opportunity. But Terry was probably the nicest bloke in the team. A great competitor, but fair.

BOBBY MOORE
(WEST HAM UNITED)

I'm going to start moaning again about the way Bobby was treated after he retired if I'm not careful, so I'll start with one of my favourite stories about him. We had been up in the West End, Bobby and I, with a few mates including Bill Larkin, who had made millions out of roasted peanuts. We were on our way back to the Baker's Arms in Stratford, one of our regular boozing haunts owned by Alan Wheeler, a former welterweight boxer who fought out of West Ham. Bill was at the wheel and well oiled. He had been on it since early afternoon. Terry Creasey, another of our pals, was in the back, and he noticed we were being followed by a police car. He told Bill he needed to be careful. 'Don't worry,' said Bill, full of bravado, 'I'll lose them down the back doubles, I'll shake them off.' He promptly turned sharp left into a dead end, and the police were now blocking us off.

Drink driving wasn't the offence it is now, but with the state of Bill we knew we were in trouble. 'Good evening, sir,' said the officer. 'And where are you off to?' Whatever Bill said in reply obviously didn't make much sense because the copper then started saying that Bill appeared to have had too much to drink, and it was all getting pretty serious. Bobby was in the back, keeping his head down, as the policeman asked Bill to step out of the car. 'Get out, Bob, let them see you,' we were pleading. Bobby did as we asked. Suddenly the mood changed – from 'You're nicked' to 'Hello, Bobby, how are you doing?' and 'Bloody hell, Bob, can I have an autograph?' These days it would have been a selfie on a mobile phone, of course. Bobby duly obliged and now we were all good pals. 'We going to win on Saturday, Bob?' said one of the policemen. 'Who else have you got in there?' He took a look in the car and we were all packed like sardines. There must have been about seven of us. 'Look, fellas,' he said, 'two of you are going to have to get out. You might get stopped again and you're overloaded.' So Terry Creasey, our team-mate Brian Dear and another of our friends, Frankie Macdonald, said they would walk the remaining distance. They set off, but the police must have had a change of heart because a minute later the same squad car pulled up again. 'Where are you going, lads?' the police driver said. When they said the Baker's Arms the coppers said they would drop them off. They did – and ended up staying with us in there until about three in the morning. They were knocking them back and dancing with the girls behind the bar. They had a great time. That is the effect Bobby could have on people. They just wanted to be around him.

Another time the chief of police took us on a pub crawl. He was the top man in the area, including Upton Park. I don't quite recall how it happened but we ended up in his company after one match, and went on a big night out around Bethnal Green. He was driving, too, and by the time we left the last place he really wasn't in a fit state. I think he forgot that red lights meant stop. We were in the car hanging on for grim death. It's got to be about the only time I was actually hoping to get stopped by the police.

But Bobby Moore the footballer? After devoting a chapter to him in my last book, I don't really know what else I can say about Bobby. Perhaps that I don't think he is given enough credit for the way he changed the position of centre-half in this country. Franz Beckenbauer is acclaimed for inventing the sweeper role, but I don't think any English central defender played the ball out of the back in quite the same way until Bobby came along. Centre-halves were all about heading it and kicking it clear. And then Bobby showed there was so much more to the role. He was the antithesis of the English centre-half really. Is he quick? No. Can he head it? No, he's not very strong in the air. No wonder West Ham nearly said no thanks. Yet Malcolm Allison saw something special in Bobby as a youth player and made sure the club kept him on.

I met Matthias Sammer, the great German sweeper-midfielder, a while ago and we were talking about the way the Germans changed their own defensive roles by switching to three at the back. They put their best passer, Beckenbauer, into defence from midfield, and he would break from there, where no one could pick him up. It was an incredibly original tactic. And they have used it many times since. Lothar Matthäus made the switch, so did Sammer – they were both great midfield players who went deeper into the sweeper role. And Bobby could certainly have operated as a sweeper had any team in England been interested in playing that way. With his reading of the game he would have been perfect with two quicker central defenders ahead, but once again English football missed a trick. Here was a player who was always in the right position at the right time, an incredible football brain and brilliant passer, who was sharper than anybody else but lacked pace. It would be wrong to say we didn't make the most of him – we won the World Cup – but Bobby's presence did not change English football the way Beckenbauer altered the culture in Germany.

Bobby's understanding of the game was incredible. I always come back to that passage of play against Jairzinho of Brazil at the 1970 World Cup. He was running everyone ragged, yet Bob just took him down a blind alley and then claimed the ball. He held him up, didn't dive in, just pushed him into an area that was safe. That was Bobby's great gift; because he was slow you would think you could run him, but the next thing you knew you'd be heading away from goal into a dead end. I'm not saying everybody could have played like Bobby Moore, but English football missed an opportunity in not getting players to at least think like him. He wasn't the greatest athlete, but the way he compensated for that was what mattered. There should always be a place in football for a man who can make the game look simple, and that was Bobby's great attribute. Rather than playing someone who is quick yet always ends up making a last-ditch lunge, sliding or blocking, why not have someone who has read the situation as it develops, and is there waiting for the centre-forward without any great drama?

A forward marked by Bobby might jump and flick it on, but he would drop and be there to let the ball fall and catch it on his chest. Other centre-halves would be nutting the forward in the back of the head, but Bobby almost used to let him have it, let him think he'd won it in the air and then step back, scoop it up, and go off and play. At throw-ins, he would step in front of his man. The opposition would be taking a throw into the box, and generally defenders would mark their opponent from behind. The striker would back in, almost trapping the defender in his place, and then the ball would come in and they would hold it, almost at the six-yard box. So Bobby started stepping in front. When he did that, the striker would think he had to reclaim his territory, so would step in front of Bob; and then Bobby would do it again. And this would carry on until the striker was 10 yards farther away from our goal. Nearly 50 years later, I am still telling my centre-halves to do that. Only the other day, with Clint Hill at Queens Park Rangers, we went through how to avoid getting pinned by the centre-forward – and it boiled down to the trick Bobby used with West Ham in the sixties. A tactic nobody had taught him, which he had worked out using nothing more than his nose for the game.

I sometimes wonder whether Bobby would have come through the ranks in modern football. Not strong enough, not quick enough – athletic prowess counts for so much these days. But then I think of his determination, his intelligence and strength of character, and I feel he would surely have forced his way through. I can't imagine that there wouldn't have been one coach – like Allison at West Ham – who could see how special he was, one that looked at what he could do, and saw that it more than compensated for his deficiencies. I think progress purely depends who is coaching the kids. As a manager you hope that you have youth team coaches capable of recognising the all-round talent of a young player. But a kid must still have that work ethic. That is what is often forgotten about Bobby; how hard he worked at his game, how much he listened to advice, how much he studied. Some people you can tell a hundred times, a thousand times, and it doesn't go in, but Bobby had a real brain for football. Tell him once and he had it. He must have been a dream to coach.

He wanted to learn, too, wanted to move his game on. Malcolm Allison helped devise what we now know as Bobby's style of play: knowing when to collect the ball off the goalkeeper, how to clip it to a forward or into a forward channel. Bobby absorbed that information, put it to work and then it was just wasted by the English game. We didn't seem to want intelligence on the football field at that time; we didn't want to think too hard about our play. Basically, we weren't as open-minded as the Germans and have been playing catch-up ever since. It was 30 years after the 1966 World Cup, with Terry Venables and then Glenn Hoddle, that we started thinking differently about the way the England team played. All those years, wasted.

JACK CHARLTON
(LEEDS UNITED)

There are plenty of contenders for the other centre-half in this team. Liverpool had Ron Yeats, a big Scotsman they got from Dundee United. When he signed, Bill Shankly told the journalists to go into the dressing-room and walk around him, to see how big he was. He'd just come out of the shower, and stood there stark naked with all those sports writers peering at him. But what a good player. He was club captain within six months of signing and led Liverpool throughout that era as they won promotion and became one of England's strongest teams. Shankly used to say that as long as they had Yeats they could play Arthur Askey in goal. Liverpool changed their strip to all red under Shankly because he thought a block of one colour looked more imposing – and which player did he get to model the new strip? Yeats, of course.

I've heard he was also the only player to beat Shankly in a penalty shoot-out. Bill used to challenge one of the first-team players every Friday, and one week it was Yeats's turn. He had never taken a penalty and Shankly was apparently a master at it – he hadn't lost all season. The goalkeeper was Tommy Lawrence, who Shankly was always having a go at for being overweight. Shankly's first two went flying in, but Lawrence saved his third. 'I got lucky there, boss,' he said. 'Yes, you did, you fat twat,' said Shankly, with all the players crying with laughter. The story goes that Big Ron then scored his first two with his eyes shut, but hit an absolute cracker into the top corner with his last to win the day and cost Shankly a tenner. Bill went straight over to poor Tommy Lawrence, while the goalkeeper was still prone on the floor. 'If it had been a fucking meat pie you'd have caught it,' he spat.

Frank McLintock at Arsenal was another fine centre-half. Arsenal were a hard team – Ron 'Chopper' Harris used to call Peter Storey the bastards' bastard – but Frank was a touch of class. He was another, like Bobby Moore, who nearly didn't get his chance. Frank's manager at his first club, Leicester City, didn't fancy him at all, but one day they had so many injuries there was no option but to put him in the team. The last person he wanted to pick was Frank, apparently, but he was never off the team sheet after that. Leicester had a good side in those days and Frank had an excellent half-back pairing alongside either Colin Appleton or Ian King. He went on to Arsenal and captained the double-winning team. But Frank was a very different kind of centre-half to Jack Charlton and many others from that time. I think all they had in common was the attitude of their teams. Leeds and Arsenal were quite similar in their aggressive approach. If one of their number got kicked, they were straight in, both of them. They'd all come over, all start poking at you. Other teams were intimidated by them.

Jack wasn't the best footballer but, by God, he was effective. I first saw him play when I was very young, about 15, for Leeds against Tottenham Hotspur. Frankly, I couldn't believe he was Bobby's brother. There was Bobby, one of the most graceful footballers who ever lived, poetry in motion just the way he moved – drop a shoulder, glide the other way, hit a 35-yarder into the top corner, all on the run. And there was Jack, who couldn't trap a bag of cement. I remember thinking, 'My God, how bad is he?' Yet he could head it, he could tackle, he could organise; he was perfect for Bobby Moore at England level really. Jack would attack the headers, Bobby would drop off. They were good cop and bad cop. Jack the aggressive, hard one who would do anything to win; Bobby his cool companion. I was too young to understand it that day, but Jack was just a really good, old-fashioned centre-half. He knew the game as well as Bobby; he just couldn't play it like him.

I found that out much later on doing my coaching badges at Lilleshall. Jack would be there, too, and half the day would be taken up with him rowing with the coaches over what we had been told. He was usually right as well. Just as Bob's understanding of the game overcame his lack of pace, so Jack's reading of it made up for his lack of technical ability. Jack wouldn't be exposed for lack of pace, but he could be caught out other ways, so he got himself into the right positions and focused on his strengths. He was great in the air, great at barking orders and getting that Leeds team set up, and he took that into his management style. His Republic of Ireland team hardly played the Leeds way, but they were very powerful, well drilled and difficult to beat.

That was Jack. He was one of the first central defenders to score goals from set plays – 9 in 34 league matches in 1961–2 and 7 the season before – and defensively he always made sure there was a screen in front of the back four. He got people at it, got them tackling and working. That is how I remember him, shaking his fist at people in his own team, bullying them into grafting harder. He wasn't the captain, but he was very much in the mould of Tony Adams or John Terry. Barking his instructions, always a leader even without an armband.

You used to hear him from all over the field. He was a big, blunt bugger, who didn't give a shit. He wouldn't mess about, he was always to the point – and he was no different on those coaching courses. There is one I particularly remember. Everything was wrong. That's wrong. This is wrong. You're wrong. He's wrong. You don't mark like that. If you want to play like that, then you can't do this. He just took over. A lot of the coaches were glorified schoolteachers and Jack would just overpower them. He was too much for all of us, really. He knew his stuff and he was a big bloke; in the end, they didn't argue with him.

The one time I did see someone get the better of Jack was on 21 November 1964 – West Ham 3, Leeds United 1. Johnny Byrne destroyed him that night in a way I never saw, say Paul Reaney, get completely outclassed by his winger. Budgie was only 5 ft 8 in, but he weighed over 11 stone and could look after himself. Jim Stannard, our goalkeeper, was pumping balls upfield and Budgie was backing into Jack, battering him and catching them on his chest. Sometimes he would volley one out to Peter Brabook and then turn and run for the return. Johnny was a fantastic player and the way he held Jack off, and his movement, was masterful. Leeds lost the league title on goal average that season, but West Ham absolutely ripped them to pieces. It could have been six. And no one would have envisaged that the centre-half who was left so exposed would be winning a World Cup medal with England two years later.

That is the other incredible element of Jack's career – how late he came to international football and what he then achieved. He had made over 300 appearances before he got his first England call-up, and two Leeds managers had already come close to selling him, including Don Revie. It is testament to his perseverance that he achieved so much in the game. That 15-year-old in the crowd at White Hart Lane in 1962 got it wrong. No, Jack Charlton wasn't at all like Bobby Charlton. But he was never trying to be.

RAY WILSON
(HUDDERSFIELD TOWN)

If Paul Reaney was George Best's most troublesome opponent, Denis Law used to say that Ray Wilson was the most difficult defender he had ever faced – and that was just in practice sessions at Huddersfield Town. It seems faint praise to call Ray a great left-back – but that is what he was. Uncomplicated, efficient, he would be 7/10, minimum, every game – the way Ashley Cole is now. He was quick as lightning, maybe not the greatest on the ball by modern standards, but his crosses were accurate and he loved to get on the overlap.

I think it says most for Ray's consistency that the mistake he made in the World Cup final – a weak header that fell to Helmut Haller to give West Germany the lead – sticks in the memory. It was so out of character, so uncommon for Ray to give the opposition a sniff. When the great defenders make a mistake everyone remembers it because it is so rare, and Ray was famous for just doing his job. I didn't see too many get past him, and while he could bomb forward when necessary, he always knew his first task was to defend. He wasn't spectacular, but every successful team needs men like Ray Wilson. He was probably the least known of that 1966 team, but that didn't mean he wasn't absolutely vital. Without good full-backs in those days, you were stuffed.

Huddersfield was a breeding ground for a lot of good players back then. Wilson and Law, obviously, but Frank Worthington came out of there too, and some decent full-backs such as Chris Cattlin, who went on to play eight seasons in the First Division for Coventry City, and Derek Parkin, who still holds the record number of appearances for Wolverhampton Wanderers. Huddersfield were more of a feeder club by then, sadly. They didn't keep any of their stars. Just before the World Cup, Ray Wilson was transferred to Everton. He was probably the best left-back in the world by that time, too.

There were a few contenders. Nílton Santos of Brazil had been the top man – and some people think the finest left-back of all time – but he retired in 1962. Wilson's only rival by the time of the 1966 World Cup would have been Giacinto Facchetti, who captained the winning Italy team in the 1968 European Championships. He played all his life for Inter Milan, and even ended up president of the club. Facchetti was a brilliant player, but I can't help thinking that when Wilson was winning the World Cup, his Italian team was going home having been beaten by North Korea. Remembering Jairzinho's performance against Italy in the 1970 World Cup, I think Ray just had the edge as a defender, too.

As I've said before, the sixties were the time when full-backs became as fast as wingers, and Ray was a product of that thinking. He wasn't an overly aggressive player, he wasn't nasty or vicious, or swearing at you the whole match; he was just quick and difficult to beat. Ray would have been faster than many wingers and it would have been interesting to see how Sir Stanley Matthews would have coped had he been up against players like that throughout his career. Stan had a good run against slower full-backs, and by the time the game changed he was coming to the end and not as much was expected of him. It would have been interesting to see Stan deal with the likes of Tommy Smith or Terry Cooper – and he never played against Wilson at his absolute peak.

Ray was certainly one of the toughest I ever faced, and there was plenty of competition at the time. Eddie McCreadie was an outstanding opponent at Chelsea, fast, with an excellent sense of timing in the tackle. I remember a goal he scored against Leicester City in the League Cup. He must have run the length of the field and, when everyone thought he might panic, he just slotted it past Gordon Banks. Very cool. Eddie was an incredible bloke. He managed Chelsea when he retired and one of his first acts was to take the captaincy away from Ron Harris and give it to an 18-year-old kid, Ray Wilkins. So he was clearly a very good judge. They won promotion under him, but he only lasted two seasons and he was gone. The rumour at the time was that he wanted a club car because the manager of Fulham, Bobby Campbell, had one. The chairman, Brian Mears, refused so Eddie quit. Then Mears decided he could have one but Eddie felt he couldn't go back on his word. I suppose there was probably more to it, but it seems incredible to give up a great job like that. The last I heard of Eddie he was a born-again Christian living in America. I don't think he has seen anyone from his old football days in years. I know Chelsea invited him to come to one of the games when they toured America recently, but he refused. He has a new life and good luck to him.

I think one of the big differences back in the sixties was that great players could come from anywhere, not just a small group of elite clubs, as today. Wilson was from Huddersfield and Eddie was signed from East Stirlingshire, who were in the Scottish Second Division at the time – and he went straight into Chelsea's first team. Cyril Knowles was another excellent left-back at Tottenham Hotspur, and he came out of Middlesbrough. Cyril was class on the ball and made that step up with no problem. If you go through that first great Liverpool team there are players from Motherwell, Dundee United, Preston North End. There was so much talent around in the lower divisions, and Scotland, whereas now it is very hard to find. Good players move much earlier, almost in their teens, so very little comes out of there. Often a kid will get picked up, move to a bigger club and then disappear in a reserve group that is full of foreign imports. He loses his way in the game, and vanishes or drops down through the divisions. When I played, every First Division team had two or three good Scottish players, now there might be ten in the entire Premier Division. I hope that is beginning to change now because there are some good reports coming out about young players in Scotland. Maybe they are getting the chance to play again – in recent years the top of the Scottish league became too focused on foreign players. It would be good to get back to the days when a great international footballer could come from almost anywhere – and Huddersfield produced as many as Manchester United.

GEORGE BEST
(MANCHESTER UNITED)

So where would I put George Best in my list of the greats? Simple. I regard him as the best footballer the British Isles has ever produced. A genius. We've never had another like him.

I can remember reading the account by Harry Gregg, Manchester United's goalkeeper, of the first time he met George. Great man, Harry – pulled semi-conscious injured team-mates out of a burning plane on the tarmac at Munich. That's bravery. These days a midfielder receives the ball with a man marking him and we say he's brave. He was also a hard man who almost used to bully opponents. He came out fast and aggressively in one-on-one challenges, and sometimes made the forward's mind up for him. Harry was not the sort of chap that a young kid fresh over from Belfast should be messing with.

The first training session George had at United ended with a practice match. George, just over 5 ft 8 in and no more than seven stone at the time, got the ball, ripped through the defence and made to shoot. Gregg went one way, and George casually took the ball past him and rolled it into the net. Harry consoled himself with the thought that it was a mistake, that he had sold himself too early and made up this kid's mind. Next attack, George went through on his own again – out came Harry, and the same thing happened. He dived one way, George went the other and tapped into an empty net. 'Do that to me again, son,' Harry warned, from his position on the seat of his pants, 'and you won't be playing tomorrow.' Yet George just laughed it off. That was what made him so magnificent. There is a fantastic clip of George playing against Chelsea. He is going through the defence, the mud is ankle deep, yet somehow he is travelling on, when Ron Harris comes across and tries to cut him in half. It is an incredible tackle by today's standards, absolutely brutal, yet he rides it, carries on and slots the ball in. George went out every game knowing there were players whose job was to hurt him. Not scare him or intimidate him, just stop him by any means necessary. He always suspected there were a couple who actively tried to break his legs. Yet they never stopped him demanding the ball, never stopped him running with it. I haven't seen anybody as brave as George. He was a one-off.

When great players retire often a myth builds up around them, but I know what George went through from experience. I grew up in the same era as him – George was the year above my West Ham United youth team that won the FA Youth Cup – and it could be really intimidating playing against these hard-nut defenders. Yet it never seemed to bother George. He never stopped wanting the ball, never stopped taking players on – too much so, some of his Manchester United colleagues thought, but if you've got that unique talent why wouldn't you use it?

Sometimes you hear a buzz about great young players because of their achievements at junior level, but there was nothing like that with George. He was fresh off the boat and straight into the first team. He didn't really bother with youth football. The player we all knew from United's junior team was Willie Anderson, a lad from Liverpool who played in George's position. George just flew straight past Willie and never looked back. Willie ended up as George's understudy, going nowhere, and signed for Aston Villa for £20,000. Sometimes that happens. Willie was a useful player and must have thought he was going to have a good career at Manchester United. Then this wonder kid from Northern Ireland comes over and that's his lot – it was a pity really, but how could they resist George? He had everything. He could dribble, shoot, he was strong in the air, a good tackler. He was the ultimate street footballer, really. That was where he'd learnt to play the game, not from any coach. Lionel Messi reminds me of him, the way he would run with the ball tight to his foot. Tap, tap, tap. He would take the ball up to defenders like that, and then swivel and go past them. You almost need to create a fresh way of measuring talent to assess George. There were so many great players in that Manchester United team but, even then, George stood tall.

He had plenty of good games against West Ham, but one stands out. We had gone up to Old Trafford to play them near the start of the 1971–2 season and I got talking to David Sadler, their centre-half, before the game. He told me there had been uproar earlier that day. 'George didn't turn up at the hotel, Harry,' he said. 'He missed the team meeting, he's been out all night. Been off with a bird, had no sleep, look at the state of him.' I must admit, the figure warming up across the other side of the pitch did look a bit dishevelled. I went straight back to our dressing-room, keen to pass on this juicy gossip. 'This is handy, lads,' I told the group. 'I've just found out that Best's been out all night on the piss. He's just turned up at the ground now, missed the team bus, missed the meeting, they're only playing him because they've got no one else.' We went out that afternoon full of confidence, and you can imagine what happened next. George scored a hat-trick and we lost 4–2. He got a header for his first goal and a fantastic shot on the turn in the middle of a penalty-area scramble for his second. For the last goal, United got a corner and George went out towards it, telling John Aston he would score from there. John played it short and George took it past about four of us from this acute angle, bomp, bomp, bomp, made to shoot, left Bobby Moore on his arse and stuck it in the far corner. I don't think I've seen a better goal. The rest of the players were looking at me as if to say, 'Thanks for that tip, Harry.' But he just had this incredible, natural ability. I should have known that one late night in a thousand wasn't going to affect George.

There were some wonderful players in that era, real crowd-pleasers like Peter Osgood, but George was the only one who could add 10,000 to a gate the way Tom Finney or Stanley Matthews had previously. Certainly, that was the deal when he came to Bournemouth late in his career. Brian Tiler, the managing director, did a deal where the away team would pay a percentage of his wages as long as we put George in the starting line-up; I really don't know how we got away with it because there must have been regulations against that type of thing. Everyone was happy, though, because a gate of 4,000 would suddenly become 14,000 with the news George was playing.

Despite this, he was always just one of the lads. I think a lot of the best players are like that. It's the ones who get the money without the ability that tend to become flash little twerps. I never hear a bad word said about Paul Gascoigne by any of his team-mates, and I was once told that it was the same with Diego Maradona. The rest of the dressing-room loved him. He didn't care that his ability was carrying the team; he just mucked in. George was like that. I imagine some people might think he was a right flash bastard, but that was never the case. He trained as if he was an ordinary player, even in America with Los Angeles Aztecs. He had his mate out there with him, Bobby McAlinden, who was his best man when he married Angie; he got him a contract with the club and they shared a house, but that was the only time I can recall George getting star treatment. McAlinden never made it as a player – he was part-time with Stalybridge Celtic when he went to America – but George liked him, and the franchise wanted to keep George happy.

How I like to remember him, though, is in front of a full house at Old Trafford in his prime. He had a style, a swagger when he played that I don't think I've seen since. And he changed football. Girls screaming at him, boys trying to dress like him. Sometimes, with all the celebrity trappings, it is easy to forget how good he was. The best: simple as that.

Keeper Bert Trautmann, who came over here as a German prisoner of war and then stayed. I don't think he could do that now, what with all the media attention and the way fans act now, but back then we appreciated what a great player he was, and he became one of us.

Roger Byrne (*far right*), pictured a year before his death in the Munich air disaster, with Busby and the other babes. They're celebrating winning the Division One League Championship. What an extraordinary, magical team.

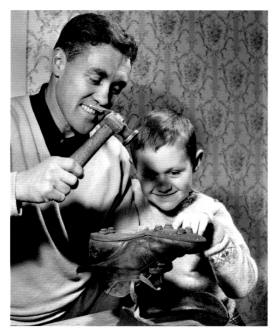

Here's Leeds United's Bobby Collins in 1962 re-studding his boots with his son. It's a wonder they used to play such great football with the equipment they had in those days. Most had big hard toe-caps and studs banged in at the bottom with the nails coming through!

Johnny Haynes, Fulham's golden boy, on crutches in 1962 after the car crash that effectively ended his England career.

The legendary Stanley Matthews, Duncan Edwards and Billy Wright warming up on England duty with a jog around Highbury in 1957. In those days they had very unsophisticated training regimes – a few times around the cinder track, or up and down the steps of the terraces for fitness.

Tom Finney taking off his boots for the last time at Preston North End in 1960. We set different standards for success then – he played for one club his whole career even though they never won anything, which never counted against him. He was still the best – and everyone acknowledged that.

John Charles – King John, as they called him, or The Gentle Giant – a lovely man away from the pitch but a monster on it, fearless and strong, a real powerhouse. I'd say he was one of the best all-round footballers to come out of Britain.

Danny Blanchflower and his Tottenham team in the dressing room, celebrating winning the Division One Championship in 1961. At first Danny clashed with manager Bill Nicholson, but together they were behind the best team Tottenham have ever produced. Bill's in the centre in the bowler, with Danny sitting on his left.

The great Gordon Banks, who used to be a coalman's mate and a bricklayer before being spotted by Chesterfield, is congratulating Bobby Charlton here on playing his 100th International in 1970.

The Charlton brothers on England duty in 1965. I was about 15 when I first saw Jack play, and I couldn't believe he was Bobby's brother. Bobby was so graceful, poetry in motion; Jack was aggressive and would do anything to win. But they were both great players in their own way, and each deserve a place on my team.

I regard George Best as a genius – the best footballer to have come from the British Isles. He had everything, and he changed football forever. Here he is before Denis Law's testimonal in 1973. Best always said about Law that he didn't need half a chance to score, he needed a hundredth. That's what gives him the nod from me.

One of the most famous photographs in football. Dave Mackay had just returned
from his second broken leg when Billy Bremner hit him with a naughty one.
I think you can see from the photograph that Billy quickly realised he'd made a
big mistake.

Bobby Moore and Jimmy Greaves. Bobby wasn't the best athlete, but he more than compensated for that – his determination and understanding of the game was incredible. On the other side of the coin was Jimmy, who people said didn't take the game seriously. God knows what he'd have been like if he did. He scored goals in torrents – hat-tricks, fours, even fives.

Training on the terraces 60s style. It was brilliant being part of that West Ham side. As well as playing with Bobby Moore and Jimmy Greaves, there were so many legends – John Charles, Geoff Hurst and Billy Bonds, amongst others.

BILLY BREMNER
(LEEDS UNITED)

It is hard to separate Billy Bremner and Johnny Giles. They were both so integral to the midfield of the great Leeds United team that it seems unthinkable to imagine them apart. But there is no way I won't find room for Dave Mackay, so it comes down to a straight choice between Bremner and Giles – and I am going for Bremner. Billy was the captain; Billy was the driving force behind that team. They were two great players, without a doubt, but Billy edges it for me. He never seemed to get injured, no matter how much he gave, and for his size his contribution to the game was just incredible. It was not unusual for him to sleep for 13 hours after a match because his effort had been so great, and while I had my run-ins with him, it never clouded my appreciation of him as a player.

It was hard to get sent off in the sixties, but I managed it against Leeds. Looking back, I am sure they knew what they were doing that day. I was having a good game – I always fancied my chances against Leeds because the left-back, Terry Cooper, was so attack minded that I often got an opening – and after 15 minutes I knew this was going to be my day. I was getting past Cooper time and again, and heaven knows how the score was still 0–0. I went on another run, got to the byline and won a corner. Bremner started complaining that it should have been a goal-kick. 'Stop moaning,' I told him. 'You're always fucking moaning.' Billy clearly didn't appreciate that because as we lined up for the corner, he stamped on my foot. I pushed him away. Then he raked his studs down my shin. I gave him a kick and he went down as if felled by a sniper's bullet. The next moment the whole Leeds team, bar Billy and the goalkeeper, Gary Sprake, were crowding in on me, hands around my throat, jostling me, pushing me back. Billy Bonds, bless him, was the only West Ham player who came to my aid – the rest just looked on. Bremner escaped, I was sent off, and as I walked past Bobby Moore, who was still in West Ham's defensive half of the pitch, the look on his face was a picture. He had his arms folded and gave a brief shake of the head, as if to say, 'Harry, son – how did you fall for that?' Yet that was the Leeds way. They were cute, often plain cynical. They won 2–0 that day, from a direct free-kick by Peter Lorimer and a penalty by Giles. 'Fouls, imagined and actual, were so frequent that I stopped counting them,' wrote the reporter from the *Yorkshire Post*. Getting played for a mug was costly in those days, too. I had to serve a suspension, and back then that meant a week with no pay. Billy Bonds organised a whip-round for me and even asked Ron Greenwood, our manager, to chip in. He didn't like confrontation, so agreed. He must have been fuming, though, coming to the rescue of a player who had cost his team the game.

Still, no hard feelings. Bremner was just trying to do the best for his team, driving them on in whatever way he could, as always. I think Giles was the brains of the midfield, but Bremner was its engine. Giles could really play. He had come to the club from Manchester United, and letting him go may have been the biggest mistake that club ever made. People think Eric Cantona being allowed to leave Leeds for Manchester United was a serious error, but to my mind that was merely the equaliser after the earlier sale of Giles to Leeds. He was such a fantastic footballer, a right-winger at Manchester United, but desperate to be given the chance to play in the middle. Even at Leeds he had to wait his turn behind Bobby Collins, but once he got it he never looked back. His touch on the ball was absolutely superb and he had a lovely passing range. Everything happened so deftly. The ball would come in and he would kill it and pass it, all in one movement. He saw everything from that central position, and with Bremner beside him they were such a great pair.

I think Billy set standards as a leader at Elland Road. Don Revie had a unique way of managing, demanding that the team stayed tight and that nothing upset his boys. Billy was instrumental in that. When Gordon McQueen signed for the club from St Mirren it was said he fancied himself a bit. Billy would have made it his business to ensure nobody's ego got in the way. 'Side before self, every time' was his motto. Even by the standards of the day he was tiny: just 5 ft 5 in. He grew up in Scotland playing against men and learning that the only way to be big enough was to act big enough – he flew into tackles harder than any player from that era. A lot of those boys could put it about but Billy was, if you like, the pound-for-pound champion. For his size, a tackle from Billy felt like being hit by a six-footer. Yes, he was nasty, but he could also play. He always wanted the ball, and always tried to run the game. He often succeeded. His passing was as well developed as his wicked streak, so no wonder the fans and his manager loved him. Whatever way you wanted to play, Billy could play. If you wanted a tear-up, he was ready to roll; if you wanted a football match, he was the best player on the field.

A few years back I watched the film *The Damned United* about Brian Clough's short time at Leeds. I know it isn't intended to be historically accurate throughout but, even so, the portrayal of Bremner was a disgrace. They made him look like a little fat sod, with a pot belly. If that was the player that was chasing midfielders all around the pitch for almost 800 games, I don't think Revie's Leeds would be regarded as one of the greatest teams of all time. At one stage they showed him smoking a cigarette waiting for Clough to come out. Shirt and shorts on, and a fag. I was so surprised I even asked Joe Jordan about it. I couldn't repeat what he said about the way that Leeds team was portrayed. I don't know why they did that. They made them look like a Sunday league team. It was nonsense – like the scene where Clough is the manager of Derby County and he doesn't even watch one of his biggest games of the season. Peter Taylor, his assistant, tells him the score. I'm sorry, I can't see that happening. Like Bremner with a beer belly, anyone who was around in those times knows it just isn't true.

I know Billy was very loyal to Revie and preferred his methods, and that he stood up to Clough. There is a story that Leeds had a pre-season game away at Aston Villa and Clough decided to give the team talk on the grass bank of a dual carriageway. It started to pour down with rain, and some of the players got up to leave. Clough asked them where they thought they were going. 'You stand up when I say you can,' he said. It was Billy who led the mutiny. 'If you think we're sitting in the rain, you must be joking,' he said, and walked off. It is no surprise that it didn't work out for Clough. They were all experienced players. They didn't have to take that.

The quote that best sums Billy up is that he was 10 stone of barbed wire. He was a warrior, a ball-winner and the scorer of the odd great goal. He had a lovely reverse pass that could wrong-foot some of the best midfielders, and he embodied the spirit of the sign that hung on the wall of the home dressing-room. 'Keep fighting,' it said. I think they always left the door half open to make sure you saw it when you visited Elland Road. It was their equivalent of the 'This Is Anfield' sign over the tunnel at Liverpool – reminding you what you were up against. I know Leeds played Chelsea the weekend after Billy died, and it was rather fitting because they had two men sent off, but still managed a 0–0 draw. The fans were singing about having 'nine men – and Billy'. He would have loved that.

It is almost impossible to overstate what he did for that team, and that club. I played Leeds in my second game for West Ham on 28 August 1965 and we beat them 2–1. I didn't think they looked much cop, yet from there they just went from strength to strength and Billy was so important in pulling the team together. A sports writer once told me a story about Billy and that spirit at Leeds. He said they were in Eastern Europe for the away leg of a European tie and they were all out after the game – players, some of the press boys, the way it used to be. The bill arrived for the night, and it was clear they were being ripped off. They'd had a good go at it, but this place must have thought they were millionaires. There was an almighty row and the next thing they knew the exit door was blocked by a big gang of heavies. Billy didn't mess about. He turned to the players and the press corps. 'Pick up a chair, lads,' he said. 'We're leaving.'

DAVE MACKAY
(TOTTENHAM HOTSPUR)

Bill Nicholson said Dave Mackay was his greatest signing, and selling him was his greatest mistake. If you look at the talent Bill brought to Tottenham, that is some statement. Dave was the manager's player, the player's player, the fan's player, the complete footballer really. Every major club he represented regards him as a legend – from Hearts in Scotland, through Tottenham, to Derby County. He won every domestic honour north of the border before coming to England, and played in a Hearts team that scored 132 league goals in one season – which at the time was a British record. Dave was a warrior, but another one of those players who could take the game in whatever direction he fancied. He could give you a war all right, but he also had incredible skill and ability. On the ball he was magnificent; off it he was a ferocious competitor and tackler, the strongest you've ever seen. Jimmy Greaves said he was the best player ever to wear a Tottenham shirt, and I wouldn't argue with that. George Best thought he was the hardest player he ever faced – but he didn't mean hard in a sneaky or dirty way. Just tough. It's a huge testament to Dave's standing among his fellow professionals.

I remember watching Dave when I was a junior at Tottenham. I followed them through all the European games and at weekends whenever I could. The team had a big Scottish contingent at the time: John White, Bill Brown, who was the goalkeeper, and Dave. They had all arrived within a few months of each other in 1959, which for those days was quite a bold move from a manager. Nicholson was proved right, though, and the Scots were essential to Tottenham's double-winning team. White never missed a game, Brown missed one and Dave missed five – but Mackay was still the pick of the bunch. He was a powerhouse, making tackle after tackle. It was just incredible to watch. I remember one game from that season against Aston Villa, which Tottenham won 6–2. I was 13 at the time. Villa weren't a bad team and they had a tough little nut playing at right-half called Ron Wylie, who went on to be manager of West Bromwich Albion. Wylie had the ball when Mackay tackled him and the poor sod must have gone eight foot up in the air. The ball came down to another Villa player, but before he knew it Dave had hit him as well, with the same result. That was Mackay. He would just plough through a midfield, tackle after tackle. You could never imagine he would come out second best.

He must have done, on occasions, because Dave had terrible luck with injuries. He broke his left leg in a tackle with Noel Cantwell of Manchester United in a European Cup-Winners' Cup tie in 1963, came back nine months later and, four games in, did it again against Shrewsbury Town reserves. Dave always says he didn't break his leg, other players broke it for him. I got to know him via Jim Smith when Jim was manager of Derby, and I know Dave believes that on at least one of those occasions he was deliberately targeted and fouled.

That is also the story behind one of the most famous photographs in football. A furious Mackay is in mid-stride, marching over and grabbing Billy Bremner by his collar, almost picking him up, as his team-mate Terry Venables looks on and referee Norman Burtenshaw dashes over frantically blowing his whistle. It was taken on 20 August 1966, the first day of the new season. Dave had returned from his second broken leg the previous campaign, his resilience merely adding to his legend. A broken leg could end a career in those days, let alone two within nine months, and while many thought this proved Mackay was indestructible, he must have felt very vulnerable when he stepped on to the field. Within the opening minutes, Bremner had hit him with a naughty one – but that wasn't why Dave was so furious. He thought Bremner had avoided tackling his right leg – the leg that had the ball – and instead had gone for his left. He thought he had set out to either break his leg again or at least make him fearful. I think you can see from the photograph that Billy quickly realised he had made a big mistake. They were two of the great competitors of the sixties, but even Billy knew that you didn't mess with Dave. The referee prevented the confrontation from coming to blows but, had it done, judging by the look on Dave's face there would only have been one winner. I'm told Dave hates that image because he thinks it makes him look like a bully – although he wasn't much taller than Billy, only 5 ft 8 in – but every football man I know loves it. Sir Alex Ferguson even had it up in his office at Old Trafford.

Everyone who played with Dave, or knew Dave, has a story about his skill. He was good and he knew it, and liked to show off. Sometimes Eddie Baily would take the training at Tottenham. He never had much time for players and would sometimes devise drills just to put them in their place. They had a wall with coloured lines on it at the training ground. The players were convinced Baily would make these sessions up as he went along. 'Right you lot,' Eddie would say. 'Get a ball each. Now,

I want you to chip it against the blue line, get it back, shoot it against the red line, take it on your chest, let it drop, back against the yellow line, keep it high, then on your head this time, head it back against the green line, wait for it, side-foot against the white line, volley up to the black line, trap it and stop.' The lads would be looking at him as if he was mad. They couldn't even remember the exercise let alone perform it. At which point, Dave would get his ball – chip, blue line, shoot, red line, chest, drop, yellow line, back, header, green line, side-foot, white line, volley, black line, back, trap. 'Like that, you mean, Ed?' he'd ask.

Phil Holder, who was a trainee at Tottenham as Dave was coming to the end of his career there, says he used to watch him in the gym repeatedly volleying the ball against the wall from 20 yards, one shot after another, left foot, right foot, never letting it drop. Graeme Souness says he saw the same. That is an incredible skill to perfect. I don't know another player who could do it. Mackay's feet were amazing.

Another memory is of that barrel chest. Dave always seemed to have mud on his hands from a slide tackle. The pitches were conducive to it then and he'd start in at the opponents from about five yards away, go right through him and always come out with the ball. He'd get up and wipe his muddy hands on the front of his shirt. It was his trademark. There was a lot of the showman about Dave. When Tottenham ran out he would kick the ball as high as he could, and then kill it on the way down with the deftest touch. It was his way of showing the opposition the technical level they were up against. 'Can you do that, lads?' he was asking. He was just this wonderful combination of brawn and brain. When he went in for a tackle, he got the ball, and once he had the ball he could do anything with it – power past people, hit a pass, hit a thunderous shot from 30 yards straight on goal. He had everything. Even after the broken leg he still went crunching into tackles, and after Bill sold him to Derby, he turned them around and won promotion playing almost as a sweeper. Anyone who pigeon-holes him as just a hard man doesn't know the player. He was a fantastic technician, too – and a member of one of football's most ferocious drinking schools at Tottenham, adding to the legend.

That team didn't just win the double, they sunk quite a few of them too. A friend of mine says he went to a match at White Hart Lane back then without a ticket, hoping to pick one up from a tout outside. He was waiting for Stan Flashman when he saw a chap he knew getting out of a taxi with Dave Mackay. Dave hurried into White Hart Lane, but his mate said the pair of them had been out at a party that weekend and Mackay hadn't been to bed since. Bill Nicholson was going to be furious. In the end, my mate got his ticket and went inside. Tottenham won. Man of the match? Dave Mackay. He was probably straight up the Bell and Hare pub or The Corner Pin with Jimmy Greaves after the game, too.

BOBBY CHARLTON
(MANCHESTER UNITED)

On 6 May 1967, Manchester United came to Upton Park in search of the league title. They were three points clear of Nottingham Forest with two games remaining – just two points for a win in those days of course – so could still be overtaken.

Their last two games were at West Ham and then at home to Stoke City, two mid-table clubs. Forest had to play away against Southampton and Fulham, both of whom had only just avoided relegation. Manchester United were the favourites, but still – might they slip up? As if. They beat us 6–1 – and I don't think I've ever seen a classier performance than Bobby Charlton gave that day. The picture on the front of the book is from that game.

We were a raw side, with a lot of youth, and Manchester United annihilated us. It was the great team – Best, Law and Charlton – and all got on the scoresheet, but it was Bobby who gave United the lead after two minutes, and Bobby whose quality and passing guided the win. He was class personified, gliding past people, the most graceful mover I have seen on a football field, able to shoot from anywhere once within the 40-yard range. He was just the most perfect striker of a ball. He would drop his shoulder and, bang, top corner. And fast. Because he was so skilful, people forget the speed Charlton had. What I remember that day is that in United's first attack Law and Nobby Stiles burst through, Law's shot was blocked and our full-back Jack Burkett made to clear. Before he got the chance, Charlton was upon him. It was like watching a gazelle taken down by a cheetah. He came from nowhere, first time shot, 1–0. It was a masterclass in taking an opportunity in the blink of an eye. One minute Jack was about to play it safe, the next we were behind. After that, United showed why they were the best team in the land. Our goalkeeper was my old friend from the Burdett Boys team, Colin Mackleworth, and he had a terrible time of it. I know he dropped a cross for their third goal but it hardly mattered – the game was only 10 minutes old when that was scored.

Bobby was the man of the match. A midfield genius at a time when there was plenty of competition. Markers couldn't control him, couldn't kick him, couldn't get near him. His passes were always so clean, his technique so faultless, and the way he switched the play was devastating. He would take half the opposition out with one pass, and did so countless times that day. What a player, and what a man. Not aggressive, not dirty, always gentlemanly in his conduct. I must admit I was in awe of him. Most young players of the time were, and perhaps that day it showed.

It makes such a difference to have a player like that in your team. I had that at Tottenham with Gareth Bale. He would get the ball, 25 to 30 yards out and – bang – find the top corner. I watched him do it for Real Madrid last season, too. All the football around the world, all this talk about possession, nothing beats the direct approach of a great player like Bobby Charlton or Bale. A team can have 28 passes to create a shooting opportunity, but a player who can hit the target from 30 yards out – that cuts straight to the heart of the game. We were raving about Bale in his last season in England, but Bobby was doing exactly that 40 years ago: the same driving runs, the same spectacular finishes. When you think what the man went through at Munich, it can't have been easy. To lose all your friends, particularly in a sports team, must have made playing very difficult. So many memories every time he stepped on the field, what must he have been thinking? How did he overcome that, seeing those ghosts? To come back and become the player he was – I think that's why he is such an icon in English football. Bobby is the only one who spans the three most seismic events in our game: the Munich air disaster, winning the World Cup in 1966 and the first European

Cup win by an English club, Manchester United in 1968. As a director, one could even say he was part of United's treble in 1999, too.

I can't say I know him very well personally, but the way he carried himself was important, too. He might have been involved in all those events and turned into a horrible bastard, but instead Bobby was a gentleman and a great ambassador for football, an ambassador for the best in the game: skill and grace and commitment. Bobby Charlton represented football played the right way as a player and a man, which is why I think he holds a special place in its history.

I was 19 when England won the World Cup and watched the match on the Burdett Estate with my mum and dad. I was in the West Ham first team by then and felt very proud because three of my team-mates were in the starting line-up, but I didn't have a ticket. Bobby Moore was a big friend of mine, but I wouldn't have dreamed of asking him to sort me out. He had far too much on his plate to be bothered hunting down tickets for me. Anyway, it was great to watch the game with Dad. We still had a black-and-white television in those days, despite my successful career. I can't remember getting a colour set for quite a few years after that. I think by the time the Redknapps came into the modern world I was married to Sandra and we had our first son, Mark.

Actually, our quest for a colour TV belongs in an episode of *Only Fools and Horses*. I was in the Dallas café opposite Upton Park station with my team-mate Roger Cross when a chap came in. He must have recognised me from the West Ham team and knew I might have a bit of spare cash. 'Harry,' he said, 'do you fancy buying a colour television?' He explained that he had a couple to sell – we didn't ask too many questions about how and why – but he needed to let them go as a pair because he wanted them off his hands. We should have smelled a rat from the start. Roger had just got married and was very keen. 'They're £110 each,' the man said. That was a lot of money – more than a week's wages. I wasn't sure, but Roger said he could have a word with his mum and borrow the cash. She had a sweet shop in Katherine Road, so was always regarded as having a few quid compared to the other parents. I thought it was expensive but in the end was persuaded. This bloke was a good salesman and told us this was a top-of-the-range piece of equipment, well in advance of most of the sets you would find in the shops. He said he would bring it round that night.

Eight o'clock, as arranged, he arrived. 'I'm sorry, Harry,' he said, 'one of the sets has got a little damaged in the van. Nothing serious, but it's got a scratch on the side.' 'Roger can have that one,' I said. 'I'll have the good one.' He brought it in, and made a big show of putting it in the middle of the room. His legs were buckling with the weight and he placed it very carefully to make sure there was no damage. 'Right,' I said. 'We'll switch it on.' 'Oh no, Harry,' he countered. 'You can't just switch a set like this on. It needs an expert, someone to do all the tuning. You might mess it up if you turn it on without knowing what you're doing. It's very sophisticated. Highly technical. You'll need help.' And, pocketing the money, off he went to deliver Roger's, with the scratch.

As luck would have it, I knew a bloke in Chelmsford who worked in television repair, and asked him to come round. The following day he arrived and we all sat down to watch the launch of the colour era in our front room. Nothing. Not a flicker. He seemed mystified. In the end, he went round the back and unscrewed the panel. 'Harry,' he said, 'is this *Candid Camera*?' There was nothing inside. Not so much as a loose screw. I had bought an empty wooden cabinet with a screen on the front. My first thought was what a mug I had been letting Roger have the one with the scratch, but we went round there and his was the same. We had been done, good and proper. Of course, we never saw our mates from the Dallas café again.

Still, that night in July 1966, Mum and Dad's black-and-white set was good enough for me. Bobby and the boys gave the East End of London one of the best nights out it had ever seen.

JIMMY GREAVES
(TOTTENHAM HOTSPUR)

We were at the training ground with Queens Park Rangers last season and Sky Sports News was showing a goal by Lionel Messi. He got into the penalty box, took his time, waiting for all the defenders and goalkeeper to commit themselves, and then just rolled it into the corner. The players were in rapture about it. I told them Jimmy Greaves scored one like that every weekend, and frequently more. He was a genius. Without doubt one of the greatest goalscorers of any era. When he got the ball in the penalty box, the world stopped; it was like somebody had hit pause on the television screen. The action around him carried on, but Jim appeared to be operating in another dimension; slower, calmer, making his mind up oblivious to the surrounding frenzy.

The centre-half would come flying across; Jim would make out as if to shoot. The centre-half would throw himself into a desperate slide to try to block; Jim would stop the ball. The centre-half would go whizzing past; Jim would switch it to his other foot. The goalkeeper would anticipate the direction and dive full-length; Jim would place the ball, gently, into the other corner. As it nestled, just about reaching the back of the net, there would be bodies lying everywhere. It was just amazing.

Jimmy could side-foot one with the same devastating effect others got from a 30-yard shot. Strikers often want pace on the ball to get it past the goalkeeper, but Jim never seemed to worry about that. His accuracy did the work: moving the ball half a yard to manoeuvre it around the blocking player, always finding the corner. So cool.

It was said Jimmy didn't take the game seriously. God knows what he'd have been like if he did take it seriously then, because he was that good. I saw his debut at Tottenham. He had returned from half a season at AC Milan and there was speculation about whether he could adjust back to English football, would he be the same player, would he score? I'll never forget it: 16 December 1961, I would have been 14. He scored a hat-trick, the first a fantastic scissor kick. It was as if he had never been away. He scored in torrents of goals. Hat-tricks, fours, even fives. He scored more than 20 league goals a season in each of the first 12 years of his career – and that includes the opening campaign with Tottenham that didn't start until December. There was once a question-and-answer session with Jimmy and someone in the audience asked if he would have scored more had he not been lazy. Frank Blunstone, one of Jimmy's team-mates at

Chelsea, was on the stage and he cut in and told this bloke that nobody scored five goals against Billy Wright's Wolverhampton Wanderers if they were lazy.

Jimmy's debut matches were phenomenal. Nigel Clarke, a sports writer from the *Daily Mirror*, told me he saw his first game for Chelsea against Tottenham. He said when he scored his first goal there was almost a pause before the cheer, like an intake of breath, because the fans were gasping at what they had seen. Jimmy was just 17 but the crowd instinctively knew this was a special talent. In his last season as a Chelsea youth team player, Jimmy had scored 114 goals. A year into his first-team career, on 30 August 1958, Chelsea beat the champions Wolves 6–2 and Jimmy scored five. He destroyed the great Billy Wright that day, while still a teenager – ripped him to pieces. The numbers are amazing: five against Wolves, five against Preston North End, five against West Bromwich Albion, four against Newcastle United, four against Nottingham Forest – and that was just for Chelsea. Even his time at AC Milan was successful in terms of scoring – he got 9 goals in 10 Serie A matches, an incredible return for the time.

Jimmy only went to Italy for the money, and he never liked it. He wasn't one for tactical talks or hard training and hated the discipline that was expected from Italian players at that time. He said he paid out so much in fines he had to get his win bonus just to break even. He even got fined for not supporting his team-mates in a punch-up with the Inter players during the Milan derby. My favourite story concerns some girls who used to hang about outside Milan's training ground. Jimmy thought they were fans, so one day, seeing them walking up the lane towards the camp, he offered them a lift in his Jaguar to come up and meet the players. It turns out they were all prostitutes. Jimmy says that misunderstanding cost him a fortune.

Jimmy was another player who operated completely on instinct. He would have learnt his dribbling on the school playground or in the street, not from any coach. He certainly didn't think about it. If you thought about some of the goals he scored you wouldn't be able to pull them off. There is a famous one against Manchester United for Tottenham in 1965 and it is almost like watching a kid playing against his mates. Greaves turns, takes two out of the game, glides past another, runs past – not around – the goalkeeper and taps it into the net. There is such confidence in that goal, such simplicity. It is not something that could have been learnt from a coaching session. I went to the same Chelsea sessions that Jimmy would have attended. They took place in a car park, same as at West Ham – and even if the coaches had been the greatest, most innovative, in the world it would have made no difference. You cannot coach what a Best or Greaves did. You can't coach a player to pick up the ball and beat four men.

This was probably the last era in which the best footballers were allowed to play with complete freedom of expression. The last era when the streets were not full of cars and when every bloke who took a kids' team on a Sunday didn't fancy himself as José Mourinho. Last season, I went to watch my little grandson play at a park where there are lots of small pitches, side by side. I was watching his game and, when there was a break in play, I'd turn and look at the other game. One side had a goal-kick and the whole team dashed up the field to the halfway line and waited as the goalkeeper kicked it as hard as he could. At the end of the game, their coach came over. 'Harry, can we have a picture with you and the kids?' he asked. 'Of course,' I said. So I started talking to these kids. 'I saw a bit of your game, boys,' I said. 'Look, goalie, when you get the ball, pass it. Give it to one of your defenders. Then they get the ball and pass it to another defender. Then try to pass it forward, go forward by passing the ball to each other. Don't just kick it as far as you can. Pass it, then you'll all be involved, passing to each other. Am I right, coach?' 'Yeah, yeah,' he replied, but his expression said, 'Fuck off, Harry, we only wanted a photograph for the clubhouse wall.' But I wanted to make my point. 'Pass the ball,' I told them, 'don't worry if you make mistakes, it doesn't matter. If you make a mistake, you learn. But you've got to try to get the ball and play football. And sometimes when you get the ball, try to beat a man. Have a go, try to dribble.' Will it make any difference? Probably not. It's a shame what happens in kids' football these days. The coaches give up their time, and that's wonderful, but I think they are more bothered about winning than trying to get the kids to play. I'm not sure how much anyone learns or improves that way. It's all about winning, clearing your lines, booting it. You see a kid start dribbling and the other parents are shouting to get rid of it and stop being greedy, all because he hasn't passed to their little Johnny. It's frightening. The goalkeeper kicks it to this wall of bodies on the halfway line. Yet you can tell the naturals, the street footballers, a mile off. That's why Wayne Rooney stood out straight away, that's why Luis Suárez was a revelation in the English game.

Yes, when Messi went to Barcelona he obviously learnt more about the game; but when he gets the ball and goes past three men, that's him, that's his instinct. It was how we all learnt in the fifties and sixties. Keep it tight to your boot and off you go, and Jimmy Greaves was just a natural at that. Nobody taught him to feint to shoot and then delay – he worked that out before he came to Chelsea. He worked that out in the park. It was his gift. The pity is that if a player like Jimmy came along now, with all his natural talent, he would be told to hassle their holding midfield player, and if he didn't do it to the coach's liking, that brilliance would count for nothing and he'd be out. The best players are no longer left to play.

I'm not sure Jimmy even worked too hard on his partnership with Alan Gilzean at Tottenham. He just knew where he needed to be when Gilzean had the ball. Suárez strikes me like that. At times he will make a run that you know is straight from the streets of Uruguay – a player operating purely off his wits, as Jimmy did.

When Robbie Fowler broke into the Liverpool team he drew some comparisons with Greaves, and the *Sun* newspaper thought it would be a good idea to get the two of them together. It was a priceless interview. At one stage Jimmy asked Robbie if he did his work – did he get back, did he cover his man? Robbie, who was a diligent player anyway, gave him the answer he thought he wanted to hear. 'Oh yes, Jim,' he said. 'I always do my work, stop their defenders coming out.' 'Don't do that!' Jimmy exploded. 'You've got nine other players on the pitch for that. How are you going to stay fresh and ready to make a run and score, if you're knackered from chasing the left-back fifty yards? Let them do that, and you wait to score. They can't do your job, that's why they play where they do.' I imagine Robbie's face would have been a picture – but that was how Jimmy saw the game.

He did score goals with 50-yard runs – I remember one against Newcastle – so he wasn't interested in chasing all over the field defending. He stopped playing for England because he wasn't getting picked by Alf Ramsey and just wasn't interested in being a squad player and listening to the tactical talks. Jimmy loved playing, and only playing. I don't think he really cared for football much beyond that. He is more of a cricket and rugby-union man. I know that, when Jimmy retired, he had the opportunity to write a coaching book on how to score goals, but told the publisher he didn't have a clue how any of it happened. 'I turned up and the ball turned up,' he said. 'I don't know why I was there.' Malcolm Macdonald got the job instead. He was a brilliant goalscorer, too, but one who worked far harder on his game – to the extent of keeping notes on opponents. That wasn't Jimmy's style at all. I remember seeing John Bond work with Ted MacDougall at Bournemouth and Ron Greenwood with Geoff Hurst at West Ham. Approach runs, getting across defenders, pulling away – but the bottom line was that neither of those players were in Jimmy's class. They needed direction, they needed instruction; but even then they still couldn't score goals like Jimmy. You could have spent every morning with him and it wouldn't have made any difference. He came into football fully formed.

I got to know him when he came to West Ham in 1970 – two goals on his debut away at Manchester City, same as always – and by then he was past his best. He was no longer part of the England squad and was a heavier drinker than most. Even then, however, you could still see flashes of that old magic. What I remember most about Jimmy was his pre-match ritual. He'd still be in his suit 15 minutes before kick-off. He'd then disappear to the toilet, have a fag, come back and put his kit on. Warm-up routines were not as they are now – some clubs didn't even bother with them at all – but Jim didn't even have oil rubbed into his legs like the rest of us. He'd put his boots on, tie them up, then stand by the door. I can see him now, kicking his feet out, 10 times each leg, ready to go. No running, no stretching. Just go out and score a couple of goals. It was all so matter-of-fact, as if this was what he was supposed to do and everything else was unnecessary. When they were at Chelsea together, Jimmy used to give the young Terry Venables a lift to games, as they lived on the same side of London. Terry says that they would stop for a pre-match meal and Jim would have a full roast dinner, everything you are not supposed to eat before exercise, and then go out and score another hat-trick. I think that's what other players loved about him. He was so laid back, so natural, so completely his own man. We all thought he was great at West Ham, even though, looking back, he was heading for trouble. He was a world-class footballer, but a world-class bloke as well. We all loved being around him.

With hindsight, knowing Jimmy became an alcoholic, it is easy to recognise the signs. Even by the standards of the famous West Ham drinking school, he was hitting it big time. He would go up to the Slater's Arms pub opposite Romford dog track after training, and stay there until the landlord, Jack, called time. A session might start at one in the afternoon and last all day. We didn't know about alcoholism then – we just thought Jimmy liked a drink a bit more than the rest of us. We thought he had everything. A lovely wife, a huge house with seven bedrooms, a successful business – he had a lot more going for him than many footballers – as well as being a great player. We didn't know his drinking was at another level. We had some guys who could really put it away in our team – Frank Lampard, Bobby Moore – a lot of days or nights would end up in the pub, so Jimmy's habits didn't seem particularly unusual. Every club had the odd player whose reputation preceded him. We just thought Jimmy fell into that category.

One of the things I most admire about Jimmy, actually, is the way he has fought back from those days. He became disillusioned with football, and then had problems with addiction, but he fought it and hasn't touched a drop since 28 February 1978. In that time he has been a television personality, a newspaper columnist and now conducts entertaining one-man shows. And just like Jimmy the player, he does it all in his own inimitable way.

DENIS LAW
(MANCHESTER UNITED)

One place left, but it isn't going to either of the forwards that won the World Cup final with England. I should explain why. Roger Hunt was an excellent striker for Liverpool. He wasn't a natural goalscorer, but he was a hard worker, very determined – the sort that was most appreciated by those he played with. Bobby Moore spoke very highly of him, while acknowledging he didn't have the skill or guile of, say, Jimmy Greaves. He was a great player in a great Liverpool team, and was their top goalscorer eight years in a row – but it was an era with a lot of extraordinary players, and I don't think Roger was ever quite in the class of the very best. He was a great team man, but lacked that individual skill that sets a player apart. Geoff Hurst was also a fantastic striker and nobody has equalled his feat of scoring a hat-trick in a World Cup final – and maybe nobody ever will. Yet as special as that performance was, Geoff had to work so hard to become that player. The strikers I have chosen – Jimmy Greaves and Denis Law – were geniuses. Geoff took his chance like no man in history, but he didn't have the ability of Jimmy or Denis, he didn't bring that guarantee of goals. Jimmy, for me, was the pinnacle, but Denis wasn't far behind him and both men could turn a bad performance into a win. Jim didn't score every time, but if you got three chances he would put two away, and Denis was the same. George Best said that Denis didn't need half a chance – he needed a hundredth. That is what gives these two the nod from me.

Denis was a class act around the box. Lightning-quick reactions, razor-sharp thinking. His most famous goal, the back-heel for Manchester City against Manchester United, is proof of that. Denis saw opportunities that others didn't, and he knew it. There was a swagger about him, a cockiness. He came from a poor family, didn't have shoes until he was 12, didn't have football boots until he was a teenager, and people from that sort of background learn to live by their wits. That is what Denis did as a footballer, too. A sniff of a chance and he would go for it, with no thought of danger. Sir Matt Busby said Denis scored the bravest goal he ever saw, for Manchester United against Everton. He said they had a left-sided corner, which Bobby Charlton took and swung in towards the near post. There was a giant Everton defender there looking to hoof it clear, but with his great big boot at the top of its backswing and about to come down, this little figure in red darted in and scored with a diving header. He could have got his teeth kicked in, or his skull, but he didn't care. That was Denis. Brave as anything. He was 5 ft 8 in but was fantastic in the air, often out-jumping big brutes of centre-halves.

He showed promise instantly. Andy Beattie, who was the manager of Huddersfield Town when Denis went for a trial, said he was the most unlikely looking footballer he had ever seen. He was skinny and scrawny and had NHS spectacles and a squint. But Andy said he knew he could be great, the moment he saw him kick a ball. Sir Matt Busby felt the same. He was trying to recruit Denis from the day he witnessed his talent in Huddersfield's youth team, destroying a Manchester United side that included some of his famous Babes. Another good judge reckoned Denis from the start, too – my dad. He saw Denis play for Huddersfield at the age of 19, in an FA Cup replay against West Ham. The game took place in the afternoon because there was another replay on in the evening, Arsenal at home to Rotherham United. My dad went to both games – but the player he was raving about when I came home from school the next day was this kid called Law. The pitch was frozen solid, but he was outstanding and Huddersfield won 5–1. 'I saw a proper player yesterday,' Dad told me. 'He had everything – his balance was amazing.' He must have made a big impression because I've heard the same from other people who were there or were told the same story by an older relative. The whole of the East End was talking about this kid called Denis Law after that, and he signed for Manchester City two months later.

Like Jimmy Greaves, Denis went to Italy to play for Torino, but didn't like it, and that was when Matt Busby finally got him for Manchester United. I think that is the Denis that everyone remembers. Sleeves pulled down and the white cuffs clasped in his hands, like he was freezing. At the start, they had to tell him to stay high up the pitch because he wanted to be involved in everything. He would sometimes almost tackle a team-mate because he thought he knew a better way to get a move started, and in the end Busby banned him from the Manchester United half. I think that was the season he scored a goal a game and ended up the European Footballer of the Year. He was magnificent in that period of his career. Not a dribbler, but a live wire nonetheless. He'd be the player the dribbler would look for at the end of his run, the player most likely to finish the move. The way he arrived in the box showed the most brilliant timing, and he was non-stop, always on the move, always causing problems. He had that electricity around him and when he got the ball everything came alive. At any other club, George Best would have overshadowed everybody, and I suppose it is a tribute to the players around him that we still refer to Best, Law and Charlton. It shows you how fantastic Denis was, to be acknowledged in that company.

He wasn't the typical striker of the time, either. Although neither of my selections, Greaves and Law, were tall men, the fashion was for big imposing strikers. Ron Davies was a particular favourite of mine. He had a tremendous scoring record wherever he played – Chester City, Luton Town, Norwich City and then Southampton – and whenever you headed down to The Dell, Southampton's old ground, your defenders knew they were in for a real battering from Ron. I remember one game in 1971. Ron Greenwood, my manager at West Ham, decided we would get the train from Waterloo rather than stay overnight. We got on board late morning, with a big long carriage almost to ourselves. It was Ron's idea that we could have our pre-match meal on the train, eggs or tea and toast, walk from the station to the ground to stretch our legs and still be in the dressing-room by two o'clock. This was going to be the way forward. It was all going nicely until the railway waiter came out with a boiling hot pot of tea, just as the train made a sudden lurch to the left. Over went the tea, straight on to about four players, including our goalkeeper Bobby Ferguson. They all got scalded, they were all screaming and Rob Jenkins, our physio, was having to rush around with balms and cold flannels. People had bandages on their arms and legs, great big patches full of cream and soothing ointments. It had taken about 10 minutes to sort it out, when this bloke appeared with a replacement pot of tea. Another lurch, to the right this time, and he did it again – now all over the lot on the other side of the carriage. Ron went mad. 'Get out, get out, you bloody idiot!' he shouted, and then there were eight of the team looking like they've just come home from the Great War. God knows how we must have appeared as we hobbled off the train, players covered in bandages, creeping along because the material from their suits was now rubbing on the scalded areas. What a fantastic preparation that was – half the team had second-degree burns. Somehow, we went 3–0 up that day – but Southampton came back to draw 3–3. Ron Davies was up front with Mick Channon, and what a handful they were as a pair.

Andy Lochhead at Burnley was another that could always guarantee you a tough game. I think he was probably Bobby Moore's least favourite opponent. A big Scotsman with a bald head, and as hard as nails. He was at you from the start. I remember one game up there, we kicked off and knocked the ball back to Bobby. Lochhead started chasing him down like a lunatic. Bobby didn't fancy that, so he laid it to our other centre-half, John Cushley, but Lochhead wouldn't give up. Now he began charging at Cushley, who thought, sod that, and played it as quick as he could out to John Charles. Again, Lochhead carried on and just as John was about to play it down the line he launched himself at him from about five yards away. It was like he was competing in the long jump. He hit John about knee height and just left him in a heap. Today it would have been the quickest sending off of the season. He'd have been gone within 30 seconds of kick-off. Back then, it was just regarded as setting the tone for the rest of the game. Let them know they were in for a tough match. And being Scottish, Lochhead always had it in for Bobby, too. It was the joke of the dressing-room that Bobby used to get it from the Scots because he was England captain. That was probably the one thing Lochhead and Law would have had in common.

I think Denis described it as the worst day of his life when England won the World Cup. I can't understand that. I know there is rivalry in football between our countries, but some of the England players would have been his mates. How could you want your mate to lose the biggest game of his life? I know Denis thought Jimmy Greaves was the best striker he ever saw, so he must have had respect for English players. I was really disappointed when I read how Denis felt. He said he went out to play golf while the game was on, and threw his clubs into the locker in disgust when he heard the result. Don't worry, Denis. You might not have loved us, but we loved you.

THE SIXTIES: THE TEAM

**GORDON
BANKS**

Leicester City

PAUL REANEY	**BOBBY MOORE**	**JACK CHARLTON**	**RAY WILSON**
Leeds United	West Ham United	Leeds United	Huddersfield Town

GEORGE BEST	**DAVE MACKAY**	**BILLY BREMNER**	**BOBBY CHARLTON**
Manchester United	Tottenham Hotspur	Leeds United	Manchester United

JIMMY GREAVES

Tottenham Hotspur

DENIS LAW

Manchester United

. . . .

CHAPTER THREE

THE SEVENTIES

For me, the 1970s begin with the best World Cup I can remember: Mexico 1970. I think that was probably the finest England team – yes, better than 1966 – and certainly the greatest Brazilian side we have ever seen. They may be the best national team ever. They won every match they played, from the qualifying group to the World Cup final – a run of 12 straight victories. Played 12, won 12, scored 42, conceded 9. Some record. On the way to lifting the trophy they beat Paraguay, Colombia and Venezuela (all twice), plus England, Romania, Czechoslovakia, Peru, Uruguay and Italy. No minnows in that lot, really – and every opponent from either South America or Europe. They had two 1–0 wins, against Paraguay, when they had already qualified, and England, and apart from that never scored fewer than two goals in any game. And like many people, I'd put Carlos Alberto's goal – Brazil's fourth – in the final against Italy as the best the competition has seen. The passing, the movement, that slow build, the vision of those players knowing precisely where their team-mates are, and then that explosive finish.

It truly is a thing of beauty. Tostão works hard, tracks back, mops up, and then Brazil play four short passes around the back waiting for their forwards to get in position. Clodoaldo goes on a little run in his own half, beats about four Italians and lays the ball to Rivelino, who pushes it down the left side to Jairzinho. He passes it inside for Pelé, who spots Carlos Alberto arriving like an express train on the right, waits until just the perfect moment and slips the ball inside to him and – first time – wham! Enrico Albertosi in Italy's goal had no chance. Nobody did, really, against that team.

England came as close as anybody, though, and I think that is part of the reason why the 1970 team is rated so highly. Even though we lost, the match against Brazil felt like a new era was beginning in English football and it is a terrible shame that it was not pursued. There were so many good technical teams at that tournament – Italy were outplayed in the final, but they had some great players like Luigi Riva and Sandro Mazzola. Their semi-final against West Germany that ended 4–3 is recalled as the Game of the Century. It had everything. A last-minute equaliser for Germany and five goals in extra time. Back home, we all thought England should have been in that game, though. We were 2–0 up against Germany in the quarter-finals and lost 3–2. That was probably the beginning of the end for Sir Alf Ramsey. He went after England failed to qualify for the 1974 World Cup, but there was an increasing backlash after losing the Germany game. We had played so well to go two up through goals by Alan Mullery and Martin Peters, and Alf plainly thought the match was won. England's defence had only conceded a single goal in the tournament group stage – and that was against Brazil. The myth, however, is that he makes two substitutions and Germany score three goals – that wasn't the way it happened at all. He was already preparing to take Bobby Charlton off when Franz Beckenbauer scored in the 69th minute – and I suppose his mistake was carrying through with that decision. Yet Germany had already equalised through Uwe Seeler when he removed Peters. He wasn't trying to save him for the semi-final as is widely claimed – he just thought he was exhausted and wanted Norman Hunter to shut Germany down in midfield. Gerd Müller won the game for Germany in extra time and I don't think Alf ever recovered his standing.

He had my sympathy. We've all been there. Every manager has tried to shore a game up, or win one, from the substitutes' bench, always with the best intentions. We all have our reasons, but when things go wrong, if you were winning and you lose, you are the biggest fool in the world and every change you made was the wrong one. Sometimes a substitution will not have had the slightest impact on the game, yet you win and get praised. That's how it goes. Everyone thinks you are a genius if you win – but the substitution has often made no difference. And look at it another way: if the substitute has won the game, why didn't you start him? If the manager was such a bright spark, surely he would have kicked off with the XI that ended up winning the match? I heard last season that one of the reasons Norwich City sacked Chris Hughton was that his substitutions didn't make enough impact. What rubbish. One of the reasons subs don't much make impression at Norwich is because they're Norwich. If the player can't get into Norwich's team, how good is he likely to be? You'll find your substitutions make a lot more impact when you're Manchester City manager and Sergio Agüero or Edin Dzeko is coming off the bench. Funnily enough, Norwich's substitutions didn't seem to make too much impact after Chris left, either. So maybe there was more to it than that.

Whatever the reason England lost in 1970, that was still a fine team, and I think it is a pity that English football was then overwhelmed by the Charles Hughes era, when it was all about scoring with less than five passes and direct play was considered the way to go. Hughes was a former PE teacher who became the assistant director of coaching at the Football Association in 1964 and rose to a position of great power and influence in the game. Under him, we missed an opportunity, thinking we could teach the Brazilians about football rather than the other way around. We told ourselves that Brazil were getting it wrong with all these passes, when there really was a chance to come home from Mexico and try to take our football forward – keep our strengths but try to add some of that Brazilian flair. I think the 1970s changed English football – it is the beginning of the game we see now with so many foreign players. At the start of the decade, we were the reigning world champions and able to hold our own against anybody. By the end, Ossie Ardiles, Ricky Villa, Arnold Mühren and Frans Thijssen had come to our game, and it is the beginning of the thought process that leads to foreign players doing the skilful jobs because our own players are considered not up to it. We were too slow to change. Even now, there are very few British coaches bold enough to try to play a very technical game. The long ball, the quick fix, will always be easier.

Yet I remember 1970 as a real highpoint for football in the country. It was a cracking summer. All day you looked forward to the football at night, and we had a World Cup panel on the television for the first time, which was good fun. It was something new. Malcolm Allison, Derek Dougan, Paddy Crerand and 'beautiful' Bob McNab were the first ones, on ITV. I don't know where Bob's beautiful tag came from – and he was probably the quietest of the lot. Malcolm, typically, was the most outspoken. After England lost to Germany he said Alan Mullery was unfit for international football, and Mullery was so incensed that when he came back to England he insisted on joining the panel. The pair had a tremendous row and Mullery threw one of his England caps at Malcolm. Can you imagine that happening now?

'I am a better player than you ever were,' Mullery told him. 'You're entitled to your opinion, but you never, ever change your mind, you see.' 'If you're going to compare yourself with Overath and Beckenbauer and Ball and Bell, I don't think you're as good a player as them,' Malcolm replied. 'I think you're a good passer of the ball, a good one-paced player – but no acceleration. And I don't think you're good in the air.' 'Is that a problem, no acceleration?' Mullery counters. 'There are stacks of midfield players with no acceleration. I'm as quick as Bally is. I'm not as good a player – but I'm as quick as he is, any day.'

Malcolm was the manager of Manchester City at the time. It would be like having Brendan Rodgers in the studio last summer and having him going at it hammer and tongs with Frank Lampard. It just wouldn't happen now. But football on television was completely different back then. When Brian Clough was sacked by Leeds United, they had his predecessor Don Revie waiting in the studio for him that very night. Incredible. It would be like setting up a live interview with David Moyes the night he was sacked by Manchester United and having Sir Alex Ferguson sitting there – if Moyes and Ferguson hated the sight of each other that is. The whole thing lasted 25 minutes and for the last 10 of them Austin Mitchell, the interviewer, could barely get a word in as the two went at each other. Even now, it is a remarkable piece of television – not least because Revie was the England manager. Can you imagine the Football Association letting their man do that now?

Revie hated Clough and wanted Johnny Giles to get his job. Clough had taken over, got the sack, and clearly inside Revie was doing cartwheels. Obviously, he had been talking to his old players all through Clough's time; they would have been ringing him every minute of the day: 'You'll never guess what this fucking idiot's done now.' You can feel the crackle in the air in the studio the moment that red light goes on. They even call each other 'Clough' and 'Revie', not Don and Brian. Clough talks directly into camera, but it is Revie that is the more aggressive. Now, everything is so slick. These days there would be a team of PR people advising against a studio head-to-head – yet in the interview, Revie actually admits he rang Mitchell and wanted to come in sooner to dispute a statement Clough had made a few weeks previously. Television was a new medium. Everyone was finding out how it could be used. And it was great for the rest of us because we had really interesting coaches like Malcolm Allison or a great manager like Clough analysing the games.

Now, so much of what is said is sanitised. Back then, we loved television's new relationship with the game. Before, no one had ever come on and talked about matches like that – you were used to watching with just a commentator and it was all very staid.

So we loved hearing the panel and guys like Malcolm sounding off – we looked forward to ITV's coverage for that as much as the football itself. I don't think I've ever enjoyed a World Cup so much, and that last goal in the final to cap it off felt like the cherry on the cake. It was a privilege to watch that Brazilian team, and I think we were all rooting for them by the end. If England couldn't win it, then we wanted Brazil because they literally played fantasy football: fantastic skills, fantastic ability, fantastic goals, everything about them was special.

We'd never seen anyone do the Roberto Rivelino move before. He would take the ball up to an opponent put his foot on the inside as if to go outside him and then, at the last moment, step over it and move off in the opposite direction. We couldn't believe what we were seeing. Defenders were going six yards the wrong way, and everyone at home was asking the same question: how did he do that? I can remember the panel slowing the footage down so they could study how it was done. Now everybody tries it – Ronaldinho, Lionel Messi, Cristiano Ronaldo – but Rivelino was the first to do the flip-flap, as he called it. This really was a great, great World Cup.

Even footballers try to imitate the greats. I think when we reported back for training that summer, everyone was trying, secretly, to see if they could do the stepover like Rivellino. I mastered it in the end, but not at the speed he managed it, so I'm not saying I used it in too many matches. I think the greatest coaching vehicle in the world for anyone – particularly kids – is to observe good players and see what they do. All the coaching in the world is sometimes not as valuable as watching a good player in his position. My grandson Harry plays right-back for Bournemouth's youngest academy team, so when we go to Bournemouth together I get him watching the right-back, to see where he plays, where he stands, where he goes. We might not be watching the best right-back in the world, but even if he just learns what the job of the right-back is, that's a good coaching lesson. Suddenly, little Harry knows about forward runs and overlaps, and how to position himself around the other defenders. The better the players, the better the lesson. I remember as a youth player, Ron Greenwood, the West Ham United manager, would get us tickets to go to all the big games. He wanted us to watch Arsenal, Tottenham Hotspur, Chelsea – if there was a game on in London he encouraged us to be there. 'Go and watch the good players,' he would say. I remember in 1963 he took a few of West Ham's best kids to see the European Cup final between AC Milan and Benfica at Wembley. Benfica had a brilliant right winger called José Augusto who became a legend at the club, and all through the match Ron was talking to the four of us about the players that were in our positions. There were some real greats on show that night: Cesare Maldini, Gianni Rivera, José Altafini, Eusébio, Mário Coluna. Milan won 2–1, but to watch them all play was an education in itself. As was the journey home. Ron cut up a lorry by mistake and the driver caught us at the next traffic lights. Suddenly, we were exposed to a whole new vocabulary. 'You fucking stupid cunt, I'll break your fucking neck,' the driver was shouting. Ron looked mortified as the cream of his youth team heard this. To us, he was still Mr Greenwood.

Yet everyone came back from that World Cup and into coaching pyramids that were basically run by schoolteachers. When you went on a course at Lilleshall it was all run by men like

Charles Hughes. There was no flair – it was football as taught by PE instructors. Some had been out to Brazil but the material they returned with didn't make any sense. I remember one day when we were being told that Brazilian footballers hone their skills on the beach. That was where they learnt to control a football and it was how we should do it, too. Where the manager of, say, Derby County was going to find a beach when his training ground was about 70 miles inland, I don't know. I'll never forget there was a silence as we digested this brilliant insight, and some years later I heard it repeated in the company of Jim Smith. 'The beach?' he said. 'In that case, why aren't Torquay, Southend and fucking Brighton and Hove Albion top of the league?' They had no answer to that.

Instead of a great leap forward, we came to the end of an international era, with nothing to replace it. Bobby Charlton retired at the end of the 1970 World Cup; Bobby Moore played his last game for England in November 1973; Alf Ramsey was sacked in May 1974. It was clear we were falling increasingly behind. England won their qualifying group for the 1972 European Championships, but were completely outplayed by West Germany in the play-off game at Wembley and lost 3–1. Günter Netzer was the star of that night – he ran the midfield in a way no English player could – but the German team were shockingly superior in every way. They did things that had never occurred to us. Their full-backs, Horst-Dieter Höttges and Paul Breitner, switched. Franz Beckenbauer played as a *libero*, orchestrating the play from behind the defensive line. They played a 20-year-old, Uli Hoeness, as a deep-lying forward. The manager who came up with this innovation was Helmut Schön, who would go on to win this tournament and the 1974 World Cup. 'England seem to have stood still in time,' he said. 'They gave us a fight, but we were far superior technically.' How often have we heard that since?

The rest of Europe was moving towards total football, and we were going into an era when we stopped trusting our most skilful players. Alan Hudson (2 caps), Tony Currie (17 caps), Stan Bowles (5 caps), Rodney Marsh (9 caps), Peter Osgood (4 caps) – England had players that, technically, could have made any team in the world. We just didn't pick them. I cannot think of a bigger waste of talent in English football than Hudson's two caps or Osgood's four, although knowing Alan, I can imagine why he wasn't picked. If you look at the men that managed England through his era – Ramsey, Joe Mercer, Revie – they were a type. They wouldn't have liked his lifestyle and they wouldn't have liked him. Alan could be his own worst enemy. He could have an argument anywhere and if he didn't respect a manager he wouldn't hide it. I can't think Alan would have had much time for Revie, and the feeling would have been mutual. I do recall, though, that one of his two appearances was in 1975 and ended in a 2–0 home win over West Germany, who were the reigning world champions. Hudson was magnificent that night. So maybe Revie should have persevered.

Alan was a world-class player with a list of flaws a mile long. At Chelsea, he used to have big rows with Dave Sexton, who was one of the nicest men in football and a great coach. Alan was a maverick. He could easily have walked out of the England team hotel the night before a match and gone to the pub, if that's what he fancied. In terms of ability he was second to none, and he had a natural level of fitness that was quite astonishing considering his lifestyle – but no England manager was going to stand for that.

I took Alan to Seattle Sounders with me in 1979 when he was only 27. He was an Arsenal first-team player but had fallen out hugely with Terry Neill, their manager. I met the two of them at Heathrow Airport to get the forms signed before I returned to Seattle. The signature on the paper and deal done, Terry put his hand out to Alan to wish him all the best in his new career and got the worst abuse I've heard in my life. It started with 'fuck off' and went from there. 'Shake hands with you?' Alan said. 'You ain't got a fucking clue, mate.' Terry was the perfect gentleman – he just stood there and took it, didn't say a word – but I can remember thinking, 'Oh Lord, what have I done?' Alan looked as if he was going to be a whole load of trouble – but nothing could have been further from the truth. He was a brilliant player for us, but a brilliant drinker, too. World class in fact. He could go for two days without sleep, or food, and still be the best trainer. I've never seen anyone quite like Alan.

We might play on a Tuesday. He'd be the best player on the pitch, run the game, then go back to his house drinking, and have a party. That would go all night – Sandra and I wouldn't stay because we had a young family back then – but Alan's crowd would only be warming up. A little group of them would then go down to the lake the next day for a barbecue. Alan would buy a gallon of gin, vodka, Coca-Cola and sit there drinking all day. They'd go for a swim, have a bite to eat – not much for Alan, as I recall – and then go straight out for the night, drinking hard again. The following morning we'd be back in for training, so he'd have a few hours' kip and then run harder than anybody. He'd been drinking for two days but no one could keep up with him. At first I organised heavy running sessions specifically to keep Alan fit, because I knew how big his drinking was, but really there wasn't any need. We had a running track at the training ground and Alan could do 200 metres and 100 metres faster than anybody. Then he would go out when training was finished and repeat the session. I'd watch him sometimes and he didn't used to run, he'd glide. He wouldn't have eaten for two days – a pure liquid diet – but there was not an ounce of fat on him and he could run and run. Of course there were rows – Alan could be hard work at times – but they were usually over very quickly and I think his reputation went before him a bit, like a few from that era.

Tony Currie was another. He was a beautiful footballer and if he'd been German he would probably have had three times as many caps; he might even have been our Netzer. Tony had great control, scored fantastic goals and could play a killer pass. He had a great feel for the ball, was a real master of it, and I think could be more disciplined than guys like Hudson or Bowles. He would beat two or three players, look up and see the pass or curl the shot, but I'm not sure he had the defensive mindset that managers of that period wanted. He scored the Goal of the Season in 1978–9, for Leeds United against Southampton, a beautiful low bending shot that was typical of his style.

Ramsey had more faith in him that most other England managers, and it was Tony who absolutely peppered Poland's box in 1973 when we were looking for that winning goal to take us to the World Cup. Revie clearly didn't fancy him as much, and Ron Greenwood picked him at first but then preferred

Trevor Brooking, who had similar ability but forged a unique understanding with Kevin Keegan. In most countries at that time Tony would have been the stand-out player in the national team, but we went through a spell when everybody became obsessed with the other side of football – what does he do when he hasn't got the ball? Guys like Tony and Alan were probably marked down for their defensive work. It was madness really.

I'm sure Tony lived life to the full, as Alan Hudson did – but there was probably less opportunity for mischief in Sheffield than the King's Road. They were proper lads, Hudson's Chelsea team. Big characters like Osgood, Charlie Cooke, Dave Webb – they needed a lot of controlling. You now realise how good a side like Leeds United must have been back then, though, when you go through the individuals in that Chelsea team and realise they never won the league. Maybe there were just too many mavericks for it to work – but every team seemed to have them, including Queens Park Rangers.

Rodney Marsh and Stan Bowles succeeded each other at Loftus Road. They were brilliant footballers – but completely unpredictable. We always imagine the best ball players to be small, but Rodney was a giant for his time, over six foot, yet with a great ability to go past people. I've always felt it was a shame he is associated with that failed transfer to Manchester City – he doesn't deserve to be tagged as the man who cost a team the championship. City were four points clear and coasting when Rodney joined them from QPR in March 1972 – and they ended up in fourth spot. Rodney, by his own admission, didn't play well, but one player alone isn't responsible for such a significant drop in form. Rodney is still a hero at Rangers. He inspired the team through two promotions, reaching Division One, and they won the League Cup as a Third Division side. He really had a special talent but, like Hudson, always found a way of talking himself into trouble. Rodney is credited with one of the most famous one-liners in football – and it may even have cost him his England career. In one game, Alf Ramsey told Rodney he would be watching him particularly closely in the first half, and if he wasn't working hard enough, he would pull him off. 'Bloody hell, Alf,' said Rodney, 'at City they only give us an orange.' I've heard that tale a thousand times, with a thousand different culprits, but I'm told Rodney was the one. (And it was Ray Parlour who sat down with Glenn Hoddle's spiritual healer, Eileen Drewery, and asked for a short back and sides – although I've heard that credited to Robbie Fowler and Paul Gascoigne, among others.) When Tony Book took over at Manchester City, Rodney was in open rebellion. It got back to Book that Rodney had described him as fucking useless. 'If you think I'm fucking useless, this is never going to work,' Book said. 'Do you want to take it back?' 'Actually,' Rodney replied, unrepentant, 'I don't think you're as good as that.'

As players Marsh and Bowles, who both played number 10 for QPR, were quite similar. Fantastic one moment, and then fading out of the game. That is the most frustrating type of player for any manager – and I had another one exactly like that last season in Ravel Morrison. If he'd played consistently at his best, he might have gone to the World Cup; on his bad days you wouldn't have put him in our reserve team. Maybe it's something about QPR. They seem to have had a long line of mavericks here.

There is another story about Rodney at Manchester City, when they were due to play Valencia in the UEFA Cup. They met up for the away leg, everyone in their club gear, and Rodney arrived wearing jeans, a T-shirt with a toothbrush in the top pocket and sandals, carrying a pair of football boots. 'Where do you think you're going?' said one of the coaches. 'Spain,' said Rodney, and carried on walking. He was a real one-off.

Stan was no different. I remember seeing him play for Crewe Alexandra at Brentford back in 1971 and, although he finished on the losing side, he looked different class. You could see then that he would be a top player – but like a lot of those with the most ability in that period he never got the international recognition he deserved. He is still idolised at Loftus Road, but he lives back in Manchester now so we don't see much of him. I don't know if he bets as much as he once did, but his gambling was legendary. He would play snakes and ladders for £50 a corner in the days when that was real money – the most Stan earned in his career was £600 a week. He would be watching the racing at five to three when everyone else was preparing to go out and play – but once he was on that pitch, what a player.

I think these guys had real personalities, and that's why the fans loved them. They were characters. I can remember the first time I met Frank Worthington, who was playing for Huddersfield Town against West Ham. He can only have been about 17 but he came bowling straight up to Bobby Moore. 'All right, Mooro?' he said. 'Here, sign this for us.' And handed him an autograph book. That took some front – particularly as he then went out and played superbly against him. Bobby loved it. 'Class, wasn't he, Harry?' he said. 'Had a bit of style.' And he did. Frank had a unique way and a prolific scoring record at clubs that were never fashionable. And, typically, won a paltry eight caps. He also scored one of the greatest goals ever, for Bolton Wanderers against Ipswich Town in 1979. It is worth seeking out on YouTube. Sam Allardyce takes a long throw from the left, which is flicked on at the near post and comes to Frank with his back to goal on the edge of the penalty area. It is an April pitch, very springy, and the ball bounces up. Frank controls it with his head, and then plays two keepy-ups before, with the third, flicking it over his head, taking four Ipswich defenders out in one move, running round and meeting it on the volley to shoot low into the bottom corner. Apparently, Terry Butcher had been giving Frank a hard time all game, very niggly, and after he scored that goal, Frank couldn't resist a little dig. 'You should have been sitting up there,' he said, pointing to the stand. 'Why?' Butcher asked. 'Because you'd have had an even better view of it from up there,' said Frank.

I just don't think those guys fitted in with the England managers of the time. They certainly wouldn't have appealed to Alf, and while the guys at Leeds could be a bit lively, Revie would have had control over them in a way he wouldn't over Alan Hudson. I think there was a distrust of some of the Southern players from the Northern managers, too, so that wouldn't have helped. I can't imagine Revie being a big fan of any of those Chelsea boys. And then Frank with his cowboy boots – they were just different, those guys. People talk about Brian Clough being a maverick sort of England manager, but I'm not sure he would have changed in this attitude to the tearaways. People forget he took Bowles to Nottingham Forest and they fell out almost instantly. Stan had only been there five days when Clough said to Trevor Francis, 'What are you doing mixing with people like him? I thought you had more class and sense than that.' Stan thought he was joking – but there was no smile, and no punchline. He lasted six months and was sold to Leyton Orient. Clough barely played him.

Looking at this team I've picked from the 1970s, it's striking that there are no Arsenal players in there. They won the double in 1971, the first club to do so since Tottenham in 1961, yet when I go through that team now I am even more impressed by their manager Bertie Mee's achievement. It's a good team, but not a great one. I'm looking at players like Peter Storey, Pat Rice, Peter Simpson, even Charlie George, and I wouldn't have any of them ahead of the ones I've picked here. I think two of the Arsenal players that came along later, Liam Brady and Graham Rix, would have been the stars of that double-winning team. I suppose it shows the value of the team as a unit. I'd still back my lads all day, though.

PAT JENNINGS
(TOTTENHAM HOTSPUR)

I first saw Pat playing in the Northern Ireland youth team in what we called the Little World Cup, against England at Wembley in 1963. The competition had a real name – the UEFA European Youth Tournament – and only countries from one continent were involved, but we weren't as familiar with international football then and it felt like a World Cup to us. I went to all the games that England played, and Northern Ireland made the final.

They beat the Republic of Ireland, Belgium, Czechoslovakia, and drew with Sweden and Bulgaria to get there. There were no penalty shoot-outs, so they went through in the semi-final against Bulgaria by drawing lots, which seems ridiculous now. England won 4–0, but I remember everybody being impressed by this big lad in goal for Northern Ireland. A week later Pat signed for Watford.

I got to know him a few years ago when I was managing at Tottenham and he was coaching there. At first he told me didn't want to come over to England. He didn't want to leave his parents in Newry. Pat was a quiet man then, so I can imagine what he must have been like as a teenager. Bill McGarry was one of his managers at Watford and he reckoned the last word Pat ever spoke was 'Goodbye' when he left his parents' house. He wasn't as bad as that, but he certainly wasn't an outgoing type, just very softly spoken, calm and sensible. He was a class act off the field as well as on it, and chatting with Pat was one of the reasons I used to look forward to going to work at Tottenham. He used to come in two or three days a week to work with the goalkeepers, and it was always a pleasure to talk football with him. He doesn't shout his mouth off, but his views about the game are spot-on and I always valued his opinions. He kept goal the same way. He never made a fuss, he was never showy, but what he did, he did magnificently. For a time he was probably the best goalkeeper in the world.

That Northern Ireland youth team of 1963 wasn't bad. As well as Pat there was Dave Clements, who had a big career at Coventry City, but it was just too early for George Best. I think it's a real shame that players like George and Pat never got to play a real World Cup at their peak. Pat did make it to Mexico with Northern Ireland in 1986 and played their three group matches, but he turned 41 on the day of the last one, against Brazil. It was a fitting end to his international career – but what a pity he couldn't have been part of it, say, 12 years earlier when he was at the height of his powers with Tottenham. Even so, it must have been more fun managing Northern Ireland through those years than it is now. Best up front, Jennings in goal – you might get away with that combination. I think they would certainly have qualified had the World Cup been in its present, 32-team, format. These days they are too far down the rankings to get much luck when the draw is made. They always seem to be up against West Germany or one of the really big boys. Maybe they'll have more chances now the European Championship is up to 24 teams – but they haven't got many around like Pat any more.

Pat's background was in Gaelic football and I think that gave him a disregard for getting hurt. He was very brave in the way he came for the ball, and very athletic, always throwing himself about. Not in a dramatic way – but Pat wasn't scared of taking a tumble or going in where it hurt. Gaelic is a very hard game, so Pat probably didn't think too much of getting the odd bang on the football field. Bill Nicholson took him to Tottenham in 1964 as part of a big rebuilding process when the double team began to fade. Alan Mullery, Cyril Knowles, Alan Gilzean – they all joined at around the same time. Pat was the replacement for Bill Brown, who was another double winner and a local hero. It took about two seasons, but by 1966 Pat was Tottenham's first-choice keeper. It would have been hard because there was huge expectation at Tottenham after what had gone before, but they won the FA Cup in 1967 and Pat was a huge part of that. He wasn't very big by modern standards – about 5 ft 11 in – but he looked big, and acted big; he was the first goalkeeper I remember that really dominated his area. Anything near that six-yard box and you knew Pat was coming for it. When I met him later in life I said that I couldn't believe he wasn't 6 ft 4 in. He always seemed huge to us, and was famous for being able to pull a cross out of the air with one hand. He made it all look so easy. Never flapped. Never got ruffled. I remember a game against Liverpool at Anfield in the 1972–3 season when he got cheered off by The Kop having almost cost them the league title. He was brilliant, Tottenham got a draw and at the time it looked as if he might have handed the prize to Arsenal. Liverpool came through in the end – but it shows the sort of man Pat was, that the Liverpool fans could still appreciate him, despite the cost to their team. I'm not sure it would happen now.

In fact, I think it shows how highly Pat was regarded that in 1977 he left Tottenham for Arsenal without there being a lasting feeling of resentment towards him at White Hart Lane. Sol Campbell did it and got slaughtered – and it seems he'll be hated by Tottenham fans for evermore. Yet there is a lounge named in Pat's honour at White Hart Lane now; he is a coach at the club and a match-day host. And he always strolls into any supporters' list of Tottenham legends.

Selling Pat to Arsenal must rank as one of the biggest transfer mistakes Tottenham have ever made – and there's quite a list. I think the club thought his best years were behind him – so it must have come as quite a surprise to see him still holding a place in Arsenal's first team six years later, as he became the first player in English football to pass 1,000 senior appearances. Pat reached the FA Cup final in three consecutive campaigns with Arsenal, winning once, and saved a penalty from Mario Kempes in the final of the 1980 European Cup-Winners' Cup, but sadly ended up on the losing side because Liam Brady and Graham Rix missed.

Manchester United, Aston Villa and Ipswich Town were all in for Pat when he left – but, unsurprisingly, a typical piece of Tottenham politics pushed him the way of Arsenal. Pat knew he was leaving but still went to the ground to say goodbye to the rest of the team, who were departing for a pre-season trip to Sweden. The directors were going, too, and Pat says that as they passed him, one by one, they all blanked him. It was then he decided to consider an offer from Arsenal. Until that point he had resigned himself to commuting up and down the motorway – but getting such cold treatment after 13 years at the club drove him to sign for Tottenham's big rivals. He is very straight about it – he did it for convenience and in the hope of embarrassing the Tottenham bigwigs. Over the next eight years he did just that – yet he still got applauded every time he went back to Tottenham. The fans never blamed him for what happened.

The negative reaction to former players is something quite new in football. There was plenty of bad behaviour among fans in the seventies, but players did not seem to be targeted the same way. The crowd fought each other and obviously some grounds were livelier than others, but there never seemed to be that animosity towards those who played the game. When Pat left Arsenal he even came back to Tottenham to keep himself fit and ready for the 1986 World Cup.

I know Bob Wilson, who Pat replaced at Arsenal, says he was the best of all time. He puts him ahead of Gordon Banks or Peter Shilton. The one I feel sorry for, really, is Ray Clemence. In any other era he would have been England's number one, but at either end of his career he coincided with the two greatest goalkeepers this country has had. I do remember Ray was coach at Tottenham, though, when Ian Walker broke into the team as goalkeeper and in one of his first games took a cross with one hand, Pat Jennings style. It is fair to say the views Ray expressed on the subject that day indicated he too thought there could only ever be one Pat Jennings.

PHIL NEAL
(LIVERPOOL)

Until Ryan Giggs came along I cannot imagine too many would have matched Phil Neal for medals: eight title wins, four European Cups, four League Cups, the UEFA Cup and UEFA Super Cup. He is still the most decorated English footballer in history, but holds a record even more fantastic than that. Between 23 October 1976, when he played in a 1–1 draw away at Leeds United, and 24 September 1983, a 1–0 defeat at Manchester United, Phil Neal did not miss a single Liverpool game in any competition: a run of 417 consecutive matches. He then lost three games to injury, after which he did another 127 in a row. I can safely predict that in these days of squad rotation we will never see that record broken by an outfield player at an elite club.

Phil seemed indestructible – he certainly behaved as if he was. Derby County had a telegraph pole of a centre-forward around that time called Roger Davies. He had come through the non-league ranks, worked as an apprentice engineer, and had been picked up by Derby for £12,000. He wasn't the most subtle or technically gifted player, but he was always difficult to play against and in one game caught Phil with an elbow and broke his cheekbone. The injury was so bad it needed an operation to realign Phil's face, and the specialist said he should rest for a month – yet four days later he played for the club again, having told Paisley he was fine. And no protective masks back then, either. He just marched out and, fingers crossed, hoped he would get away with it. On another occasion he broke a toe – the fifth metatarsal that ruined Wayne Rooney's World Cup in 2006 – but played on with a tiny plaster cast made by Ronnie Moran. He went up a boot size and a half and could barely walk in normal shoes, but somehow Phil played on. He had injections into the damaged area to enable him to kick a ball and tackle. There are very few players in the modern game who would go through the pain barrier like that.

Liverpool nearly missed out on him, too. On Paisley's last scouting trip to see Phil play for Northampton Town, he took along a director, Sidney Reaks, probably to convince him that he was worth the money. Just 20 minutes into the game, the Northampton goalkeeper got injured and Phil spent the rest of the night in goal. Fortunately, the men had already seen enough and Paisley paid £66,000 for Phil as a replacement for Chris Lawler at right-back. He could have played left-back, too, and within days started the Merseyside derby. Back then, players could take those dramatic steps up, and Liverpool were the best at judging it. They just had the knack of pulling players from the lower leagues and turning them into superstars. They scouted Phil and saw in him a cultured, classy full-back, far superior to his surroundings. Phil was good on the ball, passed nicely, took penalties and scored so many important goals the Liverpool players nicknamed him Zico.

He was another of those 7 out of 10 players. He wasn't one for cavalier charges up field, but as a manager you recognise the type – and guys like him are often the first names on the team sheet. If you think back to the Liverpool team of that era, so much of their strength came from the back. Phil Neal, Alan Hansen, always unruffled, never under pressure, always composed on the ball. Just passed it and passed it. You never saw Neal panic and whack it anywhere, there was always a ball into a channel, something the rest of the team could work from. Liverpool simply had an air of calmness, and that stemmed from Neal and those players at the back. He always looked composed, playing the game as if he was completely in control.

I always thought it was a shame for Phil that to a certain generation he is remembered for the documentary about Graham Taylor's ill-fated World Cup campaign as England manager. Phil Neal is Taylor's coach and comes across in the film as a bit of a yes man, always agreeing with his boss, seconding his opinions or parroting what has just been said. I know Phil thinks he was misrepresented at the editing stage but, whatever the truth, it is never easy fulfilling the assistant-manager role, because the boss it always going to back his hunch in the end. In the first high-profile job that I had, with West Ham United, Frank Lampard was invaluable to me because he had strong opinions that he wasn't afraid to share. You don't want to be rowing every two minutes, but you do want your assistant to speak up if he spots something going wrong, and if you ask him about a substitution, for instance, you want his call, not what he thinks you want to hear. You're looking for genuine feedback, not just agreement – and my guess is that there was more to Phil's partnership with Graham than what we saw. Frank was someone I could bounce things off all the time, even during the games. He is a wealthy individual, invested wisely during his playing days, and didn't have to be nice to anybody to stay in a job. It made a difference. He didn't stay in football long after West Ham because what appealed was working for me, and at Upton Park. I'm sure Graham got Phil in as the type of coach that would be admired by the team for his achievements as a player, and he should have felt confident enough to use that experience. If Phil read the game as a coach as well as he did as a player he could have been tip-top.

PHIL THOMPSON
(LIVERPOOL)

Wimbledon's Crazy Gang were never the greatest respecters of reputations, but even by their standards full-back John Kay was relentless, and known for a vicious sense of humour. One tackle by Kay on Peter Haddock, a defender playing at Leeds United, left manager Howard Wilkinson saying his leg looked like it had been run over by a tractor. After that, Kay revelled in the nickname 'The Tractor'. He moved from Wimbledon to Sunderland in 1987 and in one game against Birmingham City broke a leg – his own this time. Despite being in terrible pain, Kay sat up on the stretcher and pretended to row it off the pitch and down the tunnel. It's fair to say he was a nutcase. And it was Kay who during one of the first matches between upstarts Wimbledon and the mighty Liverpool is said to have taken a distinct interest in Phil Thompson's pronounced features while waiting for a corner to be taken. 'Do you know what, mate?' Kay told the Liverpool captain. 'Walt Disney couldn't draw your fucking face.'

Wimbledon's attitude was the reason they made such an impact on the top division, so I'm not knocking it – but Phil Thompson deserved a little more deference than that. We are talking about one of the great centre-halves in one of the great teams. He might be craggy, he might have a famously prominent hooter, but he was also a leader, a winner and a serious competitor. I don't know if Kay got the last word that day, but if I know Phil, there was an elbow in the gob waiting somewhere along the line. He could play, but he was aggressive too. They were a beautiful team, Liverpool, but they also had a knack of finding or producing some real hard cases – Tommy Smith, Ron Yeats, Emlyn Hughes, Phil, they could all look after themselves. Mark Lawrenson was a lovely footballing centre-half, but there are plenty in the game who will vouch for the fact he was the hardest tackler, too. In some ways those Liverpool players were like Brazil stoppers. They were up against great strikers every day in training – Kevin Keegan, John Toshack, Ian Rush, Kenny Dalglish – and they could be made to look pretty silly if they weren't at the top of their game. It's the same in Brazil – growing up playing against some of the finest footballers in the world, no defender wants to be made to look a mug. People are often surprised that Brazilian players are quite cynical – but playing against the likes of Ronaldo or Rivaldo, wouldn't you be? The alternative is getting a chasing.

Phil started off as a central midfield player and only moved back to centre-half after his first season. He was physically strong, but not a big man and far from a routine defender. Hughes and Alan Hansen, his two main partners, were more conventional in their approach, while Phil played it like a continental. Bob Paisley thought he was one of the best readers of a game that he saw, and he was very comfortable on the ball. Graeme Souness told me that Thompson was actually a better technical footballer than Hansen and, as he played with both, I'm not about to disagree. He was an organiser, too, and different class when the pressure was on; you never saw that generation of Liverpool players rattled. In the 1978–9 season, he was part of a defence that let in only 16 goals in 42 matches.

A lot of people of my generation remember the 1974 FA Cup final as one of Phil's greatest matches: Liverpool 3, Newcastle United 0. Kevin Keegan scored twice, but before the game all the talk had come from Malcolm Macdonald, who had scored in every round and was promising to do all of that and more to Liverpool. Bill Shankly, in his last competitive game as Liverpool manager, put the 20-year-old Thompson on him, and Phil marked him out of the match. Malcolm did get some tiny revenge, though. Sometime later they were on an England trip together and sitting down at dinner he discovered that Thompson couldn't stand the smell of garlic. A dish with a strong garlic smell came to a table nearby and Thompson was extremely uncomfortable. After that, the story goes, Macdonald would eat cloves of garlic before every match against Liverpool, and breathe on Thompson the moment he got near. He claimed to have an extra half-yard through the rest of his career using this method. Makes you wonder how Phil was so good in Europe, though.

I think what also sets Phil Thompson apart in Liverpool folklore is that he was a local lad from Kirkby who had stood on The Kop since he was a kid. Liverpool had a brilliant scouting network at that time – in fact, I've never seen one better – and just had a way of spotting these players in the lower leagues and bringing them through. They would go to Bury and get a player like Alec Lindsay or Northampton for Phil Neal; and while Emlyn Hughes came from Blackpool, who were then a top division club, Bill Shankly bought him after only 28 appearances.

These players would go straight into the team, too. It makes me think that maybe English players could still do it, given the opportunity. There were no foreign players in the English game back then, so you had to rely on your instincts and make these promotions. Given the opportunity, belief and support from the manager, and the comforting environment of a good team, English players showed they could make the step up from the lower leagues to, in some cases, the European Cup final.

One of the unsung heroes of Liverpool's success is Geoff Twentyman, the chief scout for close to 20 years, whose discoveries ranged from Neal to Alan Hansen (£100,000 from Partick Thistle) and Ian Rush (£300,000 from Chester City). Twentyman was a player at Carlisle United when Bill Shankly became manager there. He moved on and had a modest career with Liverpool, and he left just as Shankly was arriving as manager in 1959. It wasn't until 1967 that the pair reunited, when Shankly offered him the position of chief scout. Liverpool were a very different club then and Twentyman's brief was to find the best players that they could afford, not established stars on huge wages. He and Shankly had very similar ideas on what constituted a Liverpool player, and there are stories of Geoff ending a scouting mission having watched only the warm-up because he wasn't happy with his target's level of professionalism. Another factor was what Twentyman and Shankly called a Northern soul – they didn't like Southerners – and it wasn't until Paul Walsh joined Liverpool in 1984 that Twentyman recommended a Londoner join the ranks. Excluding such a large swathe of the populace didn't harm Liverpool's fortunes, though. Twentyman's strike rate was nothing short of astonishing: Kevin Keegan, John Toshack, Steve Heighway, Ray Clemence – and he was always in on the ground floor, so Liverpool were bidding when other clubs were just waking up to the news of a young prospect at Scunthorpe or Skelmersdale United. Liverpool bought Gary Gillespie from Coventry City, but Geoff was already monitoring him at Falkirk. Not every trip ended in success, though. Twentyman's first recommendation to Shankly was Francis Lee, but Liverpool could not afford him; nor did they follow up Geoff's interest in Andy Gray, Trevor Francis or Martin Buchan. Yet his strike rate was phenomenal.

Liverpool looked at players differently. Often they had already come to a conclusion about a player's technical ability and were more worried about character. Does he take the warm-up seriously? Is he a bit flash? Paisley wouldn't sit with the managers or scouts if he was watching a player. He, or Twentyman, would buy a ticket and stand behind the goal, get talking to the local fans, ask what a certain player was like. These days managers are so famous that this could never happen. Imagine José Mourinho turning up at Southend United and trying to remain incognito. He would be mobbed. Not that Chelsea would be buying players from Southend any more, of course. Scouting has completely changed in the modern era.

I still go to watch players and it makes me laugh, sometimes, sitting with those old boys. Half of them spend the match gossiping – what is going on at this club, who's getting the sack, who's been tapped up, who is going where. Then there is usually a moan about the facilities, about how you always used to get nice sandwiches here at half time, but now they don't even lay out a plate of biscuits. Then, 15 minutes before the end, they all get up and go to beat the traffic. In the meantime, most of the big money scouting is done on video via agents. If you need a right-back, an agent comes on and tells you he has a 20-year-old from Estonia, who is going to be the best full-back in Europe. He sends a link, you go into the club cinema and a minute later everything you need to know about him is up on screen – the games he's played, the goals he has scored, match footage, the lot. You can go from never having heard of a player to watching him play a full game in the time it takes to make a cup of tea.

It has changed so much. When I started playing, club scouts were at every big schoolboy game in the area: East London Boys, Ilford Schools, Hackney Boys, Barking Schools, Dagenham Boys, they would be there on the touchline, grafting, talking to the parents if they thought the kid was good enough. The next week, they would be round the house, chatting them up over a cup of tea, because a good kid might have six clubs chasing him. Scouts were real grafters in those days.

When I was a youth team coach in the mid seventies, during my playing days at Bournemouth, one of my smartest moves was to appoint one of the best youth scouts. How did I come to be coaching? John Benson was the manager at the time and we had a youth team but no coach. The old kit man was doing the best he could; the kids would arrive in the morning and he'd oversee matches, eight-a-side, six-a-side, depending on how many were available, but it was very unorganised. I said to John, 'Those kids, they're wasted. They never get any instruction – why don't I take them?' We had a fantastic scout working for us called Reg Tyrell, who had been at Ipswich Town and discovered players like Clive Woods and Trevor Whymark. A lot of people reckoned Reg as the best in the country. He was a great character, always laughing. He used to wear a little trilby hat.

Reg drove Bill McGarry, the manager of Ipswich, mad. In the end, Bill used to draw a line in the grass at the training ground. 'Reg, if you cross that line, I swear I'll fucking boot your arse.' John Bond had persuaded him to come down to Bournemouth as our chief scout in the early seventies, and I ended up getting him involved with youth development as well. We ended up with about six young players who had good careers, like Steve Gritt who played 435 games for Charlton Athletic – and a couple of England internationals, Kevin Reeves and Graham Roberts. Reg found them all just by watching Sunday-morning parks games. They weren't schoolboy superstars. He got them in the old-fashioned way, standing in his cap in the rain on a touchline. That was what it was about back then: going to these out-of-the-way places, scouting and having the balls to back your judgement. Imagine spotting Phil Neal playing for Northampton, and thinking he'll have the ability to play a European Cup final in front of 57,000 people three years later – and the guts to take a penalty to wrap the game up. But he did. Go back to that 1977 Liverpool team – scouted from Scunthorpe, Northampton, Wrexham, Blackpool, Skelmersdale, Bury – what an incredible achievement to see the potential in all of those boys. There was no sitting on the fence, no uncertainty about making the step up. The scout had to go to Shankly, or Paisley, and put his neck on the line. He had to say that Scunthorpe's goalkeeper wouldn't let us down in a European Cup final against Real Madrid. And he was right – Ray Clemence was superb when the moment came.

There must have been real pleasure in making those discoveries, though – a satisfaction you just won't get from watching tapes in a dark room. Imagine the night Bobby Gould, then manager of Coventry City, first saw Stuart Pearce play for Wealdstone in the old Gola League. That rarely happens now, that feeling of revelation. I can picture Bob sitting there now, watching this six-foot, marauding left-back, who can score goals one minute and boot the right-winger into the stand the next. It wouldn't have taken a genius to see what he saw in Pearce – but he must have felt like he'd just found a diamond lying on the pavement. He made a £30,000 bid the next day and put him straight in Coventry's team. I remember Dave Webb getting Nigel Spackman from Andover's bench. He couldn't even make their team, but went on to captain Liverpool and Glasgow Rangers. Jim Smith paid £15,000 for Les Ferdinand at Queens Park Rangers after spotting him playing for Hayes.

Cyrille Regis was another great centre-forward who came from Hayes. I remember David Pleat saying there was a real buzz around this kid Regis playing in the Isthmian League, and on one particular night there was no other game in town and it seemed that every club in the country was there, watching him. Regis did nothing. All the managers and scouts were looking at him, shrugging their shoulders; nobody was impressed. With about 10 minutes left to play, one of them made a move to go, and one by one they all started to follow him, down the wooden stairs at Hayes's Church Road ground. With that, Hayes's wide player put in a cross and Cyrille jumped three feet higher than anyone on the pitch – bang, straight in the corner. Everyone froze in mid-step. That was what they had all gone there to see. If a goalscorer can do that one thing better than any other player, he'll make it. West Bromwich Albion were the first on the telephone the next day. The directors weren't sure about paying so much for a non-league player, but Albion's scout, Ronnie Allen, was so sure he offered to cover the £5,000 fee himself.

Sometimes you just have to trust people. Stuart Morgan, my assistant manager at Bournemouth in the eighties, went to watch Efan Ekoku at Sutton United. He came into my office the following morning. 'Harry,' he said, 'I've seen a player – he's something special. Different class. He's got pace, he's got ability, he's so fucking strong. We've got to take him.' Their next game was the following Tuesday night, so I said I'd go with Stuart and watch him play. If he had wanted to, he couldn't have performed any worse. I don't remember him doing a single thing right in 90 minutes. I said to Stuart, 'Have you gone mad?' 'I'm telling you, Harry,' he said, 'I've watched him twice and he's been amazing. If he isn't any good, you can sack me.' He was going to cost us £40,000. We asked Sutton if he could train with us for a week. If we liked him, they had their £40,000. Seven days later, it was still touch and go – but Stuart was insistent. In the end we took him and he was brilliant for us. We sold him to Norwich City for £500,000 – and they moved him on to Wimbledon for £900,000. He had a good Premier League career. And that was all down to Stuart backing his judgement and being trusted – because if it had been left up to me I would have walked out at half-time.

You don't get stories like that these days – unknowns straight into the first team at elite clubs. Daniel Sturridge is looked upon as a revelation at Liverpool, but it wasn't as if he came from nowhere. He was a Manchester City player, a big signing at Chelsea, and then Liverpool paid £12 million for him. If anything, it was a surprise that Chelsea let him go. He was ripping into teams from that right-sided position, coming in on his left foot. We played against him at Tottenham, and a lot of our defensive work all week was built around stopping Sturridge. He could dart in towards goal, he could go outside and get it across the face of you; he really looked a player. He didn't track back enough, though, and André Villas-Boas bombed him out. Liverpool got lucky, really. It wasn't as if they discovered him in the wilderness. Liverpool were outstanding for a lot of last season, but it wasn't a team built up like in the old days. Luis Suárez was Uruguay's striker, and a World Cup player. The only one whose arrival compares to that Twentyman era really is Raheem Sterling, who came from Watford. But he didn't walk straight into the team as players used to.

Yet that great Liverpool team wasn't just about the signings. Shankly was a real visionary when it came to scouting and recruitment. Players like Thompson came through after being spotted at a young age, and that's not easy when you have a team as big as Everton across the way. In 1968, Shankly appointed the first Youth Development Officer in English football, Tom Saunders, and the club were still getting use from him when my Jamie went there in 1991. He was an ex-schoolteacher, a wily old boy, and I think Kenny Dalglish and then Graeme Souness leaned on him a lot. He did all their overseas scouting missions in Europe, going to these places inside the Iron Curtain where they definitely didn't want you. The story goes that for one match at Anfield, the manager of Dinamo Tbilisi came over to create his scouting report, so Liverpool thought they would show how hospitality to the opposing club should be done. They invited this bloke down to the famous boot room, where he got stuck into the Guinness with Bob Paisley and the boys. By the end of it, he could hardly stand. They virtually had to carry him to his car and I doubt he remembered much.

ROY McFARLAND
(DERBY COUNTY)

Here we go again. Roy McFarland was one of the greatest central defenders in one of the finest defensive partnerships this country has produced, and Derby County took him for £24,000 from Tranmere Rovers. Apparently, Liverpool were also sniffing around, but Brian Clough and Peter Taylor went to his house and refused to leave until he joined Derby. Then they paired him with Dave Mackay and he never looked back. He was a footballing centre-half. He was strong in the air, but would get the ball down and play as well, little one-twos out of the area. Colin Todd, who succeeded Mackay, was under instructions not to cross the halfway line, but Roy had more freedom. He says the greatest piece of advice Clough ever gave him was that he couldn't bring the ball out of defence every time; sometimes it had to end up in the back of the stand. The key to being a great defender was to know when was the right time for each move, Clough said – and only he could work that out. Very true.

I admit, I have had to agonise long and hard over this one. I really wanted a place for Todd in this team, too, but I prefer McFarland, and there is no way I won't find room for Phil Thompson. Yet Todd was a quite outstanding player, and captained Derby at their peak. He was very quick, could bring the ball out and was difficult for attackers to compete with because, basically, he was built like them. He didn't have the stereotypical defender's frame at all – he was squat, with a low centre of gravity and good ball skills. He could read the game and played magnificently off McFarland, but he was tough, too – just like his son, Andy.

It shows how times have changed that Todd was an integral part of the Sunderland team that won the FA Youth Cup in 1967, coached by Brian Clough, yet also made 30 first-team appearances that season. It just wouldn't happen now. Once a young player has made the senior team, he wouldn't demean himself playing with his youth team-mates any more, and the manager wouldn't want him risked at a lower level. Yet in those days tournaments like the FA Youth Cup were there to be won, and clubs would put out the best-qualified team regardless of the players' status. I wonder if we haven't lost something there.

The most impressive aspect of Clough's Derby team is the football they managed to play on that pitch. The Baseball Ground was comfortably the worst in the country, yet they played some marvellous stuff. Not a blade of grass on it after about two months, and then like a beach in April, but it never seemed to stop them. Alan Hinton and Kevin Hector were terrific centre-forwards, and they had Terry Hennessy in a defensive midfield role, stepping up from centre-half, ahead of his time. That Derby team could all play. They moved the ball beautifully and that was down to Clough. Just getting Dave Mackay in was a genius move, and judgement calls like that happened too often with him for it to be luck.

Frank Clark was a free transfer for Clough's Forest from Newcastle United, who'd probably thought he was at the end of his career. Clark was talking to Stan Anderson, the manager of Doncaster Rovers in Division Four, when Clough got in touch. Clark signed the next day. From Birmingham City he took Kenny Burns, who was known as a bit of a thug, and turned him into the Footballer of the Year; and he took Larry Lloyd, who everybody thought had enjoyed his best years at Liverpool.

It was a pity that, later in Clough's career, some of that brilliance deserted him and what was left could be a bit difficult. During the summer in 1991, my chairman at Bournemouth called and said he'd had Brian Clough on the phone wanting to buy our centre-half, Shaun Teale. Shaun was a player I had bought from Weymouth for £50,000 two years earlier and he was going right to the top. He reminded me of Colin Todd: similar size, great spring, fast, aggressive, a good left foot. The chairman said he had told Clough to speak to me about any deal and had given him my number. 'He's going to ring you,' he said, so I waited for the call. It was a beautiful day and we were heading out to Salisbury races. I waited but heard nothing. Then, in the car on the way there, the mobile burst into life. The voice was unmistakable.

'Harry, it's Brian Clough.'

'Hello, Brian, how are you doing?'

'Yes, I'm fine. Very good, actually. Now, listen, I'm interested in your man Teale. He's one of your cockney boys, is he?'

'No,' I said. 'He's from Southport.'

'Is he?' he said. 'And how big is he?'

I said: 'He's about five foot eleven or six foot, Brian. He's not a giant for a centre-half, but he can jump like he's six foot four, he's fantastic in the air, a great header of the ball, beautiful timing.'

'All right,' he said. 'How much do you want for him?'

I told him the price was £500,000. 'I'll not give you that,' he said, 'but I'll give you £499,999.'

This was his little game. He always said he paid £999,999 for Trevor Francis because he didn't want the tag of being the first £1 million player going to his head. By now I had pulled the car over. I didn't have to think for long. 'We won't fall out over a pound, Brian,' I told him. 'You've got a deal.' 'Have a word with the boy and we will get it sorted,' Clough said. So I got hold of Shaun and he came down to our ground to await instructions on the next step of his big move. Nottingham Forest had just lost to Tottenham Hotspur in the FA Cup final and were still in the top half of Division One at that time. Three hours passed, we hadn't heard a thing from Clough. I called the club, got through to his secretary. 'I'm sorry, Mr Redknapp,' she said, 'Brian's gone to Majorca for two weeks and he's not contactable.' We never heard another word.

In the end, Shaun signed for Ron Atkinson at Aston Villa, who had also never seen him. I bumped into Ron on holiday in Spain. By then, we'd gone a month without hearing from Forest, so I knew the deal was dead. 'Who is the best centre-half in your division?' Ron asked me. 'Shaun Teale,' I said. 'Who's he play for?' said Ron. 'Bournemouth,' I told him. 'No, seriously,' he repeated, 'who's the best centre-half? Don't try to sell me your player, I'm asking you a sensible question.' 'And I'm giving you a sensible answer,' I told him. 'Shaun Teale – check him out.' I came back and three days later Ron rang me. 'I've checked him out,' he said. 'You were telling the truth, he is a good player. But I'm told he might be short of a yard of pace.' 'Whoever told you that isn't a judge, then,' I told him, 'because he's like lightning.' So Ron took him and he made close to 200 appearances for Villa. I think Clough was the loser that day.

But that was Brian. Many years earlier he did the same to Kevin Bond, who was supposed to sign for Nottingham Forest from Manchester City. John Benson, his manager, said the deal with Forest was done, so off he went. Kevin arrived at the ground at 9am as arranged and was told to wait outside Mr Clough's office. He sat there for an hour and a half. Brian's secretary kept telling him that Clough was busy. Suddenly, he came out, stopped and looked at Kevin. 'The first thing you need to do, young man, is get your hair cut,' he said. And on he walked, straight past him. Kevin, waiting another hour or two, thought, 'What am I doing this for?', got up and went back to Manchester City. He never heard another word.

It's hard to tell with Brian how much was psychological masterstroke, and how much was random acts caused by his problems with alcohol. There is a story in a book about Clough that concerns the party after Derby had won the league in 1972. Everybody was having a wonderful time, when Clough suddenly rounded on Colin Todd. 'Toddy,' he said, 'I don't like you, and I don't like your missus, either.' Todd walked out. The next day everybody got flowers and the whole thing was smoothed over, and the take on it is that Clough thought Todd was too nice for a defender and too quiet for someone he thought might captain the club. He wasn't a drinker, a smoker, a gambler, a womaniser – Clough couldn't work him out, so wanted to get a reaction from him. And maybe that is true. Todd says Clough might kick him in training too, just to get him wound up. He obviously doesn't bear a grudge, but you wonder how much was intended. It's sad, but I think Brian's problems got worse through his career.

Every manager has a different way of handling players. Rafael Benítez is known for being very cold, very sparing in his praise. When Liverpool won the Champions League in Istanbul, Steven Gerrard thought he might finally get a 'well done' out of him, after the game of his life. They had the giant trophy in pride of place on the top table, and all night Steve kept edging towards it thinking that he would ultimately get a pat on the back from his manager. Eventually he got there. Gerrard, Benítez and the trophy all within touching distance. 'Not bad that, eh, boss?' said Steve, eyeing the cup. 'Yes,' said Benítez, 'but ...' And he started bollocking him for mistakes he made in the first half. I think everybody needs to hear 'well played'. Even Bobby Moore used to secretly hope for more praise from Ron Greenwood.

I can remember talking to Stuart Pearce about the way Clough operated when we were at West Ham United together. I think all managers are fascinated by him because there was so much innovation in what he did, and so many myths have grown around him since. 'He was amazing,' Stuart told me. 'We wouldn't see him all week, and then he'd come in on Friday and walk his dog. We were playing five-a-sides one day and he said to [Forest full-back] Brian Laws, "You're wasting your time doing this – take my dog for a walk." And Brian did – twice around the training ground, while Clough watched the five-a-side.' Unbelievable, isn't it?

Last season, Chelsea beat Fulham 3–1 and José Mourinho said the first half was their worst performance of the season. He claimed that he said nothing to them at half-time, just walked in and walked out. That is straight out of Clough's handbook. It is what he's said to have done with his players when they were losing 1–0 to Southampton in the 1979 League Cup final. 'You lot got yourselves into this, you can get yourselves out of it,' he said. As a manager, you've only got 15 minutes to try to influence the game once it has begun. It takes some guts to do that.

Alan Hill, who was Clough's assistant, is a good friend of mine and he told me how Clough used to simplify the game. 'Goalkeeper, your job is to save goals. Right-back, left-back, stop their wingers. You tackle, you win the ball. You, centre-halves, you head it out of the box. Ball comes in, your job is to clear it out, your job is to get there, win headers, win tackles. You get it, give it to people who can play. Midfield players, get on the ball, make us play. Get it out to your wingers. Give them the ball, we play with two wingers, give it to them. Every time you've got it, I want that ball supplied to the wingers. Wingers, you get down the line, you get crosses in. That's your job. Beat the full-back, get the ball in the box. You two up front, your job is to score the goals. Centre-forwards score.' And that was it. He played 4–4–2, nothing else, but his observations within that framework, Alan tells me, were so clever. Little pieces of information he would come out with, like his advice to McFarland about not expecting to bring the ball out of defence every time. He must have just had a gift for football thinking, and the way to motivate players. However difficult he may have been to deal with at times, you can't achieve what he did by accident. You can't take Derby to the title and Nottingham Forest to the European Cup just making it up as you go along. There was always a philosophy there. He may have couched it very simply, but we all remember how a Brian Clough team played. The same with Sir Alex Ferguson, José Mourinho, and younger managers like Brendan Rodgers and Roberto Martínez. They have a plan. I'm not saying it always had to be the beautiful game. Wimbledon had a plan under Dave Bassett and Bobby Gould, and while if might not always have been pretty, it was effective, and they came through four divisions and won the FA Cup, so I don't think anyone can criticise it. And that was Clough's greatness, too. You knew what you would get from his teams, but his players were so good and his ideas so clearly visualised that, at its best, nobody could cope with it.

TERRY COOPER
(LEEDS UNITED)

For a time, Terry Cooper was quite simply the best left-back in the world. He had turned up with his boots in a paper bag at

Leeds United one day and just asked for a trial. He wouldn't get past the security guard at the gate at any of the top clubs now, but imagine what they would have lost. I remember first seeing Terry as a left-winger. I didn't think he was much cop at all. He was very average; no top club would have looked at him twice. As I've said before, it was hard for wingers in the sixties. You were stuck out there, the right-back booting you up in the air every time you got the ball. A lot of wingers were being made to look very ordinary by the changes in the game, including Terry. But Don Revie must have seen something in him because he switched him to left-back and suddenly it was a different ball game. That was a masterstroke by Revie, really. Now he was coming on to the ball, running forward with it, so he'd have a head of steam by the time the full-back was arriving. Terry changed the way full-backs played. He wasn't the first to go on the overlap, but he took it to a new level. His combination with Eddie Gray on the left for Leeds was just devastating.

The full-back position evolved very quickly from the fifties to the seventies. Roger Byrne, captain of the Busby Babes, liked to get forward, but more typical was a player like Tommy Banks at Bolton Wanderers, who was fast and physical and would put a winger in the stand at the first sign of danger. Ray Wilson took full-back play on, and Alf Ramsey and Ron Greenwood were both coaching players to get on the overlap, but the first player to fully exploit the potential of the role in this country was Cooper. He was our version of Nílton Santos, the great Brazilian, so eye-catching in the 1958 World Cup. Cooper was the first Englishman to play the full-back position in a way that kids watching football today would recognise. He was the forerunner of all the greats – Kenny Sansom, Stuart Pearce, Ashley Cole. And no, he wasn't the greatest defender, but full-back hasn't been a solely defensive position for close to 50 years now. After Cooper at Leeds it was never the same.

My second game for West Ham was against Leeds, on 28 August 1965. Willie Bell was their left-back that day, I played well against him and we won 2–1. Terry was the left wing. I can remember thinking that if *he* could make a career in Division One, I wouldn't have a problem. He was frighteningly bad. The next year when we played them, he was transformed. He was picking it up deep and running at us – I thought he was the best I saw all season.

For a spell he was the best around, certainly on the attack. He could dribble, he had real pace, he could hit a great cross and he had the skill and imagination to cut inside and join up with the midfield action. We all remember his wide interplay with Gray, but he could be as effective linking up with Johnny Giles. And while the defensive side of the game wasn't natural for him, he picked up tips from players like Norman Hunter, Paul Reaney and Jack Charlton, and he could certainly get by.

Having started as a winger, the aggression that most defenders had was not really part of Terry's game. He could tackle all right, but it was going forward that Terry was most effective, even scoring goals, like the volley that won the 1968 League Cup final at Wembley against Arsenal – the first major trophy of the Revie era. It was a pity that a broken leg sustained in 1972 kept him out for almost two years and altered his long-term prospects. Until then, Revie had never employed a reserve left-back, using Paul Madeley, who was a utility player across the defence, whenever Terry was injured. That had to change after the broken leg, and eventually he lost his place to Trevor Cherry. By then, every team had full-backs who were trying to play like Terry – but I'm not sure too many of them ever managed it.

LIAM BRADY
(ARSENAL)

I first saw Liam Brady in the Arsenal youth team playing West Ham at Chadwell Heath. Everybody was talking about him even then, this little Irish kid with an amazing left foot. Arsenal had a couple of outstanding players coming through at the time; the other was Graham Rix, who was in the same mould as Liam, another fantastic footballer, but a bit younger. Liam's team won the FA Youth Cup and South-East Counties League that season, 1970–71. Rix was in the next batch off the production line, and they both got into Arsenal's first team within a few years of each other. Later they combined for the winning goal scored by Alan Sunderland in the 1979 FA Cup final – that Arsenal team probably under-achieved considering the talent at its disposal.

Liam could cross with his right, but it was all about the left for him really. He had a left foot like a magic wand; he was a real artist with the ball. My old man absolutely loved him. Dad was still an Arsenal man at heart and he would put Brady right up there with the best he had seen. I was in America then, so he was back watching Arsenal and every week I'd get a call from him raving about something Brady had done. It's just a pity for the club that many of his best years were spent with Juventus in Italy; but it shows how good he was that he was probably our first player since John Charles to truly look at home there. He only left Juventus because they bought Michel Platini. It's a bit hard to argue with that.

When people look back at the great players from that era, I don't think they give Liam the recognition he deserves. Arsenal fans do – they watched him every week – but the rest of us barely got to see him before he was gone. He was only 24 when he went to Italy, and his only honour won in the English game was the FA Cup. We tend to think of Leeds and Liverpool players from that era, and clubs like Arsenal get forgotten. Liam came into the Arsenal team just as the Bertie Mee era was drawing to a close, and it was quite difficult for Terry Neill and Don Howe. Italy was the place to be then, though, and it shows how good Liam was that he was chosen as the player from English football that could end a pattern of quite negative publicity around our players. John Charles was a legend there, but Jimmy Greaves and Denis Law couldn't settle, and after that they seemed to lose interest in us. Liam changed that. He showed that a top player from the Football League could adapt, and paved the way for Ray Wilkins, Trevor Francis and Graeme Souness, among others.

In the seven full seasons Brady played at Arsenal, the club did not finish higher than fourth and even spent two campaigns in the bottom half of the table, so most of the great memories of Brady are restricted to individual big games rather than consistent displays over the season. The highlight for many Arsenal fans, for obvious reasons, is a 5–0 win against Tottenham Hotspur at White Hart Lane, on 23 December 1978. Alan Sunderland scored a hat-trick that day, but what people remember above all is Brady's fourth goal, 20 minutes into the second half.

Peter Taylor turned into him, but Brady was too quick in the tackle, nicked the ball and took two or three strides towards goal. He hit a left-foot banana shot from 25 yards that Mark Kendall, the goalkeeper, didn't even try to save. Then there was his performance in the 1979 FA Cup final against Manchester United. Undoubtedly, he was man of the match. Arsenal were leading 2–0 with five minutes to go but, to the amazement of all, Manchester United scored twice. Arsenal kicked off, lost the ball again, got it back and Sammy Nelson played a long pass up to Frank Stapleton. He fed it to Brady and it was his run, with Rix on the overlap outside, that inspired the winner, Rix crossing for Sunderland to score. Sadly, that was the beginning of the end for Brady in an Arsenal shirt. The win put the club in the European Cup-Winners' Cup the following season, and they were paired with Juventus in the semi-final. Brady was so magnificent over the two legs of the tie that the Italian club bought him that following summer, 1980.

Juventus had little answer to Brady at Highbury. They decided to try to kick him out of the game and Marco Tardelli was sent off. The match ended 1–1 and Juventus attempted to defend that away-goal lead by getting a 0–0 draw at home – a plan ruined when Brady crossed for Paul Vaessen to score a winner late in the game. Pat Jennings told me that as they walked past the Juventus dressing-room after the final whistle it was completely silent because their players were so stunned. Juventus had only lost one home game in Europe since 1968. I know Liam considers it the greatest display by an Arsenal team in his time there.

I think the impact of playing in Italy is probably lost on the modern generation. These days, Adel Taarabt gets relegated with

Queens Park Rangers and then goes off to play for AC Milan. Back then, only the greatest went to Serie A. Even the lesser known players from the exodus in the sixties – Gerry Hitchens and Joe Baker – were outstanding players in their time. A lot of those moves did not work out and it went quiet for close to 20 years before Juventus went for Brady. He was a trailblazer, really, because life in Italy was so different when compared to the standards and professionalism in England.

Graeme Souness told me a story about when he was at Sampdoria. He said they played a game pre-season against a village team, up in the mountains, in front of about 6,000 people. It was a nothing match, just preparation for the new season, and a bit of a public relations exercise because Sampdoria were in a camp down the road and were leaving to go back to Genoa the next day. Graeme said it must have been about 85°C and as he was leaving the club after the game he grabbed a small, cold bottle of Peroni from the bar to take on the coach. He got on and sat at the front, beer in hand, and it was like one of those Wild West saloons where everything falls quiet as the stranger enters. The players were all staring; the manager boarded and stared; then the president, too. He looked at Graeme coldly. 'Monday morning, in my office,' he said. That day, the president absolutely slaughtered him. 'Do that again, and you'll be out of the club,' he was told. All for having one cold beer because it was hot. He said he got no support from the players, either. Their looks had said it all. 'Oh my God, what are you doing?' Italy was a different world, then, for a British-based footballer.

I know one of the things that drove Jimmy Greaves mad about the Italian system was that you didn't get to go home after the game. There was the team camp the night before the match, and the team camp the night after. They would all go back to the training ground, stay over, warm down the following morning and have massages, and only then get to go home. Yet Liam fitted in with the Italian regime immediately. He won back-to-back titles with Juventus, the first playing some beautiful football. The second time, he took the penalty that clinched the league, even though he knew he was being replaced by Platini. It shows how much the coach trusted him – but then Chippy, as he was known at Arsenal, was always a class act. (And, by the way, he was called Chippy not because he had a lovely way of chipping the ball – but because he loved chips. I bet that too had to end when he went to Italy.)

GERRY FRANCIS
(QUEENS PARK RANGERS)

Okay, as manager of Queens Park Rangers, I might be biased, but Gerry Francis is one of the unsung heroes of English football in the 1970s. He was captain of a great QPR team that came within a whisker of winning the league, he was captain of England at the age of 23, he won Goal of the Season for 1975–6, and if he hadn't suffered a back injury at the peak of his career, I am sure he would be remembered as an England great. He reminds me a little of Bryan Robson – a player whose individual talent was undermined by the failure of his team. Gerry didn't even get a chance to play in a World Cup. He came into the England team set-up after they had failed to qualify for the 1974 tournament and his international career was over before the qualification process for 1978 began. He only made 12 international appearances but 8 of them were as captain and he scored 3 goals – not bad for a central midfield player. It is a faster strike-rate than Steven Gerrard, for instance.

Every time I come to work I walk past a photograph of that QPR team. It's on the wall at the training ground – what a set of players: Phil Parkes, Dave Clement, Ian Gillard, Dave Webb, Frank McLintock, John Hollins, Mick Leach, Don Masson, Stan Bowles, Don Givens, Dave Thomas – and Gerry, the captain. He scored 12 goals in 36 league games, 1 in 3 from midfield. He scored more goals that season than Bowles. They started the campaign with a 10-game unbeaten run, defeated Liverpool 2–0 at Loftus Road, went to Derby County, who were the reigning champions, and won 5–1. Later in the season they won 11 out of 12 matches, drew the other and were top the second week of April. They lost 3–2 at Norwich City but went back to the top again on the last official day of the season – but Liverpool had a game in hand at Wolverhampton Wanderers. These days, they make sure all the matches kick off at the same time to maintain credibility, but it wasn't like that back then. Rangers had to wait 10 days for Liverpool to play. Wolves went 1–0 up and the dream looked like becoming reality, but Liverpool equalised and went on to win 3–1. They took the league by one point – it was their first title under Bob Paisley.

Rangers played some lovely football that season, though, and a Francis goal against Liverpool epitomised it. McLintock played it into Bowles, he back-heeled it through his legs to Gerry, a lay-off to Givens, back to Gerry and he finished it quite superbly on the angle past Ray Clemence. They won't have seen too many like that at QPR. Gerry is still a big hero at the club and all the players from that team speak very highly of his ability. You don't end up England captain at 23 without being special. He scored a lovely goal against Scotland in the Home Nations match in 1975, just five minutes in at Wembley, batting through midfield and hitting an absolute screamer from 30 yards. The goalkeeper, Stuart Kennedy, didn't even move. England ended up winning 5–1.

There were a lot of fantastic maverick midfield players in that time – Alan Hudson, Tony Currie, Bowles – but I just think that Gerry was a more modern midfielder, a real up-and-back guy, and his forward runs from that position were the best. He always seemed to have space, always seemed hard to pick up. He wasn't aggressive in the tackle like, say, Bryan Robson, but he did his work and it was such a terrible shame when he got that injury in 1976. He was never the same after that, never played for England again, and he was only 32 when he drifted into management at Exeter City.

It was probably just as well that he had so many interests outside of football. Gerry always had a head for business – antiques, property, theatre shows. I think one of his companies has the rights to the musical *Buddy*. And, of course, he always had his pigeons. Gerry's whole family were into pigeon racing and breeding – though his dad was also a professional footballer – and I know Gerry had quite a successful side career as a pigeon fancier. It would seem strange to hear that about a professional footballer now. They all seem much more one-dimensional in their interests these days. Birds, yes. Pigeons, no.

GRAEME SOUNESS
(LIVERPOOL)

If English football struggled through the 1970s, Scottish football thrived – maybe that is why there are so many Scots in this team. Graeme Souness, though, would probably make the starting XI in any era. What a player. Also he just had an aura about him. He said to me that he would never go into the players' bar after a game. All the time he played for Liverpool he shunned it because he wanted to keep a barrier between himself and the opposition players. He thought if he went in and had a drink, suddenly his guard would come down and he couldn't be the Souness they feared on the pitch any more. And he was feared. Players thought he was evil. No chance of that if he was in among them, laughing and having a drink at the end of a game. He must have been one of the first players to think about image, to actively try to shape the way he was perceived by others. Keeping that aura was very important to Graeme. Any unwinding would be done in private, and with a glass of champagne, if I know him. Deep down, he isn't a miserable type at all, really. He just knew his own ability, and liked intimidating people. That was part of his job.

He always had faith in himself. It takes some guts to tell Bill Nicholson you are the best player at Tottenham Hotspur – when still a teenager who can't get in the team – but that is what Graeme did. He had been there since the age of 15 but wasn't making any headway, so he told Bill that he wanted to leave. Bill was one of those old-school managers whose attitude was, if you didn't want to play for him, stuff you, and off you went – so he sold Graeme to Middlesbrough. I still think it was an audacious statement on Graeme's part, though. Imagine having the confidence to say that, at 19, to a manager who had won the double?

Coming down from Edinburgh, it was hard for Graeme, and I know he thinks some of his experiences at the club helped toughen him up. An old team-mate of his, Phil Holder, does some scouting for me at Queens Park Rangers, and he was a young player coming up through the ranks with Graeme. Steve Perryman was Phil's big mate and they were inseparable at Spurs. Phil's only a little guy but he's a South London boy and there's no bullshit with him. That's why I like him as a scout – he tells it as it is. Last summer we were at a do with a lot of old friends near where I live, and Phil was there. The sun was shining, a singer was performing Frank Sinatra songs, and everyone was mingling and having a good time, when who should walk in but Graeme Souness. He had been in the restaurant the night before and his wife had left her mobile telephone there. I told him there was someone here he might remember from the old days – and brought him over to see Phil. I couldn't believe his reaction. He gave him a big hug, and then all the old memories started coming out. 'You and Stevie, you fucking slaughtered me every day,' he said. 'Dear lord, what a pair of lads you two were. No one messed with you.' I can imagine that of Phil as well, because he hasn't changed. Graeme said it was a huge part of his education. He had come down from Scotland, Billy Bigtime, but Phil was about a year older, as hard as nails too, and wasn't going to take any old nonsense. Steve Perryman was the same – he never took any prisoners as a player and he was going to sort anyone out who he thought was a bit flash. I can't imagine there were too many got the better of Graeme later in his career – but he said coming across Phil and Steve at Tottenham was the making of him. He loved them to bits. They were all in the same Tottenham team that won the FA Youth Cup in 1970.

Graeme knew his worth by then. He was going to be a top player. That is why he went to see Bill Nicholson when he had only made one appearance in the first team by the end of the 1971–2 season. Graeme said he was better than any of the players in the first team and if he wasn't getting picked he wanted to leave. 'That's your opinion,' Bill told him – but as the manager who had let Dave Mackay go, he wasn't about to be told what to do by some kid. I think Graeme met his match that day because Nicholson was as stubborn as anyone in football. Once confronted there was only going to be one winner – so Graeme ended up at Middlesbrough, in the Second Division, where he came under the influence of the great Bobby Murdoch, a member of the 'Lisbon Lions' Celtic team that won the European Cup in 1967. Murdoch had been Jack Charlton's first signing when he took over at Middlesbrough, and I know Graeme believes he was a formative influence on him as a footballer. Jock Stein said Murdoch was the best player he had ever managed, and he only sold him because he ran out of challenges at Celtic. They had lost the European Cup final to Feyenoord in 1970. When Stein was asked when they might win it again, he replied: 'When Bobby Murdoch is fit.' Middlesbrough won promotion in Jack's first season and Murdoch's influence was crucial, according to Graeme. He said his experience settled the team down, and he had an excellent attitude, as well as being a fantastic passer. 'He would always pull me to one side to pass on advice or to tell me when he thought I was acting wrongly,'

Souness said. He was a hard man, too, which is probably how Graeme learnt to look after himself.

By the time he came to Liverpool, Graeme was nearly the finished article. The transfer fee, £350,000, sounds like a snip but it was a record for a move between two English clubs in 1978. The time with Murdoch had added real steel to go with that glorious talent. He was the same type as Bremner and Mackay – whatever way you wanted to play it, he was happy. A pure football match, and he was the best player on the field. A tear-up, and he would be nastier than anybody. He seemed to have a particular problem with Peter Nicholas, a Welsh midfielder who played for Arsenal. In one game, Nicholas went in high on Graeme, and soon afterwards Souness put him out of football for two months. He needed six stitches on a knee injury. Willie Young, Arsenal's giant centre-half, came tearing over and Graeme thought there was going to be a punch-up. What he didn't know was that Young hated Nicholas almost as much as he did. 'Oh, come on, big man, you know he deserved it,' said Souness as Nicholas lay on the ground. 'I know,' said Willie. 'I was coming to congratulate you.' There was another match between Scotland and Wales in 1985 when the two clashed and Souness appeared to rake his studs down Nicholas's face, almost causing a riot. That was Graeme. He could be wicked if provoked, but people only went at him like that because, left alone, he could do the lot. He lives down near me on the South coast now and we have the odd game of golf. He hasn't changed – he's so competitive, it's ridiculous. I like him a lot.

And get him talking about football after, and you're certainly in for a good night. What you see on Sky television isn't the half of it. His favourite word is bluffer. This manager's a bluffer; that manager's a bluffer – and it doesn't matter who he's talking about. I know he sometimes does it for effect, just for the sake of argument. Arsène Wenger: bluffer. Pep Guardiola: bluffer – thinks he's reinvented football. He does it just to get us all going, and then sits back laughing.

I know he thinks his Liverpool team was the best, and maybe he is right. They were a fantastic side, and I think anyone of that generation remembers tuning in to *Sportsnight* in midweek, watching grainy footage from somewhere like Bulgaria, with a lousy picture you could barely see – it was half-time before the smoke from the pre-match flares had cleared – but Liverpool were the best in Europe and I think we all felt very proud of them. Graeme was a hit at Liverpool from the start. I remember he scored a cracking goal against Manchester United in one of his first games for the club, and when he was made captain in 1981, his inspiration turned the season around. They had lost to Manchester City on Boxing Day and fallen to 12th place, when Bob Paisley gave the armband to Graeme. I know it made things awkward with the existing captain, Phil Thompson, but I don't think Graeme is the sort to be bothered by that. John Toshack's Swansea City were top at the time, but there were bigger clubs in the chase, like Manchester United and Bobby Robson's Ipswich Town. Driven on by Graeme, Liverpool reeled them all in: they hit the top by the end of March and never looked back. They were four points clear of Ipswich by the end – and had won the League Cup, too.

Graeme was always best under pressure. He was immense in the 1984 European Cup semi-final second leg away to Dinamo

Bucharest, when he was targeted by a hostile crowd on account of an incident in the first match that left their captain, midfielder Lica Movila, with a broken jaw. The incident happened off the ball, and off camera, but it must have been one hell of a blow. Naturally, the Romanians were not best pleased and the reception in Bucharest was ferocious – Kenny Dalglish later wrote that he'd 'never been in such a war zone'. But the louder they got, the better Graeme played. He almost revelled in it. Stayed calm, stayed focused, let that negative energy wash over him and steered his team to the final. Just brilliant. It was the same in the final, against AS Roma at their home stadium in Rome. It was Souness's idea, as captain, to lead the team out on to the pitch to get used to the atmosphere, provoking an inevitable tirade of boos and jeers. Having shown the home crowd that they were not afraid, Liverpool won the match. That was Graeme's thing: show no fear.

I remember we were all having dinner in Spain once – myself, Jim Smith, Trevor Francis and Graeme – and Trevor brought up the name of Claudio Gentile, the notorious Italian hard man, who did such a horrible man-marking job on Diego Maradona at the 1982 World Cup. 'He scared you, Gentile,' Trevor said. 'I remember he waited for you down the tunnel – ' But Graeme didn't even let him finish the story. 'No, he didn't,' he snapped. 'Not a fucking chance.' He really had the hump about it.

He managed as he played, too. He was a brave, bold influence on Rangers – and it would have taken real guts to challenge and change the culture of that club by signing Mo Johnston, a very high-profile Catholic player. I don't think another manager would have done that – and so much of Rangers's success during

Graeme's time and after he left was built on this new freedom. Fans were burning season tickets in the street when the deal was announced, but that wouldn't have bothered Graeme in the least. The only person I know he's scared of is his wife, Karen.

JOHN ROBERTSON
(NOTTINGHAM FOREST)

Bill Shankly said he could pass the ball with the accuracy of a snooker player potting the black, but John Robertson was on his way out at Nottingham Forest when Brian Clough and Peter Taylor arrived. He was the most unlikely professional footballer anyone had seen. He was overweight, smoked liked a trooper and, in Clough's words, was living out of a chip pan. He ate all the wrong foods, wasn't interested in staying fit, wasn't interested in football really – and dressed scruffily, which Clough hated. Yet he must have seen something, a glimmer, in training because Clough decided it was worth persevering with him if he could clean his act up. Peter Taylor delivered the message, as I understand it. He took Robertson to one side and just slaughtered him – told him everything Clough had said about him in private. Taylor concluded: 'It's clear you have problems – but we think you can play.' Robertson knew it was his last chance to sort himself out or his career would be over. And what a player he became.

Clough's description of him in his autobiography sums up the incredible transformation that occurred. 'John Robertson was a very unattractive young man,' he said. 'If, one day, I felt a bit off colour, I would sit next to him. I was bloody Errol

Flynn in comparison. But give him a ball and a yard of grass, and he was an artist, the Picasso of our game. He became one of the finest deliverers of a football I have ever seen – in Britain or anywhere else in the world – as fine as the Brazilians or the supremely gifted Italians.' People remember Clough buying players like Trevor Francis or Peter Shilton, but the bulk of his signings involved taking incredible gambles on players that were not in the least household names. Robertson wasn't a signing, but he was evidence of the unique way Clough thought about football and footballers. No matter his talent, had he just given up on Robertson he would not have been the first. Even a great manager like Sir Alex Ferguson has sometimes just decided a player simply has too many problems to handle, and washed his hands of him. Paul McGrath, one of the greatest central defenders of the modern era, fits that category. Alex didn't think he was worth the trouble. Yet Clough persevered with Robertson and won two European Cups. He scored the winner in one, and made the winner in the other. Apparently when he signed Francis he told him to get the ball to Robertson and the rest would look after itself.

I think once people saw what Clough had done with Robertson, everyone wanted a winger like that. Not necessarily a flying machine, but intelligent with the ball. He was Forest's playmaker but he started wide – that was what made him special. Even at Bournemouth we were trying to replicate what Forest had. I took a little winger called Mark O'Connor on a free transfer from Bristol Rovers because he reminded me of Robertson in lots of ways. He's the under-21 coach at Bristol City now, but before that he was with Tony Pulis. Tony took him everywhere – Gillingham, Portsmouth, Plymouth Argyle, Stoke City. I wouldn't be surprised if he ended up at Crystal Palace, too. Mark was a clever player, he knew exactly where he should be, like Robertson. He could toy with defenders, get it, roll it in front of them; he joined the play very quickly. He was quick enough over 10 yards, but not lightning, so it was the way he used to work the ball that made things happen – and Robertson was the same, just a step up in class. He had a fantastic football brain, and it showed in the way he orchestrated Forest's attacks.

John was one of the first playmakers we saw that would start wide and come in to link up with the front man. It was a real thinking formation. A lot of the great players in recent times have done that – Gheorghe Hagi, Zinedine Zidane, Lionel Messi, Thierry Henry – but when John did this it was revolutionary. Clough gets a lot of credit for intuition and psychological ploys, but not so many people talk about his coaching – yet he did a quite wonderful job with Robertson. He wanted him to play with the whole game in front of him, side on, so that when he got the ball he had the complete picture. Too many people these days come and get it off the full-back and they are moving towards the ball with their back to the game. They should be side on, so when it comes to them they can see the full-back, their own team, who is in the best position, everything. If it's tight they can turn it round the corner first time, if it's not they can hold it, and they don't even need a call because they have the game right there, in vision. Clough got Robertson playing like that and coached him to be the most influential winger in Europe.

The minute Forest got the ball, John would hit the touchline and then all you could hear Clough shout was, 'Show me your arse, show me your arse!' He wanted him heels on the touchline, backside facing towards the stand and the dugout. He didn't want him facing back or forwards, he had to play sideways on so he could see the game. I remember watching Manchester United's game against Olympiakos last season – the away leg that they lost 2–0 – and seeing Ashley Young receive the ball blind, with his back to the opposition goal, and back-heel it straight into touch. Clough would have gone spare. It showed so little awareness, not only of where he was on the field, but of where the rest of the players were, too. Had he been side on he could have made the smart decision, the way Robertson would. Body position is so important in football. Robertson still got up and down the field, but he did so showing Brian Clough his arse because that way, when he received, Forest began to play immediately.

He was a great character, too. In season 1979–80, Nottingham Forest played Liverpool five times: twice in the league, in the FA Cup and over the two legs of the League Cup semi-final. Liverpool won the title that season and Forest won the European Cup, and matches between the teams were always big events. Forest won the home league game, lost in the FA Cup, but had knocked Liverpool out over two legs of the League Cup, with Robertson scoring from the penalty spot in each match. The Anfield league game was scheduled for seven days after the second League Cup tie and as Forest were warming up, The Kop were given them all kinds of stick. Someone threw a tennis ball at John, who did no more than trap it in the air and play keep-up with it to the penalty spot. He then put it down gently, and in front of the Liverpool crowd, rolled it gently into the corner, just as he had done in the cup ties. What a reply.

John was always a bit of lad, though. He did start trying to live right, but the Forest boys always hit the town on Wednesday if there was no match, and I don't think he ever stopped smoking. There is a story about one trip away with Scotland when he spent ages chatting up this girl at the hotel. In the end, she told him her room number and he arranged to call later. He knocked at around midnight but couldn't get a reply, so he went back to his bunk and tried to get through on the telephone. He asked to be put through to the room number she had given. 'Why do you want to call Jock Stein at this hour?' the night porter asked. Luckily for John, Scotland's manager was a heavy sleeper – or there could have been real trouble.

KEVIN KEEGAN
(LIVERPOOL)

I was watching a game down at Bournemouth when I first saw Kevin Keegan in action, and my first instinct was to telephone Ron Greenwood at West Ham and recommend him. I knew Bournemouth wouldn't be able to afford him and he was obviously destined for greater things. 'Scunthorpe have got this kid, Ron,' I told him. 'He's fantastic – you should have a look at him.' Kevin was playing in midfield then, often on the right, like me, and maybe Ron thought West Ham were well staffed in that department. I don't know if he ever acted on a word I said, really – our relationship wasn't the best by that time. Kevin joined Liverpool at the end of that season, so maybe West Ham made an inquiry and were told it was too late. I can't see how Ron wouldn't have seen the promise in Kevin at that time. Still, it is all about opinions. The other player I recommended to West Ham was David Speedie during his time at Darlington – and he didn't end up at Upton Park, either. I was the manager of Bournemouth by then and we had tried, and failed, to sign him. Darlington wanted £30,000, which was too rich for us, but he would have been a snip for West Ham, where John Lyall was now the manager. Never mind – just add it to a list of ones that got away.

I was right about Keegan, though. What a player – and what a career. Brilliant at Liverpool, brilliant in Germany with Hamburg, won the European Cup, twice European Footballer of the Year – he turned into a truly amazing player. I know he took something Bill Shankly said to heart. 'Even if I was a road-sweeper,' Shankly told him, 'I'd have the cleanest street in town.' And that was Kevin's attitude to football. He threw himself into every job he ever had, particularly his role at Liverpool. Once he had been spotted – by Geoff Twentyman, naturally – the work he put into his game was just phenomenal. It is said Kevin made himself a great player, and some might find that a little disrespectful, but he was at Scunthorpe for a reason and I think it's perfectly feasible that the great player we now recall bears no relation to the one that came into football at the age of 17. He went for a trial at Coventry City and didn't make it, so he must have worked very hard to improve from that point. Scunthorpe spotted him playing for his works team, Pegler, a plumbing manufacturing company in Yorkshire.

So Kevin wasn't a player that was born with silky skills. He wasn't like Kenny Dalglish, for instance. I saw Kenny play at 14, and everyone there instinctively knew we were watching someone destined to be one of the great players in British football. Kevin was different. Obviously, earlier in life, professional clubs had looked at him and thought he came up short. In the same way I can remember seeing Jamie Carragher as a young player for Liverpool and not rating him at all. He is another who worked extremely hard to get to the top.

By the time I saw Kevin for Scunthorpe the player we know was beginning to form. He was busy, busy, busy – a threat all the time. Bournemouth's defenders couldn't get to grips with him, couldn't mark him, and it was easy to see why Shankly took one look and decided to make him a forward. Central defenders at that time were used to having people that stood up against them, and suddenly there was this little lad who was always on the move, buzzing everywhere, causing problems. Did I think he would be the European Footballer of the Year? Frankly, no. But I could see he was way better than Scunthorpe and could probably make it at a First Division club – by then Kevin's energy alone set him apart.

The idea at Liverpool was that Keegan would replace Ian Callaghan on the right side of midfield. Ian had been a wonderful player but was coming to the end of his career and was injury prone. Liverpool sorted out the Keegan transfer while preparing to meet Arsenal in the 1971 FA Cup final. The story goes that they were going to bring him through gradually, but Shankly played him in a practice match against the first team the following season and he created such havoc, he went straight into the starting line-up; and 12 minutes into his debut, he scored.

If I had to compare Kevin to a modern footballer, it would probably be Luis Suárez. Not in terms of his technical ability, because Suárez's skill level is quite amazing, but in terms of his work-rate and the way his threat as a goalscorer never ceases.

He was a pest, the way Suárez is a pest; the test was constant because he was always on the move, a perpetual motion machine for 90 minutes. It is the same with Suárez: defenders do not get a second's rest. You don't know where he is because he never stands still, constantly changing positions, wanting the ball, playing it and spinning, impossible to mark. Again, it was a wonderful bit of scouting from Geoff Twentyman – Liverpool seemed to pluck players from thin air in those days.

Of course, it must have been hard to go there and not do well for someone like Shankly. He was such a strong character. I was told he wouldn't even talk to injured players, would just ignore them completely until they were fit again. Brian Clough was the same. He wouldn't even have injured players at the ground. Liverpool's training was legendary, too. It didn't change in close to 30 years. They would have a warm-up and play nine-a-sides. Before European matches foreign coaches would come to watch them in open sessions, go away disappointed, and then sneak back in the afternoon, thinking they could peer through the fence and all the secrets would be revealed. There was nothing to see but an empty training ground. They weren't hiding anything at all. There were no secrets; they really did just play nine-a-side. And it hadn't changed from Shankly's time to when Kenny Dalglish was manager. When my son Jamie signed for Liverpool I was fascinated to hear what Liverpool did to produce such wonderful teams. 'What did you do this morning?' I'd ask. 'Nine-a-side,' he'd say. 'No, before that,' I'd press, 'you must do something else.' 'No, Dad, it's the same every day,' he would insist. 'Two-lap warm-up, nine-a-side. Kenny plays, Ronnie Moran plays, all the coaches play. We have proper games, Dad. Good games. But that's it.' And that is how Keegan would have trained 20 years earlier, too. I don't imagine it changed that much until Gérard Houllier took over.

Key to Keegan's greatness is that he formed one of the great forward partnerships with John Toshack. It was a classic pairing, really, the big 'un and the little 'un. Toshack, strong and fearless, winning the headers; Keegan buzzing around him, feeding off those scraps. As a model, there's not too many better than that – it was a perfect combination then and, really, it still is. Look at Burnley in the Championship last season – Sam Vokes, the big Welsh striker, knocking it down to the quicker and more mobile Danny Ings – or go right back to Jimmy Greaves and Alan Gilzean, or John Radford and Ray Kennedy at Arsenal. If you can get a partnership like that going you've got a chance.

Kevin was the bridge between the era when fans and players still felt connected and the modern era when players are superstars, living in gated mansions and earning money that is beyond the imagination of the ordinary man. He was probably the first footballer to work carefully on his image, and although he was a household name he was rarely in the newspapers for the wrong reasons. He wasn't like George Best – there was never any scandal around Kevin. He made Liverpool's number seven shirt famous – although the next player to wear it may have been even better.

KENNY DALGLISH
(LIVERPOOL)

I go back a long way with Kenny Dalglish. In 1966 I used to take him to training when he came in for a trial at West Ham. I've read that he was rejected by Ron Greenwood, but I don't think that's true. Ron would have loved to sign him, but knew we had no chance. Every club in Britain was clamouring for Kenny's signature by that time.

Kenny would have been 15 when he came to us for two weeks, and was staying in digs about a minute up the road from our training ground in Chadwell Heath. I had a little green Austin 1100 and would collect him and another Scottish lad, Jimmy Lindsay, who had come down from the same Scotland Schools team and ended up signing for us. The boys were both forwards – Jimmy eventually played as a midfielder – and had good reputations. Scotland had put a strong team into the Victory Shield, the schoolboy equivalent of the Home Nations tournament. One Saturday morning during Kenny's brief time at West Ham we had a practice match and Ron Greenwood played him in with the first-team players. One of the lads laid a ball to him and it was like fast forwarding through the next 20 years of British football – he took it perfectly, dropped a shoulder, turned and curled it into the far corner of the net. Our reserves didn't know what had hit them. Both sets of players just stopped and applauded. I can remember talking to Ron about him after that game. 'Will we get him?' I asked. 'No chance,' he said. 'We've tried. Everybody wants him, but he's going to Celtic.' He was right. Kenny signed as a professional there a year later.

I don't remember him being very talkative then, but I'm not sure I would have understood a word anyway. The strength of Kenny's Glasgow accent is legendary. When Liverpool wanted to sign my son, Jamie, Kenny rang up to speak to us about it. I could hear my wife, Sandra, on the phone but I didn't know who she was talking to. 'I'm sorry,' she kept saying. 'I can't understand your Scouse accent.' She must have said it about four times. In the end, I heard her say the name Kenny. I took the phone, just in time to hear Kenny saying in the broadest Scottish tone you'll ever hear, 'Can ye nae understan' me?' That's my missus. She's got to be about the only person who doesn't know Kenny Dalglish is from Scotland. 'I thought he was from Liverpool,' she said. 'No, he manages Liverpool – he was born in Glasgow,' I replied. We got there in the end.

Kenny was just a fantastic player. Absolutely world class. He could hold the ball as well as any man twice his size; he could bring team-mates into play or take it on himself. He didn't have pace, but that didn't matter. His pace was in his head. He was the attacking equivalent of Bobby Moore, in that he read the play better than anybody. And, despite his size, he was so strong. David O'Leary, who was an outstanding defender with Arsenal, said it was impossible to get the ball off Kenny at his peak. He said Kenny would almost crouch over it with his legs spread and his elbows poking out, so that whatever angle the defender came in from, he'd have his backside in the way of the ball. Bob Paisley said Dalglish was the best player he ever worked with at Liverpool, and praise doesn't come much higher than that. There were some great strikers around in that era, but I'd say Kenny was the pick of them.

Trevor Francis was the first £1 million footballer – whatever Brian Clough says – at Nottingham Forest, but I'm not sure he was ever better than in his earliest years at Birmingham City. He was this country boy, from Plymouth in Devon, but he broke into the first team at the age of 16 and had scored four goals in a game against Bolton Wanderers before his 17th birthday. He scored 15 goals in 22 games in his first season – a phenomenal feat for a youngster. He could pack a ground like the greats of the 1950s – over 50,000 at St Andrew's in 1972 when they won promotion. He was so prolific in those first seasons that one edition of BBC's *Sports Report* began with the news that he *hadn't* scored. He was fast, brave and prolific. Talk to him now about that game at Bolton and he'll still say that he came off injured and his replacement missed a sitter. 'I should have had five,' he'll moan. I've talked quite a bit in this chapter about scouting in this era, and I think the chap who discovered Trevor for Birmingham should get his own statue at St Andrew's. No, I don't know who it was either. That's my point. Those blokes worked in anonymity back then, digging out these gems of players from obscure parts of the country, regions where nobody was expecting to find the next Jimmy Greaves. How did Birmingham get him and not Plymouth? How did Plymouth miss the one true great to be born on their doorstep?

I find it amazing that England failed internationally through the 1970s, because I do believe it was a golden age for strikers: Kevin Hector, Alan Clarke, Martin Chivers, Mick Channon, Malcolm Macdonald – these are players that would walk into most teams today. Can you imagine if Roy Hodgson had that lot to choose from in Brazil last summer?

Yet Dalglish, I feel, stands alone in his generation. Liverpool must have wondered how on earth they could replace Kevin Keegan, but Dalglish turned out to be an upgrade. Liverpool played Keegan's Hamburg in the UEFA Super Cup shortly after the change had been made and won 6–0, which I think says it all about his ability to slot straight into a successful team. He came down from Scotland, but there was no talk of needing to adapt. It was as if they knew, and he knew, that there was only one man for the job. He scored 30 goals in his first season, including the winner in the European Cup final. It allowed them to maintain this fantastic period of dominance in the English game. Somehow they could always identify goalscorers that were perfect for the Liverpool way – Ian St John, Roger Hunt, Keegan, Dalglish and then Ian Rush. In the second phase of his Liverpool career, Dalglish turned from the best goalscorer to the most imaginative goal provider – so the next decade belonged to Liverpool, too.

THE SEVENTIES: THE TEAM

PAT
JENNINGS
Tottenham Hotspur

PHIL
NEAL
Liverpool

PHIL
THOMPSON
Liverpool

ROY
McFARLAND
Derby County

TERRY
COOPER
Leeds United

LIAM
BRADY
Arsenal

GERRY
FRANCIS
Queens Park
Rangers

GRAEME
SOUNESS
Liverpool

JOHN
ROBERTSON
Nottingham
Forest

KEVIN
KEEGAN
Liverpool

KENNY
DALGLISH
Liverpool

CHAPTER FOUR

. . . .

THE EIGHTIES

The eighties was the last decade before the Premier League and probably the last time there was room to fail in football. Not consistently, obviously. Managers would still get sacked if they regularly fell below expectations. But there would be time to build a team, and one bad season didn't end with a P45. John Lyall managed West Ham United from 1975 to 1989. There were good years and bad years. One season the club got relegated – but John's vision fitted West Ham's own and they gave him time to get it right. Eventually, he brought them back up. Now, lose five games and you're under threat. Get relegated and the whole regime changes – players, coaches, scouting staff. People say that the money has changed football – but it was still a business even then. I think the culture has changed. Once one chairman sacks a manager, they all want to sack a manager because they want to be seen to be doing something. Yet West Ham's board were doing something under Lyall. They were buying players and trying to improve the team that way. That's action, just the same.

I think chairmen are terrified, literally terrified, of relegation now. The Premier League is football for such big stakes and everybody thinks they cannot afford to be out of it. Plus there are more foreign owners, billionaires from around the world who have never known anything but success and cannot understand why they are not winning the league. Listen to them and everyone is going to be in the Champions League or Europe in the next few years, no matter how ropey the team is. I'm not sure owners talked like that 30 years ago – and the league was a lot more open with considerably more movement. Now, nobody seems happy. Everyone should be doing better, getting greater value for the fortune they have invested. And, yes, it is a fortune – but if it's only one tenth of what Sheikh Mansour has spent at Manchester City, the chances are you'll have one-tenth of the team. I do fear one day we will be lucky to have any clubs that are locally owned, and that is going to make it difficult for our domestic game, for our managers and players to thrive.

Looking at the other teams I've picked for this book, this is the last one that does not include a foreign player. Once the Premier League begins, everything about our domestic game changes. Foreign players, foreign coaches and foreign wages to keep up with the biggest clubs in Europe. I'm not knocking that – suddenly managers are earning as much as the top players, but has the quality gone up? I'm not convinced. If you look back at the achievements of men like Brian Clough and Bob Paisley, I don't understand why owners suddenly lost faith in British managers.

Should Brian Clough have been England manager during this period? I think so. I feel his record at Derby County and

Nottingham Forest should have been enough to promote him, instead of either Ron Greenwood in 1977 or Sir Bobby Robson in 1982. Sadly, he didn't fit the bill. Appointing Don Revie was probably as bold as the Football Association were ever going to get, considering the controversy around his Leeds United side, and when that backfired, Clough's chances were almost certainly over. From there, until the appointment of Terry Venables in 1996, I think they were after a safe pair of hands. I'd love Clough to have managed England, but knowing the type of FA people he would have had to deal with, it seems an impossibility looking back. On his first day, he would have cancelled all the free trips for the blazers, on his second he would have questioned why they needed to be at matches at all, and before the first game he would have been kicking them off the chartered plane. It would never have worked – but what a wonderful manager. He really knew how to put a team together, how to match players up, get them working as a unit. That is what he was best at, the simple stuff. Get players doing what they are good at, and in that way get the best out of them.

Bob Paisley was another who would be in any list of the greatest managers of all time. When Carlo Ancelotti won his third Champions League title last season with Real Madrid, it was good that a younger generation were reminded whose record he was equalling. Liverpool had a unique style and was run in a unique way back then. There are a lot of coaches, players and owners who wouldn't recognise it as an elite club in the modern sense, considering the way it just ticked over, built on wonderful traditions. Every day the same, every training session the same, the ball zipping about in those famous nine-a-sides, great players like Alan Hansen and Ian Rush taking it as seriously as any game. A warm-up and then half an hour each way.

What was their secret formula? Good players. They kept producing them, kept finding them, putting them in the right positions, and then that Anfield atmosphere made them feel 10 feet tall. The managers just carried on the tradition of the boot room – the same philosophy handed down from Bill Shankly. It went right through the club – and modern managers like Kenny Dalglish carried it through. Yet Liverpool was ahead of its time, too. For all the tradition it had a continental set-up because Peter Robinson, the chief executive, conducted all the football business. Bob and later Joe Fagan ran the football team, and made the football decisions, but Peter was in charge of the club. When my son Jamie signed for Liverpool, Kenny Dalglish met us – but Peter Robinson did the deal, and Kenny still addressed him formally in front of us as Mr Robinson. At a lot of clubs the manager would have been weighed down with the business, but Liverpool knew how to compartmentalise the club. They trusted the scouts to find players, the chief executive to sign players, the coaches to guide players and the players to play. It was a winning formula, and every successful club since has deployed a version of it.

This was also the last decade when the prizes were spread around, particularly the FA Cup. Between 1978 and 1988 there were 9 different winners of the FA Cup in 11 seasons; in the next 19 years, 17 of the FA Cup finals were won by four clubs (Liverpool, Manchester United, Arsenal and Chelsea) with Tottenham Hotspur and Everton – who probably make up the big six – accounting for the other two. I am pleased to say my club, Portsmouth, broke that stranglehold in 2008 – and Wigan have also managed it. You look at some of the clubs that won the FA Cup in the eighties and wonder whether they will pass that way again: Wimbledon, Coventry City, West Ham United. It's a shame. It isn't healthy when football loses its uncertainty. Everybody fielded their best team in the FA Cup then, too. You didn't toss the cup off because relegation wasn't the death sentence it has become now. The league was important but it wasn't all-consuming, and the cups mattered. These days, many people think fourth place is akin to winning a trophy, and small clubs associate a cup run with relegation. If Sunderland or Hull City had gone down last season everyone would have blamed it on getting to Wembley, which is ridiculous.

It was also the decade in which football was touched by tragedy. On the day of the Heysel Stadium disaster, 29 May 1985, I was playing cricket in a charity match with Alan Ball and a few other ex-players. We were doing it to raise money for the family of a policeman who had died in the line of duty. We would play the game and then go back to the police clubhouse to watch Liverpool versus Juventus in the European Cup final. We got there and saw it all unfold on television. 'Someone's been killed,' said one of the club members. We didn't believe him at first. Then you saw the footage and realised how terrible it was. I still can't believe they played the game, or that Michel Platini celebrated Juventus's goal. They must have had an inkling something was wrong, even if they were unaware there were so many dead.

Bournemouth were at home to Stoke City on 15 April 1989, the day of the Hillsborough disaster. We lost 1–0 but that is about all I remember of the match. I think everyone in football felt numb with shock. We knew the game couldn't be the same again. It felt that way after the Bradford City stadium fire in 1985, too. Bradford were in the same league as us, Division Three, and I can remember the silence on the coach as we drove back from Leyton Orient, having heard the news. Terrible times.

It was a decade when football was beginning to change in every aspect and I witnessed the new wave arriving, first-hand, at Lilleshall. Bobby Robson had brought two Dutch players over to Ipswich Town, Arnold Mühren and Frans Thijssen, and Mühren in particular was a disciple of a Dutch skills coach called Wiel Coerver. He had developed a pyramid method of instruction by studying the best players in the world, and it was the first time anyone had really applied academic techniques to basic skills. I'm not saying it was going to turn anyone into Lionel Messi, but it would certainly improve technical levels. We were all at Lilleshall, just about every young coach in the country, when Coerver came over – and it was the most fantastic couple of days. 'Tomorrow we have a man arriving from Holland,' we were told. 'He teaches dribbling skills and he is going to put on a session for us.' I think Bobby was instrumental in getting him in because his Dutch players spoke so highly of him. It was a revelation. Coerver turned up with some Dutch kids in tow. He was older than most of us, but looked super fit. He laid out loads of balls and all these boys started doing stepovers. Then they speeded it up. Double stepovers. Passing people on the run and doing it. He had them playing games where the skill level was just mind-blowing – then he asked for volunteers. That was my favourite part. George Graham was straight up there – he fancied his chances. The kids would do a skill and then Coerver would ask us to replicate it.

There were some sights that day. I had my assistant manager, Stuart Morgan, with me. He was a good coach but as a player let's say skill wasn't his strong point. If Coerver had a course entitled 'Clumping the striker off the ball at corners', Stuart would have been his man. Stepovers, not so much. As for Jimmy Sirrel, the old manager of Notts County, his stepover was so slow I think the half-time whistle would have gone by the time he completed it. We were in tears of laughter watching some of the guys – people were stepping on the ball and falling over. Yet the one thing we all agreed on was that here was a way forward for English football. All the different skills that were shown to us that day could be applied in the game. The plan was that we would all be given videos to take back to our clubs and use as the basis for youth training. Instead of running them into the ground, the kids would learn new skills and could then go away and practise in their back garden or over the park, just as they do in Holland. Of course, it didn't happen. There was a big argument over the rights and the videos never got ordered. So the only people exposed to the brilliant coaching of Wiel Coerver were a load of middle-aged football managers, not the next generation of young players.

Yet I'll never forget those kids that he brought over. It is no coincidence that the Dutch produce wave after wave of beautiful footballers when they are working with coaches like that. The skills they had – they were sending people five yards the wrong way with a twitch of the foot, doing drag-backs at full pelt. And none of it got used. It was so hard to introduce new ideas into Football Association courses back then. Up at Lilleshall all the lads would have a chat and talk about different ideas, but there were very few new techniques to be learnt. I can remember us all asking if Wiel could stay another day because everybody loved it so much – and the second session was as good as the first. Then he disappeared from our game. It was as if he had been smuggled away for letting the cat out of the bag. What a waste. His methods should have been put to all the clubs in this country. Take it or leave it. Here's what you do with the kids, here's what you show them; give them a ball each so they get hundreds of touches in training. You could have taken his methods anywhere, even into Sunday league clubs, and the kids would have loved it. Yet we had our own ways and, sadly, there were too many PE teachers without the imagination to understand what Coerver was doing. So many of the coaches at Lilleshall came through the same route, and a lot of it involved non-league football. Basically, our coaches were being taught by people who couldn't play – and that cannot be healthy.

I know I say skill is mostly natural, but that doesn't mean coaching is worthless. You can definitely put Wiel Coerver's methods into a session; you would certainly improve any kid by doing that for 30 minutes each day. I introduced it at Bournemouth as soon as I returned. Each time I took a coaching session, instead of warming up without the ball running round the pitch, I would tell them to have a little stretch, then spend about half an hour with a ball each. Stepover. Take it away with you. Stepover. Take it away to the right. Double stepover – bang, bang. Every morning. I don't think we spend enough time like that – or we hadn't done, until Coerver opened some minds. I used to go and watch our kids every Tuesday and Thursday night and they might be doing doggies and fitness work for two hours.

They're young, fit men. They can run anyway. Skill is what the game is about – as the players in my next XI would know.

PETER SHILTON
(NOTTINGHAM FOREST)

Peter could have made my team of the decade for the sixties, seventies or eighties, really. He was that good. I know Ron Greenwood couldn't make up his mind between Peter and Ray Clemence, but Shilton just had the edge for me. Brian Clough thought him the better man in every aspect, but I think that's harsh on Ray. Clemence only suffers in comparison to one of the greatest goalkeepers of all time – maybe the best there has been. It is a myth, though, that Peter and Ray alternated throughout Ron's time in charge as England manager. Ray was his first choice for most of it and played over half of Greenwood's 55 games in charge. Joe Corrigan, another excellent goalkeeper, played in eight. Peter was only capped 19 times by Ron, and 5 of those were the last matches of his reign, when he finally made Peter his number one at the 1982 World Cup. Before that tournament Ray had played twice as many England matches under Ron for England. In many ways, it shows how good he was that, for a time, he kept Shilton out of the England team. Without Ray, I don't think Peter's caps record could ever be broken. It stands at 125 – but imagine how many he could have got.

Peter had a presence about him. He was a goalkeeper who was just dedicated to his craft, an exceptional worker, an exceptional trainer, absolutely obsessed with his game. I'm not saying he was perfect. He liked a drink, he liked a bet – he'd be the first to admit that. But when he was about his business he could be quite fanatical – that probably comes from growing up as the understudy to Gordon Banks. He studied Gordon and his game expanded from there – he couldn't have had a better start in life, really. As I've said, you can have all the schooling in the world but to go in every day and see the greatest goalkeeper in the world, as Banks was at that time, is the best education around.

I think everybody knew Peter was destined for greatness from an early age. At West Ham, we had a young goalkeeper called Steve Death. He wasn't big but he was a real prospect, and he was the second-choice England schoolboy goalkeeper when Peter was number one – poor Steve couldn't get a look in. It just shows you the gulf in class, really. Steve was a great kid, but he couldn't get in the team at West Ham ahead of Bobby Ferguson either and ended up going to Reading, where he had a fantastic career and played well over 500 games. He held the record for the longest time without conceding a goal – 1,074 minutes – before Edwin van der Sar broke it in 2009. Bit of difference between going that long at Manchester United and at Reading, though. Yet while Steve couldn't break through at West Ham, Shilton displaced Gordon Banks at Leicester City. It shows you how good he must have been.

Shilton was exactly six foot but looked much bigger. He managed to give that impression by spreading himself and working the angles brilliantly. He had a way of setting himself that made him appear hard to beat and, apart from Diego Maradona, I don't remember too many besting him in a race to the ball. He was very quick off his line.

I remember watching the game against Argentina at home in 1986. Like the rest of the country, watching it in real time I had no idea he'd handled it. I just couldn't believe Shilton had been beaten from there – it was so unlike him. It looked like a fantastic, incredible jump and it was only when the replay was shown that we all thought, 'Hold on.' I know Terry Butcher wanted to strangle Maradona after the game, and I don't think Peter has ever forgiven him. Maybe I've led a sheltered life but I'd never seen anything like that before – a player get away with punching the ball into the net. I believe Peter has had the opportunity to meet Maradona since, to shake his hand and forget it, but he won't. He thinks he should have apologised – which he never has.

And, yes, I can understand why people think the attitudes in the professional game are strange at times. It isn't the handball that Peter objects to, but the lack of an apology. If Maradona had said sorry it would have been okay. Do I get that? I guess so. Professionals are trained to win at all costs and if someone gets away with one, we tend to think that all's fair in love and war. Just own up – admit it in the bar later. Maradona never did that. He acted as if what he did was some sort of divine intervention, and that sticks in the throat a little more. It was as well he scored one of the greatest World Cup goals to effectively win the match soon after, otherwise I think the bitterness would have lasted even longer.

The one thing I cannot comprehend, though, is when people say it was an instinctive reaction. Handball is a foul in football. How can sticking your hand up be instinctive, then? Every instinct as a footballer should be telling you to get your hand out of the way. I won't accept that it was instinctive. Maradona knew what he was doing, and he intended to cheat to try to score. A slip fielder wouldn't try to catch a hard cricket ball with his foot – so why would a footballer attempt to divert a ball with his hand? I saw the same excuse made for Rafael of Manchester United last season, and I thought it was rubbish then, too. He's just rash, that's his problem. He hasn't got instincts any different to the rest of us. I had his brother, Fabio, at Queens Park Rangers and he was the same. He'd rush in and kick a player up in the air after the ball had gone. It seemed to be his greatest talent.

I know Brian Clough credited Peter Shilton with winning the league for Nottingham Forest – he reckoned he was worth 12 points a season – but the relationship between the manager and the goalkeeper was unconventional to say the least. On one occasion, Clough was due to meet John Holmes, Peter's agent, and his partner Jeff Pointon. He kept them waiting outside his office and then his secretary announced that Clough was ready to see them. They entered the room and both went flying head over heels. Clough had rigged a squash racquet handle up by the door to trip them over as they came in! On another occasion, before the 1980 European Cup final – which Nottingham Forest won – Peter complained that the training pitch in Madrid wasn't suitable for his practice routines. Clough announced he knew just the place and instructed Peter Taylor to take Shilton there. They ended up on the grassy centre of a large roundabout, surrounded by chaos and tooting traffic horns. Clean sheet the following night, mind you.

It is a shame that, after retiring from football, Peter has had financial problems. The gambling took a toll. In 1996, after Peter left Leyton Orient, he was with me at West Ham for a spell as a back-up goalkeeper. He must have been 47 by then, and things weren't easy. I got him a little club car because he didn't even have transport to get him back and forth to training. He was borrowing a motor from somebody at the time. He didn't play for us but I enjoyed having Peter around, working with our goalkeepers along with Les Sealey who was my goalkeeping coach. I'm glad to see he's getting back on his feet now. I often see him at charity dinners or fund-raisers and the like. It's easy to tell us apart – he's getting paid and I'm not.

I'm a real sucker for that stuff. I just find it so hard to say no. I'll ring a bloke back and hear his story and the next thing I know I'm driving home from Ipswich at two in the morning, or stuck at the worst hotel in living memory, because I think I should do something to help. And once you've said yes one time, they've got you. The League Managers Association must see me coming. Every time they have a function I get roped in to speak. I wouldn't mind if it was shared around – but you never seem to see Arsène Wenger there. Just me. Would you do a dinner for 20 people, Harry, they'll give a lot to the charity if they could meet you? Of course. Then you get to the dinner, and they say they're having a raffle. First prize: dinner with me. But they're at a dinner with me! Oh no, this is a more intimate one – only five people. And on it goes. I swear, if I don't learn to say no soon, I'll end up having to go round and cook somebody breakfast one day.

David Armstrong, the old Middlesbrough and Southampton player, is one of the worst for calling in a favour. He's always hitting people up for prizes and he gets hundreds of people to his events. I can remember doing one when I was manager of

Bournemouth. I went down there with my mate Jimmy Gabriel, another Southampton old boy who, like Peter Shilton, hadn't been doing so well and was struggling to find work. David got me up on stage with Lawrie McMenemy to draw the raffle. Everyone had to sign a tenner, and the first prize was a weekend for two at the five-star George V hotel in Paris, flights included. Dave could get prizes off anybody. He could get you a night out at Buckingham Palace if he put his mind to it. Jimmy was at a table with a lot of his old Southampton team-mates – Denis Hollywood, John McGrath, Hugh Fisher, all good lads. Dave had put all the £10 notes in a big barrel, and I thought it was an opportunity to do my mate Jimmy a turn. A weekend in Paris would be lovely for him and his wife, Pat – she had been quite ill and they could probably use a holiday. I pulled out a tenner at random. 'Great news,' I said, 'it's one of your favourite players of all time at Southampton – Jimmy Gabriel!' And I made sure to chuck the £10 straight back into the barrel, where it couldn't be seen. The crowd went mad. They were all singing his name: 'Jimmy! Jimmy! Jimmy!' Meanwhile, Jimmy was at the back of the room waving his arms at the stage. 'No, no,' he was shouting, 'it's a mistake – I didn't have a ticket.' Oh my God. What was he playing at? He did me like a kipper. Now, I had to improvise. Fortunately, nobody could hear Jimmy's protests above the noise – and I still had the microphone. 'What's that you say, Jimmy?' I said. 'What a fantastic gesture, ladies and gentlemen, Jimmy wants to have the prize re-drawn. Round of applause for Jimmy Gabriel.' I could see Jimmy looking puzzled and I was trying to catch his eye and mouth to him 'shut up'. In the car on the way home, the first thing he said was, 'I don't know what happened there, Harry. I didn't have a ticket.' 'I know you didn't have a fucking ticket, Jim,' I hissed. 'I just made out it was you because I thought then you could take Pat away for a weekend because she hadn't been well. I thought it would be nice for you and her to go to France.' 'Oh,' he said. 'That would have been nice. I would have liked that.' What can you do?

There was another occasion when I went down to Southend, in Essex, because some people I knew who had a casino in London were opening a new club down there and they wanted me to visit on opening night. I was the manager of West Ham at the time and when I arrived it turned out Lester Piggott was also a guest. Being a horse-racing man I was pleased to meet Lester and we all went up to the Mayor's office for a reception, which wasn't really my cup of tea, or Lester's. We were clinging to one another a bit by this time and the plan was to drive to the new place in a horse-drawn carriage along the seafront. The owners wanted to put on a bit of a show, and the council and Mayor's office were clearly all behind it. Off we went, with a big black horse up front like they have for funerals. Lester and me, the Mayor and Lady Mayoress. She was loving it, acting very regally, waving at people like the Queen. Suddenly I spotted a gang of kids running alongside the carriage and I could see they had these giant water pistols, the huge ones that look like machine guns. It was early evening during the summer school holidays and they looked like proper scallywags, too. By now, Lester had also seen them and we both leaned back into the carriage to escape the inevitable barrage. Not the Lady Mayoress. She was enjoying her moment too much and the poor woman copped the lot.

Her hair collapsed like a bad soufflé – it was as if someone had doused her with a bucket of water, which in a way they had. I'm sorry, but Lester and I were struggling to control our laughter. We didn't know where to look. These little sods ran off hooting and hollering, too. In the end, Lester got out and just lit a cigar. What could you do? The whole plan was a bust.

It was good to meet one of my racing heroes, though. I was always a huge fan of Lester's – he was the greatest jockey and, in my opinion, there is no one quite like him. Alan Ball had a few horses and it was always his dream for Lester to ride one. In the end, he booked him for a race at Salisbury with one he thought was a real prospect. The horse finished way down the field and by the time Alan had scurried over to the unsaddling enclosure, Lester had dismounted and was walking over to his next ride. Alan chased after him, desperate to hear the wisdom and insight of racing's greatest pilot. 'Lester, Lester,' he said, finally getting his attention. 'What do you reckon?' Without breaking stride, Piggott looked at Alan and in his sneering nasal tone uttered one word. 'Glue,' he said, and walked on. Not another sound. That was the end of Alan's little dream. I dare say his Southampton team-mate Peter Shilton backed a few like that, too.

STEVE NICOL
(LIVERPOOL)

'Where have you been all my life?' Alan Hansen's words to Steve Nicol, apparently, after their first match together. It's the same old story. Liverpool spot a kid at Ayr United, buy him for buttons – £300,000 – and turn him into one of the most versatile players in Europe. Steve was a right-back who could also play on the right or in the centre of midfield. He was the butt of the jokes in the Liverpool dressing-room, apparently, but it was no laughing matter when the game started. He was a serious player: powerful, fast, imposing, technically outstanding. He had a reputation for not being the brightest, but he certainly didn't lack intelligence with the ball at his feet. I read Kenny Dalglish's description of his arrival at Anfield in 1981. It bears repeating.

'Until then, the three Scots already at Anfield, Alan Hansen, Graeme Souness and me had been pretty well able to look after ourselves. We had built up an understanding that the Scots were the master race. We would quote historical facts to the English players to prove it. Some of the most important inventions and discoveries in the world came from Scots, the television, the telephone, penicillin, the steam engine and tarmac. Their names are part of history – John Logie Baird, Alexander Graham Bell, Alexander Fleming, James Watt. Not to mention those other wonders of the world, golf and whisky. Per heads of population, the Scots are the most educated race in the world. We did well flying the flag of Scottish supremacy, until Nicol came. Everything we had built up, he destroyed in ten minutes.'

He had all sorts of nicknames. Chico after one of the Marx Brothers, and Chopsy because he liked chips, which in his broad accent were pronounced 'chops'. The Liverpool lads from that time said he had the worst diet of any footballer they'd seen. Endless packets of crisps, chips with everything – and he smoked, which drove Kenny Dalglish mad. This was probably the last era in the English game in which a player could live unhealthily and get away with it. The next decade saw the arrival of the Premier League and the influx of foreign players. It all changed from there.

Yet, no matter how he prepared, Nicol was never found wanting as an athlete. He had size 12 feet that would pound the right flank like no other player of his time. When you think of the other players about in that era, Mike Duxbury at Manchester United, Gary Stevens at Everton, I think Steve was in a league above. Certainly his versatility set him apart. He ended up in central midfield and was outstanding in that role, too. He was two-footed, a strong presence in the air and a very courageous defender. When Phil Neal was at right-back he played on the right wing, and at one time he deputised for Hansen at centre-half when he was out injured for a spell. Hansen said that when he returned to the side he felt as if he could play with a cigar on when Nicol was to his right.

Was he as daft as they make out? Well, he held down a manager's job with the same club in America, New England Revolution, for nine years, and now has a good number with ESPN over there, so he can't be that stupid. I think every club needs one guy who hasn't got the guile of the others – there are always some pretty sharp lads in football dressing-rooms – and messing them around is good for team spirit as long as it doesn't go too far. When my son Jamie was at Liverpool, Jason McAteer was in the Steve Nicol role. There are so many stories about Jason – although I have no idea how many, if any, are true – footballers like a good story. One day, away with the Republic of Ireland team, the players were out at a local Italian for a bonding exercise. They were all ordering pizzas. 'Do you want yours cut in four or eight?' the waitress asked Jason. 'Four, definitely,' he said. 'There's no way I'll eat eight.' Another one, which Neil Ruddock swears is true, has Jason filling in a credit-card application form and getting to the line that says 'position at company'. 'What should I put?' he asks earnestly. 'I'm usually a midfielder, but he keeps playing me at right wing-back.'

Graeme Souness swears that Nicol turned up for his first away trip with a teddy bear tied to the top of his travel bag, which must have kept the lads going for a few months, but he was most certainly one of the boys once he settled in and was even known to sneak a fag on the team bus on the way home after a game. These days, players have often come through an academy system and are therefore attuned to the professional way of life from a young age. But Steve had been a building-site labourer back in Scotland and only played for Ayr part-time. He smoked, liked a drink, enjoyed his chips and his fatty snacks like any other working-class lad. And he wasn't going to stop that just because he now played for Liverpool.

I think sometimes that experience of life outside the game makes a character stronger. Although Steve Nicol missed Liverpool's first penalty the night they won the shoot-out for the European Cup against AS Roma, what impresses me is that he wanted to take one at all. Here was a kid, on as a substitute for Craig Johnston, having played just over 20 matches for Liverpool, and he volunteered to take the first penalty against Roma in their own stadium. They don't make them like that any more.

Picking this Eighties XI, and other teams from the Premier League era, I notice this one is the last to include Scottish players, and I think that's a real shame. Nicol and Hansen, maybe Gordon Strachan, were probably the last of the greats – the last truly magnificent Scottish players to operate at the pinnacle of the English game. Looking back through the other teams, there are Scotsmen at the heart of it all – Souness, Dalglish, John Robertson, Denis Law, Dave Mackay, Billy Bremner, Bobby Collins – but the driving force in the Scottish game begins to dwindle at the end of the Football League era. It surprised me that it dropped off so quickly. We went from every good team being built around a Scottish influence to a time when Darren Fletcher of Manchester United was probably alone as a Scotland international in a top English side. It can't have been prejudice on the part of the coaches – not with men like Sir Alex Ferguson around. I think their league simply became overstuffed with second-rate foreign players and their kids just couldn't get through. Once that happens, people stop putting such emphasis on looking and scouting. The production line has never stopped in terms of Scottish managers, but for a time nobody searched north of the border for players any more.

That's a pity because there was a raw talent in some of those Scottish lads that you won't always find at academies. I'm thinking of another Scottish right-back from around that time, Ray Stewart at West Ham. He came from Dundee United, who were a reasonable team, but even so there was something untutored in the way he used to smash his penalties as hard as he could off a proper run. The West Ham fans called him Tonka because, like Tonka Toys, they reckoned he was indestructible. West Ham, in particular, seemed to have a good connection to Scotland once Ron Greenwood signed Bobby Ferguson and John Cushley in 1967. We were a team of London boys at the time and at first with their accents it was like they came from another planet, but they soon fitted in. Like Liverpool, West Ham had a long tradition of Scottish players: Neil Orr, Don Hutchison, Frank McAvennie, Christian Dailly, even a goalkeeper called Alan McKnight, whose name sounded a little too much like McNightmare – and he did have a few. Yet where are the Scots in Sam Allardyce's team now? Where are they for Brendan Rodgers? I would love to see a resurgence of Scottish players in our game – and I just hope the sort of men who unearthed Nicol and Hansen haven't given up.

ALAN HANSEN
(LIVERPOOL)

Reading the game, understanding the game, always in the right place at the right time, Alan Hansen was just a class act. What you have seen on *Match of the Day* for the last two decades or so was how he played. Never rushed, always cool, very laid back. No matter how frenetic the match, Alan looked like he had time. He was a centre-half who could play, could pass, could come out with the ball and build the attack. Again he was player that Liverpool picked up from an inferior level of football, yet put straight in the team. Hansen won promotion with Partick Thistle, played one season in Scotland's Premier Division and came to Anfield. He signed in the summer and was in the starting line-up the following September. He didn't play every game of that 1977–8 season, but he was regarded highly enough to start in the European Cup final against FC Bruges of Belgium that Liverpool won. In the end, he took over from Emlyn Hughes. In season 1978–9, Liverpool conceded just 16 goals in 42 matches – only 4 at Anfield – and kept 28 clean sheets.

Goalscoring partnerships are important, but no more so than getting the centre-halves right, and Liverpool have had some fabulous pairings over the years. Hansen and Mark Lawrenson are two of the best there have been at any club in the world. Liverpool broke their club transfer record to sign Mark from Brighton and Hove Albion, and I think that shows the sweeping changes in our game now. It is unthinkable that a signing record would be created with a move like that in the modern era. At the end of last season, in the entire Premier League, only one club, Crystal Palace, still had a lower league player as their record signing – Dwight Gayle from Peterborough United for £4.5 million. That record is bound to fall, too. The rest are either expensive foreign imports – and not always successful ones, if you consider Dani Osvaldo at Southampton and Erik Lamela at Tottenham Hotspur – or established Premier League players like Andy Carroll, Darren Bent or Peter Crouch. I doubt very much if the modern Liverpool are hunting for the next Lawrenson at Brighton, either. And is their defence better for it? Not on last year's evidence.

I think the talent is still there in the lower divisions, but people just haven't got the time to make it work, or the freedom to take a risk. When so many managers are losing their jobs they will go for the tried and tested, the comfort blanket of a big foreign name with proven success. There aren't the opportunities in the modern game because everybody is looking over his shoulder. If there was more space to breathe, managers would bring some of those players through and we would see that the talent is there. It might take time, but given the opportunity I still believe talent exists in the lower leagues. I remember going to West Ham from

Bournemouth and taking little Matthew Holmes with me for £40,000. He did great, and was runner-up in our Player of the Year Awards in his first season; we used him all over the place and ended up selling him to Blackburn Rovers for £1.2 million. So they are out there, but if I hadn't gone to West Ham as manager, who would have taken a chance on Matthew? He'd have been in the lower divisions all his career.

If managers are constantly under pressure they are not going to gamble. They'll always look for the instant fix. I'm not advocating picking up second-rate players from second-rate leagues, but either clubs like Partick, Brighton and Ayr United have just stopped producing players overnight – which seems unlikely – or we've stopped looking; because those guys came in and won European Cups.

It was a great pity that Liverpool didn't win the league last season with the number of English players they had in the team. We've been told for so long that English footballers aren't good enough, and then suddenly there were six of them – plus Joe Allen, who is Welsh – at the top of the table. I know Manchester City have a long-term project with their academy, but Manuel Pellegrini, their current manager, doesn't seem too interested in developing English players. Half of the English lads at the club spent all summer trying to get away. I really fancied Liverpool at one stage last season, particularly at home. Once they had beaten Manchester City, with Vincent Kompany struggling to contain them, it really looked possible. In the end, though, what they missed was steel at the back. The modern team used Luis Suárez the way the great Liverpool side used Kenny Dalglish, and they have Steven Gerrard where the great team had Graeme

Souness – but what they don't have is Hansen, Lawrenson, Steve Nicol, the great defenders that got them over the line in so many matches. The best Liverpool teams only needed one goal because their back four were not going to leak. That makes life so much easier.

There were some good defenders around at that time. Terry Butcher was a fantastic competitor and Mark Wright had a lot of style, but I don't think anyone had the aura or control of Hansen. As a manager, sitting there watching him you would have felt comfortable. In fact Bob Paisley said he gave him more heart attacks than any other player because he would insist on playing the ball out when others would just have lumped it clear, but all I remember is his air of calm. There was never any panic, no last-ditch tackles. He reminded me of Bobby Moore. I never saw Bob throw himself into a diving header or make a lunging tackle because he'd seen the danger ages earlier and was in the right place. Hansen was the same. He would cut out a pass or a cross, fill in the space at the near post and catch it on his chest, like Bobby. And play from there. And that's what he is like away from football, too. He's an easy person, a wonderful golfer – three handicap – and very laid-back company. Jamie goes golfing with him in Florida every year, and I was with him at the World Cup in 2010, working for the BBC. He's a good chap.

We were based in Cape Town, which was lovely, but then England had to play Germany in Bloemfontein. What a strange, hick town that was. I don't know where Alan was – somewhere classy, no doubt – but I ended up staying in a bungalow with a pal of mine, Clive Tyrell. Clive's just like his dad, Reg, who I worked with at Bournemouth – he always makes me laugh. He was an apprentice at Chelsea as a kid but it didn't work out. I lost my licence for six months for speeding and Clive was my driver in that time. I ended up taking him to South Africa to say thanks. We played a lot of golf, had a great time. In Cape Town it was marvellous. Lovely big hotel suite – he had a bedroom, I had a bedroom. Perfect. So on we went to Bloemfontein, where it is fair to say conditions were somewhat different. When we pulled up outside this bungalow I couldn't quite believe it. 'Sorry,' said the chap from the BBC, 'there are no hotels.' That night the temperature must have dropped 15 degrees and, try as we might, we couldn't find the heating. It went from lovely during the day to freezing. I don't think I've ever been colder. The result the next day didn't do much to warm us up, either. Hansen wouldn't have stood for it, I know that. And he wouldn't have got beat by four, either.

PAUL McGRATH
(MANCHESTER UNITED)

What a player he was, but what a player he could have been. Without the injuries, without the drinking, who knows what he would have achieved in his career. Ron Atkinson rated him as better than John Terry and Tony Adams – put together. I don't know about that, but he was a quite exceptional footballer. He had incredible pace and was equally at home in a back four or running midfield, as he did later in his career with Aston Villa. He was a great player – but we probably never saw how good he could have been because of the way he lived his life. When I tell stories about lads who liked a drink, it is usually with fondness because those days were fun, and most of the lads could handle it. Paul was different; twice he tried to kill himself and on one occasion he consumed a bottle of Domestos. There was little merriment here. Paul, sadly, was a man with serious problems.

He was brought up in orphanages around Dublin at a time when they were not many black faces about: a hard life. He didn't touch a drop of alcohol until he was 18 but then discovered a real taste for it. Like a lot of alcoholics he used it to give himself confidence and to escape reality. He admits there were times when he played while still drunk, even falling over the ball once in a pre-season friendly. Yet when he was right, and his game was right, there was no one to touch him. I think by the time Sir Alex Ferguson came to Manchester United he was almost beyond help, and Alex just associated him with a poisonous drinking culture that was ruining the club. He sold him to Aston Villa where, for all his troubles, he became a club legend. He played every game in the 1992–3 season when they just missed out on the title. He was magnificent on occasions for Villa – inspired, I think, by a determination to prove Ferguson wrong. Aston Villa beat Manchester United in the League Cup final during his time there and Paul was exceptional that day. I know Alex never stopped admiring him as a player, but he couldn't control the man – and at that time what he had to do above all at United was establish control. Players like McGrath and Norman Whiteside had to go.

The way Paul lived would have made his injury problems worse, no doubt of that. Tony Cascarino roomed with Paul for Villa, and on Ireland trips, and he says he was one of those fellas that could be out every night, no matter where they were in the world. If they were in a hotel in Norwich on a Tuesday, Paul had somewhere to go; and the same in Oslo on a Monday. He always knew the places, but that lifestyle takes its toll.

At Villa, they had a physiotherapist, Jim Walker, who devised a way of nursing Paul through the week with his knee problems. He would do a bit of bike work, have a bath and a massage, sometimes collect the balls from behind the goal, just to be involved with the team. Paul reckons he would have retired four years earlier if it wasn't for Walker – in fact, Manchester United's first plan before they sold him was to have him quit and claim the insurance. He was only 29, but his knees were that bad. Yet more than five years later he was playing for Ireland at the 1994 World Cup finals and marking Roberto Baggio of Italy out of a game.

Paul just had everything. He was a big lad. Strong, quick, powerful. Ledley King was similar some years later. A lot of the same attributes, and terrible problems with injury. He couldn't train all week, either, and the day after he played his knees looked like you had inflated them with a bicycle pump. In the end, he didn't train at all through the week. I think that shows amazing commitment and discipline – not to train, and then still play at the level Ledley and Paul McGrath achieved.

I was close to taking Paul at the end of his career. He came in to train at West Ham, but he was struggling with injury. He worked hard and tried to get fit for us, and he still had that pace, even with the dodgy knees. Not many could get the better of him in practice matches, but in the end he had to face the truth. To be fair, he was completely honest. He called me up. 'I don't think I can do it now, Harry,' he said. 'I don't want to let you down.' So that was that – but he was as good as gold in the brief time we were together.

Of the other central defenders from that time, Des Walker had fantastic pace as well, but I don't think he had Paul's technical ability. When they did away with the back-pass rule in 1992 it made a huge dent in Des's game. He would use his speed to nip in front of the striker, mop up the ball and knock it back for the goalkeeper to pick up. Then they changed the laws so that the keeper couldn't handle it from a back pass and that was a real problem for Des. Suddenly, he was being required to play his way out of trouble, and that wasn't his style at all. A man like McGrath was far more comfortable in that position, and that gives him the edge.

KENNY SANSOM
(ARSENAL)

They used to call him 'White Shorts' at Arsenal because Kenny often left the pitch as spotless as he went on it. It wasn't that he lacked the courage for a tackle, more that his timing and reading of the game were so perfect he did not need to go flying in. He carried on where Terry Cooper left off really, as a great marauding left-back. Stuart Pearce took over from him, and then Ashley Cole – it's a position where English football has been strong for a few decades now. They had a very good left-back at West Bromwich Albion at the time called Derek Statham, but he couldn't get a look in. He only made three appearances for England, which shows you how strong Kenny, who made 86, was in that role. He was just a fantastic player and I can remember the coaches at Crystal Palace raving about this kid they had discovered. Every now and then you find one and think, 'If we can't make him a footballer we should pack up.' They felt like that about Kenny at Palace. I know Sir Alex Ferguson did about Ryan Giggs at Manchester United, Arsenal did with Jack Wilshere and I did with Joe Cole at West Ham. Kenny was a certainty, apparently. He was a brilliant trainer, came back in the afternoon, worked non-stop on his game, always striving to be the best. I can remember seeing him in those early days – he stood out a mile. He had a low centre of gravity, was great going forward and you couldn't get past him. Strong in the air, too, for a small guy. Now he's battling alcoholism. With a guy like Kenny you really do wonder where it all went wrong.

In his book he says he didn't have a drink until he was 21 and then he couldn't leave it alone. He was a big gambler, too. Maybe it's the punter in me, but I look at an ex-player like Kenny and wonder what I could do to help him. Could you help him? Could he change? I don't know. Maybe he is beyond help, but I have never understood why a great club like Arsenal doesn't get hands-on in situations like this. Get him involved with community projects, give him something permanent in his life. It's sad to see a player who has done so well left to fade away like that. We see it with Paul Gascoigne and a lot of others from this era. Looking at this team now, a lot of these players have had problems – Peter Shilton, Paul McGrath, Kenny, Paul Gascoigne, even Bryan Robson. I think the next generation made more money from the game, so could ride it. If you look at a player like Tony Adams, he's had his troubles with addiction, but he has stayed relatively comfortable. I don't think everybody will end up that way, but at least they have a little more protection. You look at Kenny now, and he's got nothing. I'm not saying that isn't his fault. There are plenty of players from the same period like Gary Lineker or Ian Rush that have been successful. Yet not everybody has a future as a television presenter, and clubs could do more to help their ex-players. I think it's easy for people to say, oh it's his fault, he's lost his money gambling. I'm a gambler, too, but I'm a lucky one because I have been able to control it. I love a bet, it gives me a buzz. I enjoy a glass of wine, too. But when I see boys who have lost all their money, or have drunk their lives away, I don't feel superior. Addiction is an illness. Even now, with all the money being earned, I still think there will be lots of players who will end up potless. One of my old Portsmouth players, David James, was declared bankrupt this year and he was a fine professional.

I don't think Kenny would have been a heavier gambler than some of the lads these days – he just didn't have the same level of income. He might have earned £300 a week and lost that in the betting shop by the time he got home on Friday night. And, with football, that financial lifeline gets cut at a very young age. Kenny had a good career but he was still only 36 when it was all over. Suddenly, he didn't have a job. What is he going to do? What does he know? What's the next move? There is nothing out there beyond coaching or the media. It would even take three years to learn to be a taxi driver in London. You hear about chaps taking pubs, but I've always seen that as the road to ruin. A lot of the boys I know went in that direction and it turned out to be a marriage breaker. They start drinking, telling all the old tales – that turns into too many late nights, and in the end the wife packs up and leaves. Not ideal.

Yes, I know, somewhere along the line you have to do something for yourself. It's no good expecting a testimonial or a handout every year. But some people just do need help more than others. Players like Kenny Sansom and Paul Gascoigne are clearly higher maintenance than some of their contemporaries. They need more direction in life, a greater sense of purpose. They need a proper job in football. Not something part-time or just on match-days, a job that they get up to every morning.

I've never worried that my own betting was getting out of hand because, throughout my life, I've only gambled what I could afford. I have never been in a situation where the family was affected, nor do I bet amounts that are going to change my life. I'm a heavier gambler now than I used to be because I'm earning more – but what I'd call a good bet, and what was a good bet to Kenny, are probably two different things. I tell my players that football is a window of opportunity in which a fortune can be made if you're good enough – but look after your money because when it's finished there is no second chance. I'm not saying everyone listens. I saw John Hartson lose just about everything during his time at West Ham.

I think footballers live on the adrenalin of big matches and that gambling is a way of maintaining that buzz. They say the reason drugs are so prevalent in the music industry is that there is a rush associated with performing, and when the concert is over a rock star wants to find a way of maintaining that high. Obviously, professional sportsmen can't take drugs without risking severe punishment, so gambling fulfils that function for them. They replicate that excitement by having a bet.

I don't get to the races as much as I used to. I loved it as a day out, but these days you get some people who won't leave you alone. It's different if you're in a hospitality box, but to go walkabout – I'm afraid I can't do it any more. I prefer a quiet life. But I'll still have my bets – on golf, cricket, anything I'm watching really. They're changing the rules now to ban all football betting because of some recent scandals, but I think that is an over-reaction. What harm is there in me having a bet on a game in Serie A or the Champions League? It won't spoil my enjoyment – I can watch football without having a bet – but I just think it's a stupid rule. Banning bets on matches that take place in my league, I can understand. But why shouldn't a Premier League player be able to place a bet on a match in League One, or a lad at Bournemouth pick a winner between Arsenal and Chelsea? When I see new rules like that being made I am glad I am not at the start of it. The people in charge haven't a clue – particularly as all of football's governing bodies now have betting partners themselves.

If they are going to benefit from those commercial deals maybe they could use the money to help out guys like Kenny Sansom, by putting the proceeds into an addiction centre or rehabilitation. That would make more sense than banning gambling one minute, and teaming up with bookmakers the next.

GLENN HODDLE
(TOTTENHAM HOTSPUR)

Glenn Hoddle was such a beautiful footballer. The scorer of spectacular goals, and a simply fantastic passer. At Tottenham he had a great understanding with his fellow midfield players, like Ossie Ardiles, and again with striker Clive Allen. The game always seemed to unfold at his pace, he had a way of appearing to have time on the ball and always knew where the other good midfield players were. It was as if he had pictures in his head, he saw what was on and knew where the ball was going before it arrived. He reminded me a bit of Johnny Haynes. Glenn would hit a pass and everybody would be thinking, 'How did he see that, how did he know that player was there?' He never seemed to be obviously searching for it, either. He would look up – he always played with his head up – but it was never as if he was hunting a pass. He knew what the next move was before the ball even came. That is how the best play – and Glenn was one of the greatest midfielders this country has produced.

Some of the goals he scored, the little free-kicks and the clever things he did are evidence of an outstanding football brain, and it is a real pity that there is a generation that will remember him only for the controversies around his time as England manager. Even then he was on the right lines – but the off-the-field stuff surrounding his beliefs did for him.

I worked with Steve McClaren at Queens Park Rangers last season and his contribution was excellent. I think it is a real pity that failure in the England job taints a manager almost for life. Steve should never have been my temporary coach at QPR. He was too good for that, as he then showed with Derby County. But at the time he was glad of the work, just to get his foot through the door. A lot of clubs still wouldn't touch Steve because the fans would have been up in arms, and it needed one like Derby, where he is still highly regarded from his time as a player, to show that faith in him.

Glenn had been out of league football for eight years before I took him to QPR – how had we lost a football mind like that? It isn't right – and it makes the England job increasingly an older manager's game. The downside is so great these days that it's now becoming a position you take at the end of your career when you can't be tainted and aren't really looking for more work. For a young man, while it may seem irresistible, it may also come to be considered too great a risk. Unless you do very well – and even the quarter-finals wasn't considered good enough for Sven-Göran Eriksson in the end – people are going to be on your case, and it might render you unemployable. Why would a bright young coach take a chance like that?

Roy Hodgson is old enough not to be affected by this now. He isn't thinking of going too far from here. He's managed Liverpool and Inter Milan, as well as Switzerland, he's taken Fulham to a European final – he's had a fine career. He's not looking to get the Sunderland job when he stops working for the Football Association. In fact he probably sees this as his last managerial role in football. It's different for a younger guy, and I think it took a lot for Steve to get over the fall-out of managing England and failing to get to the European Championship. He had to go to Holland and work with Twente Enschede to escape the negativity at home – and ended up winning the Dutch league. So he's clearly no fool. It is a job that has chewed up two of our best young coaches in recent years and that is not right.

I'm not saying Glenn didn't get his chances after England. He did a very creditable job at Southampton, and also took charge of Tottenham and then Wolverhampton Wanderers – but he deserved those jobs because it wasn't as if he flopped as England manager. Steve did fail to get England to the European Championships in 2008, but Glenn qualified for the 1998 World Cup and was unlucky to lose to Argentina on penalties. I'm sure he would have got us to the 2000 European Championships, too, given time. Statistically he was one of the most successful

England managers ever. Yet every job he went to after England there seemed to be a stigma attached. Tottenham were a mid-table team, with middling investment, and Glenn's league finishes suggest this – but somehow it wasn't enough. How could the club show so little patience with a man who as a player pretty much *was* the club for 12 years?

Glenn was another player who was wasted by England really. In the 1979–80 season he scored 19 goals in 41 league games from midfield – yet only started 4 games for England. Even then, he scored two goals – but never kept his place. That seemed to be the story for Glenn. No England manager ever really showed enough faith in him, and it was as if he constantly had to prove himself. He played 53 games for England but it was a stop-start career. He made his debut against Bulgaria, started, scored, England won 2–0, and he then had to wait four matches and six months for his next game, against Wales. Then another three games before he was used again, then another three. He played his first game on 22 November 1979, and his fifth on 25 March 1981 – and in that time England played 15 matches. He was at the top of his game. It was a terrible waste of a great player.

I feel we've squandered Glenn's insight as a manager, too. In many ways, he pre-dated Brendan Rodgers and Roberto Martínez with the approach he took to players in the lower leagues. What Glenn did at Swindon Town, the belief he showed in getting those guys to pass their way to promotion rather than just hoof it, was ground-breaking. We need more people like Glenn in the game, more coaches with his philosophy. I think we'd produce better players in this country, better technical players. Look at what Brendan has done and Roberto Martínez – Glenn was years ahead of his time. From the start at Swindon, he had a clear idea of how he wanted to play – with a sweeper, coming out of the back, passing their way through midfield and always trying to play. He was influenced by what the Germans had done with Franz Beckenbauer, Matthias Sammer, Lothar Matthäus, and he thought that was the way England should go. He was very unlucky because in the end he wasn't sacked over football matters.

Glenn probably got the England job too early, too. He hadn't really let go of his playing career. There are stories of clashes on the training field with players like David Beckham, when Glenn wanted him to replicate certain of his own skills. I think it's difficult if the manager is still angling to be the best player, too, and I'm sure he would do things differently second time around. I have always found Glenn a nice guy, with good ideas on how the game should be played, and it was just a shame he didn't get a proper run at it. I feel certain he would have developed into one of the best England managers we have had, and I'm very happy to have him back involved again with us at QPR. He's definitely got something special to offer, and he's been out of the game for too long.

PAUL GASCOIGNE
(TOTTENHAM HOTSPUR)

There should be an inquiry into Paul Gascoigne one day. How did it end up like this? How, when we could all see the trouble ahead, did his decline just happen, like a slow-motion car crash? What could we, as people in football, have done to help him?

It would be an inquiry with one difference, though. When a great player like Gascoigne falls on hard times, former clubs, old friends and team-mates often rally around in support. So the people I'd want to hear from, right at the start, are his agents, his accountants, his lawyers, all the people that made fortunes from the industry that was Paul Gascoigne. What do these people actually do to help when the money stops coming in? I'm sure there are one or two agents who care beyond that final payday, but a lot of them are only interested in the loot. They are hanging about for their percentage, and when you're skint they move on. Who is looking after Paul Gascoigne now? At one time you never saw him without an agent by his side. Now he's out there, it seems, totally alone. We shouldn't be surprised, I suppose.

Mel Stein was Gascoigne's first agent, although in those days he preferred to be called his lawyer. Either way, his services won't have come cheap. In the aftermath of the 1990 World Cup, with offers pouring in every day, can you imagine how many hours he could justifiably say he'd spent working for his client? The pair fell out in the end – which is not much of a surprise either.

I am sure Gascoigne's many advisers did their best, but in another way they are lucky that he became an alcoholic, because that way everyone blames Paul for his problems and forgets that he had a legion of experts who were supposed to look after him – lawyers, accountants, commercial and marketing gurus, PR people. Everyone looks at him and thinks he's pissed his money up the wall, and nobody asks questions beyond that. Yet not every agent has the best intentions. A lot of people who make fortunes – bankers, investors – have money as their business. So for most people earning at that level, managing their accounts is not much different to their nine-to-five job. Sadly, in terms of numbers and accounts, footballers don't know what day it is. Some footballers earn £300,000 a week. How many people pull that in, without any financial knowledge? Sports people, pop stars, film stars. Unless the people around them are honest, they are vulnerable, an easy target. I'm not exempting myself from this; as my court case showed, I'm near the top of any list for naivety.

Of course, owners are always moaning about agents, too, but they forget how players used to get ripped off before they came along. You'd walk into the manager's office, get given an extra fiver and be told to send the next one in – there was no negotiation, no bargaining. We were just boys who had wanted to play football from the age of six – while the bosses had all the power. Sure, there will always be the odd book-smart lad – but most of us weren't interested in anything beyond playing football. The school work comes a poor second. I'm not saying footballers are thick. There are plenty that are what might be termed street-wise, but they are not going to have an A* in Further Mathematics. In the old days they accepted what they were given, and now they sign up with agents and put complete trust in them instead.

I met a chap in Dubai a few years back who had built two new houses near Chelsea's training ground in Cobham. He sold one but was struggling to find a bidder for the other. The bank was on his back, and then he heard about a player signing for Chelsea for a lot of money – an English lad. He got hold of the player's agent and offered him £100,000 if he could persuade his client to buy the second house. And he did it. Took the lad there and convinced him to do the deal – and I bet the lad didn't know his friend, the one who was supposed to be looking after him, was on a six-figure kickback to make the sale happen.

Should clubs take greater responsibility, get more involved in their players' lives and welfare? Definitely. I know Sir Alex Ferguson was very keen on the junior players getting some coaching qualifications, so that if they were let go by Manchester United and couldn't get a club, they at least had something to fall back on. That's a good idea. All those years ago at West Ham, Ron Greenwood did the same. He encouraged us to take our basic coaching badges young, and we then got paid to coach at the local schools. We didn't get our full badges, but we got the next best thing, which was called a premium – but I don't know how many clubs would bother encouraging that now.

I also like the way some clubs link their academies to good schools in the area – like Crystal Palace do with Whitgift in Croydon. Colin Pates, the former Chelsea captain, and Steve Kember are teachers there, and having those connections ensures the boys get a good education, academically as well as in football. Victor Moses came through there, and if you look at the choices he has made throughout his career, you can see he's been using common sense rather than chasing the money. I read that when Moses went to the European Under-17 Championship in Belgium, a condition of his release from the school was that the Football Association paid for a teacher to travel with him and help him revise every day, because it was in the build-up to his GCSEs. Moses got three goals, helped England reach the final, won the Golden Boot – and came home and got five GCSEs. I think what is key here is that the school insists on treating the academic side seriously, too – the young footballers are not just there to win trophies for the school football team. Yes, they'll strengthen the first XI – but they'll also have a good education. I think that shows what can be achieved – but obviously not every club has the money to send its star prospects to private schools. And not every boy would be suited to that environment, either. But at least the ones that are have more of a chance.

I just don't think the advice is there, even now. This is what to do with your money. This is how to avoid going skint. For all the advances in other areas of the game, I still think players are left to rely solely on their agents.

I had Ravel Morrison at Queens Park Rangers last season. Sir Alex Ferguson said he was the most naturally gifted player he has seen at Manchester United since Paul Scholes – and then sold him because he could do nothing with him. He'd been at West Ham, scored one of the goals of the season against Tottenham, but they, too, found it hard to control him. He'd already had one loan spell at Birmingham City, but ended up with me. The kid can really play. He goes past people and makes them look silly. He's like Alan Hudson. He doesn't run, he glides.

By the time we came to the end of the season, though, he couldn't get in our starting line-up. I left him out in the second play-off match against Wigan Athletic and the play-off final against Derby County when we won promotion. Yet all season Barry Silkman, his agent, was telling everybody he's better than Gareth Bale. 'Harry,' he said to me, 'he's on a different planet to Bale.' And yes, Barry, Ravel is a very good player. But Gareth Bale? He as good as scored the winning goal for Real Madrid in the Champions League final on the day Ravel couldn't get in QPR's team. Scary, isn't it? All year I heard Manchester City might take him, Liverpool might take him – and he's an amazing talent. But his attitude makes you think about where he will be in six years' time. By then Morrison will be 27 and we may still be wondering if someone's going to get a grip on him.

There was one game last season. We had all the ball in the first half but conceded a goal from a corner, lost confidence, and were getting pegged back on the edge of the penalty box. Half time came, saved us, and I decided we couldn't go out for the second half the same way. I introduced a second striker and said to Ravel that I wanted him to play off the left. Start left, but come inside when we have the ball. His face fell into a petulant pout. The whole team were looking at him. We were losing 1–0 and, deep down, I wanted to call him every name under the sun for playing up. In the end I pulled him away from the rest, took him outside and explained as patiently as the time allowed.

'Ravel, we are losing the fucking game,' I said. 'I just want you to play there and do a job for the team. We have to win the game. It's not about you, Okay? It's about the team. People look at your face in there when I've asked you to do something, and they will all go away and think you are a big-headed bastard, because your attitude stinks. That's what people say about you. You've come here, you've done well and I treat you like a million dollars. I keep telling you how good you are, I pick you, now I've asked you to do something for me and you fucking do that. I'm not asking you to play on the left or play wide. When they get the ball, go out there, because they are playing with three at the back, so they have a right wing-back. Once we have the ball, you come inside and the only one who is going to come against you is their big, slow, right-sided centre-half. That's all I fucking want you to do.' Second half he was absolutely different class. He ran the game, everything good we did came from him, and we were all watching it thinking, 'What a talent.' You looked at that performance and thought he could get us promoted on his own if he put his mind to it. It was like watching a player with Bale's class in the Championship. He would get the ball, beating three or four players like little kids in the playground, and have a shot at goal. The keeper had the game of his life to keep him out.

The trouble is, you could imagine him getting in the England team, being asked to do a job, and reacting in exactly the same way. Ravel should look at the fact that Will Keane still has a contract at Manchester United and he doesn't. We had Will on loan last season and he's a decent player, but in terms of pure ability he couldn't lace Ravel's boots – yet United would rather have Keane on the staff than Ravel. That should be a wake-up call, no matter what he is hearing from elsewhere.

Lee Clark, the Birmingham City manager, said to Ravel that he was the best player since Gazza. His response: 'Who's Gazza?' Should that surprise us? Admittedly that World Cup in Italy is 24 years ago now, and Ravel Morrison is 21, but however long ago it was, I think he can be expected to know who Paul Gascoigne is. But it does show you that when you've gone, when you've had your day, nobody cares.

All young players should be familiar with Gascoigne's story – first as inspiration, because he was such a great footballer, but then as a warning of how quickly the fun can turn to tears. I've been lucky. I've always been in a position where I've earned really good money over the years, as a manager. Paul earned great money as a footballer – but then it was over. He was a recovering alcoholic by the time he was at Everton, and he was only 34 when he played his last game for that club.

I remember crying with laughter one night with Walter Smith, who managed him at Rangers as well, telling stories about the stuff he used to get up to. Some of it was madness. He used to go out with his air rifle and would give his mate Jimmy Five Bellies £100 to use his backside as a target. He would send Jimmy up the end of the range, get him to drop his trousers and bend over, and every time he got hit on the arse he would give him £100 compensation. He hit him on the same place twice once. Walter says you could hear the screaming from the centre of Glasgow – and also Gazza laughing about it. He once played a wicked trick on Ally McCoist, who had just bought a big and expensive new car. Gazza had been fishing, so he hid a giant salmon in Ally's motor, under the floor of the boot where the spare wheel goes, then put it all back exactly as it was. It drove Ally mad – it was the height of summer and his car stank of rotting fish. Eventually, he took it back to the dealer and they found it. What he didn't know was that Gazza had a pal who was a mechanic, and he had actually hidden a second one in the engine somewhere it couldn't be found – just like in the film *The French Connection*. Every time Ally put his air conditioning on, he got another blast of decomposing salmon. Walter said you could smell Ally coming before you could see him. He wanted to strangle Gazza.

He was hyperactive, that was the problem. He couldn't sleep. Jamie told me that during the European Championships in 1996, he might get a call at 2am and Gazza would ask if he fancied a game of table tennis. In the 1991 FA Cup, Portsmouth played Tottenham in the fifth round. Terry Venables, the Tottenham manager, was at breakfast on the day of the game when one of the players approached him, very worried. 'There's something you should know, boss,' he said. 'Gazza couldn't sleep. He's been up since 3am playing squash.' 'Thanks,' said Venables, 'but who was he playing against?' It turned out to be Paul Walsh. Terry dropped Walsh from the team, but started

Gascoigne – knowing one had the metabolism to handle it, and the other would be dead on his feet. Tottenham won 2–1, and Gascoigne scored both goals. He had an energy level that was berserk – but what a footballer. He is another one who didn't look coached. It all seemed so natural with him – the dribbling, the way he could go past people and open the game up, the fantastic goals he scored.

Considering his talent, some of the moves he had at the end of his career were heartbreaking, though. Kettering Town, Gansu Tianma in China, near the Gobi desert, Boston United. There is history over the years of players with great talent finishing up in these career dead ends. George Best was with Brisbane Lions and Nuneaton Borough; Jimmy Greaves played with Chelmsford City, Barnet and Woodford Town. They are not making the right decisions, not getting the right advice.

Yet when Paul was at his peak before the bad injury there was no one like him. At the World Cup in 1990, I think he was close to being the best player on the planet. Diego Maradona was still around, so it would be difficult to say for sure, but he was certainly the best player England had, the way he could run with the ball, putting his arm out, beating people off as he went. It is great to see people that can just go past players and do something special, who can open the door in a way others can't. In the modern game, I'd put him alongside Lionel Messi, Luis Suárez, Sergio Agüero, because he had flair that was almost South American. All the top teams are searching for that figure now, the individual who can change the game. Modern defences are so packed, defensive midfields so organised, that everyone is searching for a Gascoigne type to unpick that lock. When Ross

Barkley came into the Everton team, straight away there were comparisons with Gascoigne. We're desperate for another one to open the game up. We all loved him, whatever his weaknesses as a person.

I think the difference between Gascoigne and a lot of the players I've heard mentioned in the same breath since is that he went out there and actually did it. He didn't leave us wondering. Until the injury he sustained in the 1991 FA Cup final, every week we saw evidence of his brilliance. He went to the World Cup and was arguably the best player; he turned major matches on his own. He won an FA Cup semi-final against Arsenal in 10 minutes, having been told that he might last 35, maximum. That was a quite incredible performance. Gascoigne had a hernia operation after the quarter-final with Notts County and had only played half the midweek match against Norwich City before the Arsenal game. The medical advice was that he would last little more than 30 minutes, and Venables decided to start him and told him to see what he could do in that time. He won the game in 10. Tottenham got a free-kick 30 yards from goal and Gary Lineker's advice was just to smash it. Gascoigne did. He took a run-up like Michael Holding from the boundary and absolutely leathered it past the Arsenal goalkeeper, David Seaman. Soon after, he played a beautiful little pass inside to Paul Allen, who set up Gary Lineker for Tottenham's second goal. They won 3–1, and in the end Gascoigne lasted around an hour. My favourite story from that day is what he is supposed to have said to Venables on Tottenham's bench after the free-kick went in. 'Did you see that silly bastard in the goal?' Gascoigne asked. 'He only tried to save it.'

I see Paul reasonably often because he lives in Bournemouth now, and he always stops and has a chat. He's good as gold really. He's someone I'd love to find a spot for somewhere, if I could. If he actually wanted to come and do it, I'd like to help, get him doing something with the youth team, get him back in the game again. Yet, really, shouldn't Tottenham be prioritising that now? I can understand that clubs might not want him to coach academy kids – there could be worries about parent reaction because of his run-ins with the police – but surely there is a way of finding work for him? Would he turn up? I would hope so.

When people make wild claims about some of the young players I'm often sceptical about their credentials. Better than Bale? The next Gazza? Okay, prove it. Where are the Wembley winners? Where are the performances that people will still be talking about nearly 25 years on? I think the pity with Gascoigne is that in the end the desire to define those big occasions just overwhelmed him. In the 1991 FA Cup final against Nottingham Forest he was hyped up to an unhealthy degree and ended up with a self-inflicted injury that changed the course of his career. He damaged his ligaments and was lucky he did not do worse to Gary Charles. I think he always knew he wasn't quite the same player after that, and it really hurt him. He couldn't help himself, though.

BRYAN ROBSON
(MANCHESTER UNITED)

And now to the man Paul Gascoigne rates as the best English footballer he ever saw. I think one of the reasons Liverpool would have been popular Premier League champions last season is that a lot of people wanted to see Steven Gerrard win the league. I know many felt the same way when Bryan Robson finally got his hands on the trophy in 1993. He wasn't an integral part of the team – in fact, he only featured in 14 league games that season, and 15 when Manchester United retained it the following year – but it was considered a long overdue reward for a player regarded as so much greater than the team in which he played. What Robson truly deserved was to be in a successful England team and at the beating heart of Manchester United when they dominated English football. It wasn't to be. Robson was approaching the end of his career when Sir Alex Ferguson won the first of 13 Premier League titles, but he still got to play a part. Alex speaks very highly of him, as a man and a player, and I am glad to see United have given him a role at Old Trafford as an ambassador of the club.

If Robson had the same medal collection as Ryan Giggs it would not have been unmerited. He was a fantastic player, and a great signing from West Bromwich Albion. Ron Atkinson had inherited him at West Brom and, when he left to take over Manchester United, made sure that Robson followed him. It was a record transfer fee in 1981, £1.5 million, but Ron knew exactly what he getting. Robson could do the lot. He was a world-class box-to-box midfield player, he scored goals, he would run through a brick wall – it is no surprise that his replacement at Manchester United was Roy Keane. It would have taken a player of Keane's calibre to fill Robson's shoes. He was a proper leader as well, a warrior, the type of player that would drag his team back into the game, and that comes across off the field as well.

He's a good lad, the sort of bloke people enjoy being around. Whenever I've been in Bryan's company, I've always liked him.

I think it is a testament to Bryan's ability that Alex always puts him in his best Manchester United XI because he didn't even work with him that long as a first-team regular. There have been other central midfielders who had longer or more successful careers, yet he always finds room for Bryan. He would have been worth his weight in gold to Manchester United under David Moyes – they wouldn't have finished seventh if he had been in the heart of midfield.

When major tournaments came around we always seemed to be praying for Robson to get fit, which was a pity. The way he threw himself into games didn't help – he was a bit like Wayne Rooney in that – but I think once a player becomes injury prone it is very much a downward spiral. One injury leads to another, taking the stress off one muscle puts greater pressure on muscles elsewhere, and had he been a little more robust who knows what he might have achieved. He missed the 1983 League Cup final, the 1992 League Cup final and, having scored two goals in the 3–0 comeback against Diego Maradona's Barcelona side in 1984, missed both legs of the European Cup-Winners' Cup semi-final with Juventus, which United lost. He was chaired off the Old Trafford pitch by the fans after the Barcelona win – they always recognised his contribution, even if injury meant he didn't play more than 30 league games for United in any of his last five seasons.

Bryan could have been the first player to score an FA Cup hat-trick in 30 years when, having already nabbed two against Brighton and Hove Albion in 1983, United got a penalty. But

Robson stood to one side and let Arnold Mühren, the regular taker, do his job. Robson was always a class act. When he scored after 27 seconds against France at the 1982 World Cup, he was rewarded with a gold watch for the fastest goal of the tournament, and he wanted to sell it so the money could be divided among the team.

He was a proper lad, too. He was in the Peter Shilton-era England team and that was a hard school. Drinking, gambling, cards, they must have taken a bit of controlling. No wonder things sometimes got a little confused. There is a lovely story about Sir Bobby Robson bouncing down to breakfast one morning. Bobby was never the best with names, but this time he excelled himself. Spotting Bryan Robson in the lobby he offered a cheery wave. 'Morning, Bobby,' he said. Bryan looked up and explained carefully. 'Boss,' he said. 'I'm Bryan – *you're* Bobby.'

People knew what they had in Bryan. Although there are many stories about those sessions with Manchester United and England, it is interesting that he was one player to whom Alex turned a blind eye. He got Norman Whiteside and Paul McGrath out of the club, but he tolerated Robson. Maybe Bryan reined it in a little, too, but that Manchester United team were certainly famed for their fierce spirit. I remember one year when they won the title in midweek without playing – another result had gone their way – and Steve Bruce, who had succeeded Bryan as captain, rang all the team about 10.30 at night, got them to his place to celebrate, and they all went into training the next day straight from the party. That sort of togetherness is hard to find now, and Robson would have helped build it at United. He may not have been around for all of the good times, but he certainly deserves the accolades for helping to get them started.

JOHN BARNES
(LIVERPOOL)

What strikes me about a lot of the players in this team is the versatility. Steve Nicol could play in the full-back role, at centre-half or across midfield; Paul McGrath played centre-half or could step into midfield; Glenn Hoddle was a brilliant midfield player who late in his career moved to sweeper; and when a recurring Achilles tendon injury robbed John Barnes of his pace on the left, he became a fine central midfielder, controlling the game and schooling the younger players around him. They were all British or Irish, these players, too. We think of total footballers, the ones who can play anywhere on the pitch, as being the property of the Dutch, or the Hungarians back in the 1950s, but it shows that we can do it, too, if required. I find the way John Barnes adapted to his changed circumstances hugely impressive. Some players with his injury problem would have slowly dropped through the leagues, but he never gave up. Roy Evans created this new role for him in Liverpool's midfield, and John played it to perfection, even getting back in the England team as a central midfield player under Terry Venables.

John was so much more than just a wide man. He was an all-round footballer, with a good football brain and lots of intelligence. His goalscoring record from left wing alone suggests he could have been a striker, too, had Liverpool not had Ian Rush, John Aldridge and later Robbie Fowler to play that role. As a winger, John had real strength. He was a big, powerful lad who could pick it up and just drive through people. The moment he dropped into a midfield role, however, he showed there was such subtlety to his play – what Ryan Giggs brought to Manchester United late in his career, Barnes brought to Liverpool. He dictated matches the way a real top midfielder does. It was as if he had played there all his life.

His is a remarkable story really, because he was playing as a centre-half for his boys' club in Paddington when Watford spotted him. He joined the club in 1981 and they put him in their youth team against Leyton Orient, still at centre-half. Suddenly he brought one down on his chest and volleyed it in with his left foot, and that was the beginning of his career as a forward. Watford were on the rise through four divisions under Graham Taylor, and John came in on the end of that. Everybody was swept away by his talent, obviously, and Watford's success continued – in 1982–3 they finished second to Liverpool in the league, which is an incredible feat for a club of that size, especially in their first season in the top flight.

But it was when Kenny Dalglish signed him at Liverpool prior to the 1987–8 season that his career really took off. He was offered to Manchester United first but Sir Alex Ferguson turned the deal down, something I know he regretted until Giggs came through. That was the season Liverpool beat Nottingham Forest 5–0 in April in what must rank among the finest performances seen at Anfield. Barnes's part in that is immense. It is his lovely one-two that sets up Ray Houghton for the first, his speed of thought from the corner that creates the third for Gary Gillespie, and for the fourth he nutmegs Steve

Chettle out on the wing, rides another tackle superbly and cuts the ball back for Peter Beardsley's shot. Without doubt at the time he was among the best players in the world. When you spoke to the greatest players in his position, men like Sir Tom Finney or George Best, they used to rave about him. The only surprise that day was that he didn't score. John was prolific at Liverpool, for a wide man – 17 goals in his first season, a tally only beaten by Aldridge, and club top scorer in his third with 28 goals in all competitions including 22 in 34 league games. All from left wing.

They still talk about one of his goals at Queens Park Rangers. It was in his first season for Liverpool, and he nicked the ball off Kevin Brock in the centre circle and went on a run through the middle, all the way to the penalty area. Terry Fenwick dived in, but he rounded that tackle, landed on the other side, changed direction and somehow stuck it in with his left foot. It is hard to see how he stayed upright, but he had such incredible balance. John says it was the best goal he scored – better than that one in the Maracana Stadium, he reckoned.

I'm not sure. I think what made that particular goal special was that it was scored against Brazil, and in a Brazilian style. We were ready for one of their players to do that to us – we weren't expecting one of ours to do it to them. The slalom run, the poise, the courage to keep taking the ball on, it was a special moment. The expectation level around John for England after that probably stifled him at international level. He won a lot of caps, but I don't think he ever performed for the national team as he did for Liverpool. Maybe Liverpool were just a better side at the time, too.

Injuries troubled John from 1992 onwards, and it was Roy Evans's promotion to manager in 1994 that led to his swansong as a central midfield player – the career change that I feel sets him apart from his contemporaries. It showed how well he read the game. He didn't need to beat half the team as he did in the Maracana. He could take them out of the game with a sly little pass. He had my Jamie and Steve McManaman around him, and I know they learnt so much from watching him play. He was an exceptional footballer and I think it's a pity he's not more involved in the game today. He had a few spells in management and it never worked out, but if you listen to him he talks a lot of sense on the game. I think he could be a great influence on young players, talking to them about the need to adapt, to be versatile, to open their minds to playing different positions. A player like Ross Barkley, for instance, could learn a lot from John.

I think it is so important to have that variety in your game. At Liverpool now, Glen Johnson is one who I think could switch roles. He can play right-back, and also further forward, but I know Glen has the ability to operate as a centre-half as well. If he could get the ball and bring it out he would be fantastic, because when he's on the ball he's like a Rolls-Royce, so smooth. I had Glen at West Ham and we thought he had it all. He was a centre-half back then; it was his first position with us and he played there for England Schools, too. He's not the tallest, but neither is Javier Mascherano – and he has shown what can be done at Barcelona. Glen was quick, he had a good spring, he was strong in the air – and I've always felt he had the ability to play anywhere if he was encouraged. He certainly has the quality on the ball. Luke Shaw is another. He looks as if he could play further forward, as Gareth Bale did. A lot of coaches are switching the left-back and left-wing roles now. Danny Rose came to Tottenham Hotspur as a left-winger, but now he's at left-back. Stuart Pearce certainly liked him on the wing with the under-21s, but I think he just lacks the little bit of magic to thrive there. He's better coming on to the ball from deep, just like Terry Cooper. It would be great to see John Barnes involved with the younger England players, showing them how to make the changes to their game. I know how good he was with Jamie and I think he'd have a lot to offer.

IAN RUSH
(LIVERPOOL)

We'll get on to the goals in a minute. Everyone knows about the goals. What many managers equally admired about Ian Rush was his phenomenal work-rate. Jimmy Greaves said there was no point in strikers doing their defensive work because they would be too exhausted to go out and score – but Rush was the forward who proved it was possible to do both. He is Liverpool's all-time top goalscorer – no mean feat considering the calibre of some of their players – but was also the first line of their defence. Joe Fagan described him as an example to the rest of the team, and he didn't mean the goals but his willingness to work back and tackle. Seeing Rush do that so successfully, Joe thought, gave the rest of the team a psychological boost.

I know what Jimmy would have said about that, but he's never been a manager. Rush was the envy of every other coach in the league. He is the example we would all use if we thought our forwards were being lazy and not helping their team-mates. 'Go home and watch Ian Rush. He's the best goalscorer in the league. If he can do it, why can't you?' The game was changing and Rush changed with it. It was no longer acceptable for forwards to just stand around waiting to be brought into the game, and as soon as Liverpool lost the ball, Rush would chase the full-back or the centre-half down, as Luis Suárez does now. He was the first line of defence, with a fantastic work-rate. Now there are strikers who seem to get picked purely for shutting the opposition down – scoring goals is the secondary aspect of their game. Yet Rush had it all. He could do the donkey work – but he was also the greatest finisher.

Rush was one of the last players to be discovered by that great old Liverpool scouting network. They got him from Chester City and had to make him the most expensive teenager in British football – but what a bargain that £300,000 turned out to be. Rush didn't settle in well at first, barely played in his first season and didn't score, and it only turned around for him after he went to see Bob Paisley asking for a chance in the first team – or permission to leave. Paisley said he would alert clubs, Rush went away and redoubled his efforts in the reserve team to get a move – and started scoring regularly, which is what Paisley wanted all along. Given a chance in season 1981–2, he never looked back. Indeed, from that point until 1987 when he left for Juventus, his scoring aggregate was two goals every three games. Anyone who saw the first live midweek league game on the BBC, Aston Villa versus Liverpool, on 20 January 1984, will never forget Rush's hat-trick that night. It was a frozen pitch and everyone was finding it difficult, but Rush's poise in front of goal made it look like Wembley in the spring. It was what is called a perfect hat-trick – left foot, right foot, header – so delicate, but also lethal. I know it is generally felt that Manchester United were a more entertaining team when they came to dominate English football – but looking back at the goalscorers Liverpool have had over the years I'm not sure that is true. Ian St John, Roger Hunt, John Toshack, Kevin Keegan, Dalglish, Rush, John Aldridge, Michael Owen, Robbie Fowler, Fernando Torres, Luis Suárez and Daniel Sturridge – incredible. I don't think any club loves its strikers quite like Liverpool. Not even Newcastle United.

Torres has his critics now, but he was magnificent there. When Liverpool signed him, Sir Alex Ferguson thought they had made a mistake. 'We watched him and I don't fancy him,' he told me. 'I don't think he's got the bottle. When we play them we'll steam into him and he won't want to know.' He took a year to settle in, but the following season Liverpool went to Old Trafford and won 4–1. Torres scored the first goal and Nemanja Vidić couldn't handle him. He ended up getting sent off. He always seemed to struggle against Torres after that.

I think the reason a lot of people didn't see the great Liverpool teams as cavalier and entertaining was because they knew how to shut up shop, too. Against United, opponents always felt they had a chance to score – but if Liverpool went 2–0 up their defence was so strong and players like Rush so tireless that the game was over. If you tried to chase it, they just picked you off on the counter-attack; but because of their solidity people overlooked how wonderful they were going forward. At their best, they were a complete team. The guile of Dalglish and then John Barnes, the finishing of Rush and this rock-hard defence. It would be hard to find a weakness in Liverpool back then.

GARY LINEKER
(EVERTON)

Why Lineker and not Andy Gray? If you were going to pick an Everton striker from the eighties, surely it would be Gray, whose goals under Howard Kendall took the club to the pinnacle of the English game. And, yes, I can see that argument. But it's simple, really: just look at the goals Lineker scored in his one season at Goodison Park. It really is one of the most underrated turns of recent years.

Football is a results business, and that is why Gray and Lineker are recalled differently. Andy Gray scored 22 goals in 68 games for Everton in all competitions – an average of one goal every 3.09 matches. Lineker scored 38 goals in 52 games – an average of one every 1.36 matches. Yet who do the Everton fans remember? Gray, of course – because his goals helped win the FA Cup in 1984 and then the league title and European Cup-Winners' Cup a year later. Lineker was considerably more prolific and without doubt a better player – but Everton won nothing in his time at the club. They lost the FA Cup final and came second in the league, so Evertonians tend to forget what a special season he had.

I think Gary's record was exceptional because he wasn't always with the best teams. He scored 51 goals in his last two seasons with Leicester City, and even in his final year with Tottenham

Hotspur before going to Japan he scored 35 times. I'm grateful to Jamie Carragher for pointing out the anomaly about Lineker's time at Everton, and how poorly he is recognised, considering his performances. It is no coincidence that after one season he was snapped up by Barcelona, where he scored 41 goals in his first two seasons until Johann Cruyff, the coach, switched him to a wider role. Jamie grew up as an Everton fan, and he said all he ever heard was Andy Gray this and Andy Gray that – but when he looked at his record it was good, but not great. Lineker's was exceptional. It just goes to prove that only winning matters. Graeme Sharp had a better scoring record than Gray, too – 159 in 426 games, an aggregate of one goal every 2.67 matches.

Gary was, plain and simple, just a fantastic finisher. He wasn't a dribbler, he wasn't a special link-up player like Gray or Sharp, but give him half a chance in the box and the ball was in the net. He was razor sharp, with probably the best poacher's instinct of any player from his generation. He was one of those players like Gerd Müller, the great West German striker. I can't remember a goal Müller scored from outside the penalty area, and I'm not sure I saw too many from Gary either. If I was arranging all of the players from all the teams I have picked for this book on grounds of pure technical ability, Gary would be pretty near the bottom. Yet when you have his knack for getting goals – which is the point of the game after all – that doesn't matter. It didn't for Müller either. When he signed for Bayern Munich, the coach, Zlatko Cajkovski, told the club president: 'I will not put this bear among my racehorses.' Yet it was Müller's 35 goals that drove the club out of the Oberliga Süd into the recently formed Bundesliga in 1965 – and they have not been out of it since.

Here's Pat Jennings, who I got to know a few years ago when I was managing at Tottenham and he was coaching there. His background was in Gaelic football which gave him a complete disregard for getting hurt. Here he is with his Arsenal teammate Liam Brady, who my dad really used to rate. He'd put Brady right up there with the best he'd ever seen.

Liverpool defenders Phil Neal and Phil Thompson, celebrating their 1981 European Cup victory. Liverpool through and through, Thompson was a local lad from Kirkby who'd stood on the kop since he was a kid, while Neal holds a record for playing in 417 consecutive matches for them, never missing a game in almost seven years.

Two legendary managers, Brian Clough and Bob Paisley, at the Manager of the Year lunch in 1978. If you look back at the achievements of men like these two, I don't understand why owners suddenly lost faith in British managers. They're both on my list of the best managers of all time.

I remember the first time I saw Kevin Keegan in action, down at a game in Bournemouth. I knew he was destined for great things. He just threw himself into every job he ever had and the work he put into his game was just phenomenal.

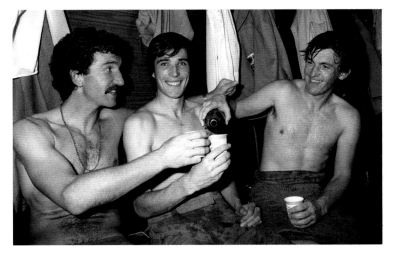

Liverpool's Graeme Souness, Alan Hansen and 'King Kenny' Dalglish celebrate their championship win in 1983 with champagne in the dressing room. Graeme told me he never went into the players' bar in the whole time he was at Liverpool, because he wanted to keep a barrier up between himself and the opposition – he wanted to be feared. It's nice to see him here enjoying a drink!

John Robertson and Peter Shilton. John was the most unlikely footballer anyone had ever seen when he started out – he was overweight, he smoked, wasn't interested in staying fit. But what a player he became. Peter was so good he could have made my team for the decade of the sixties, seventies or eighties.

Alan Hansen with the FA Cup in 1986. What you have seen on *Match of the Day* for the last two decades or so was how he played. Never rushed, always cool, very laid back. No matter how frenetic the match, Alan looked like he had time.

Paul McGrath, who suffered with alcoholism but was a genius with the ball, and Bryan Robson, the man Paul Gascoigne rates as the best English footballer he ever saw. Here they are with Sir Alex at Old Trafford.

Gary Lineker and John Barnes after a European Championship qualifier in 1987 against Turkey where they scored five between them. John was such a versatile player and was brilliant for Liverpool, although I don't think he ever performed for the national team as well as he did for the Reds. Gary was such a great finisher – he always found space. It was like a psychic ability.

Poor Gazza, unable to hold back the tears after England's penalty shoot out defeat to Germany. I'd say at this time he was close to being the best player on the planet.

The two great warrior-midfielders and famous rivals, Arsenal's Patrick Vieira and Manchester United's Roy Keane. It took Keane a long time to get his break as a player, because apparently he was a bit timid. For anyone who saw his set-tos with Vieira, that's pretty hard to imagine.

I've selected many players from the Manchester United 1999 treble-winning team for my two premiership teams – Roy Keane, Gary Neville, Paul Scholes, Ryan Giggs and Peter Schmeichel. All fantastic players, who brought about one of the most incredible feats in the history of the game.

It's hard to say who is the best English team of all time, but I'd say the game to decide it would have been Manchester United's treble-winning team versus Arsenal's Invincibles, the team that went the entire 2003-4 season unbeaten. They were only five years apart, but sadly never really met. That would have been a fascinating battle.

John Terry, a fantastic centre-half and a great leader, with Rio Ferdinand who I tipped at 16 to be the greatest centre-half in Europe – for a while, he was just that.

Having a laugh with Stuart Pearce. I managed him at West Ham when he was 37, and he was fantastic for us, but I have to say I wish I'd worked with him in his prime. He was a ferocious competitor, and I think if you asked any right-sided player for his least favourite opponent, Stuart's name would be top of the list.

Everyone knows Gareth Bale is good, but I think until you've worked with him you might not realise how good. People see him as a flying machine, but he's so much more. He wins game after game for you, and I think he'll go on to be an all-time great.

Holding the FA Cup trophy with Sol Campbell in 2008. Sol was a great captain for Portsmouth – he'd been there and done it all and the players looked up to him. He had such a strong, imposing physique – he was a monster of an athlete really.

Müller was never regarded as the most fluent footballer, but his record in the international game is unsurpassed in modern times – 68 goals in 62 appearances. He wasn't a fast runner over distance, but was typical of the sort of athlete with fast-twitch muscle reflex, because his bursts over the shortest distances were exceptional. Franz Beckenbauer said nobody stood a chance against him in training.

That wasn't quite true of Lineker who, despite possessing the same razor-sharp reactions, hated training and refused to work on his game. It is amusing to see Gary looking so fit now because during his peak years as a player his aversion to practice sessions was famous throughout football. He was a terrible trainer. He just liked to come in on Saturday and play. I know Gary's explanation is that he was superstitious about using up his luck and thought that spending all week banging in goals would somehow dry up the amount of chances he might get on a Saturday. He wanted to save his sharpness for when it mattered. Fair enough, but that doesn't make sense to me – and I have heard an alternate version.

It goes like this. Despite his magnificent scoring record, Gary was far from the cleanest striker of the ball. His goals were often scruffy, and he didn't like having to finish in training with the whole team looking at him. He thought it harmed his reputation if the rest of the players saw these shots that were hardly pristine. On Saturday, it wouldn't matter. He would get the goals and nobody would care how cleanly the ball went in – but training was different. All eyes were on him and he felt the pressure. It made him quite self-conscious, so he came up with a lot of excuses to miss training. I don't know if that is true, but if so I sympathise. With Gary's technique, in a typical shooting session from 20 yards he wouldn't have been the one pinging them into the corner, lovely and clean. Clive Allen is the sort of player who excelled at that. I worked with Clive as a coach at Tottenham and, even now, he could put it in the top corner, clean as a whistle, all day. Clive could hit the ball beautifully, showing the other strikers how to do it. I can't imagine Gary being like that. He was a darter, an instinct player. He found space, he knew where it was, almost on a psychic level. I imagine you could take him on to a pitch blindfolded and he would be able to point to where the goals were. That was why his partnership with Peter Beardsley for England worked so well. Beardsley was the schemer, the craftsman, and Gary gave his work that cutting edge.

THE EIGHTIES: THE TEAM

**PETER
SHILTON**

Nottingham Forest

**STEVE
NICOL**

Liverpool

**ALAN
HANSEN**

Liverpool

**PAUL
McGRATH**

Manchester
United

**KENNY
SANSOM**

Arsenal

**GLENN
HODDLE**

Tottenham
Hotspur

**PAUL
GASCOIGNE**

Tottenham
Hotspur

**BRYAN
ROBSON**

Manchester
United

**JOHN
BARNES**

Liverpool

**IAN
RUSH**

Liverpool

**GARY
LINEKER**

Everton

CHAPTER FIVE

PREMIER LEAGUE I

When we first heard about the Premier League, we all thought it was just a change of name, really. Division One was now going to be called the Premier League – what a load of rubbish. It was the same when Division Two got renamed the Championship. More crap, really. You're at Bournemouth playing Darlington and suddenly that's a League One fixture? We all knew the reality was Division One, Division Two, Division Three, Division Four. We considered the rest mere window-dressing – and I don't think anyone in football realised just how big the plans were for this new competition, or what it would become. The first weekend, the referees were in green shirts so the goalkeepers had to wear a different colour – it all seemed so trivial and unnecessary.

The changes were huge, though. The money coming in from Sky Television, the influx of foreign players – we all had to learn to adapt very quickly. Everybody's thinking had to change, if not overnight, then certainly within one or two years. Suddenly, we were dealing with foreign players that were brought up differently, that were totally professional in the way they lived. They weren't into the drinking culture that pervaded English football. Those nights out were part of our game – even the most successful teams had their Tuesday drinking clubs. But Italian players didn't go out getting hammered and acting stupid. They looked after themselves, they went to bed early, they were in great shape. That made a real difference to the fitness regimes. These players had higher expectations. They wanted fitness coaches, and foreign coaches too. The English guys had to change their ways. The days of walking in, shouting and screaming and throwing teacups at players were gone. There is no point effing and blinding at a player who can hardly speak English. You had to talk to them, slowly, reasonably. An awful lot of British coaches ruled by fear and bullying, and the foreign players wouldn't accept that. They weren't used to being talked to like that, being embarrassed or humiliated in front of their team-mates.

Levels of athleticism rose, too. I remember Paolo Di Canio brought his fitness coach to West Ham United. He requested we engage a guy from Milan that he knew well, and he changed so many things at the club. Players were stretching properly; times were set aside for conditioning routines. The food at the training ground changed, too. Lunches at Chadwell Heath had barely altered since my day – steak and kidney pie, loads of potatoes, anything you could get. By the end of that first season with Paolo's man everyone had their own tailored, balanced food intake, and a special dietitian supervised that regime. English football changed dramatically. Before we didn't even have goalkeeping coaches; now a player could see an acupuncturist if the fancy took him. In that first season, the Premier League clubs didn't have a fifth of the backroom staff they have got now.

Prozone is one of the biggest changes. Last season, when Queens Park Rangers were due to play Blackpool, our most recent scout's report had them operating with four at the back and two holding midfield players. In the old days, that would have been all that was available. Now we've got machines that can call up game after game, personnel, the most detailed statistics, changes in the gameplan – so we knew that for most of the season they had played three centre-halves, and pushed the full-backs on – and that would be how they intended to play if everyone was fit. The aids for a manager are incredible now. When I began, we might have one report on the opposition. That aside, you just played – sorted your own team out and went from there. If they had a player you fancied was good you might tell one of the lads to watch him, give him an idea of what to expect – but there was no detail. Don Revie at Leeds United was the only one who went into depth, and his dossiers were the talk of football. Other managers were still not convinced that they were a good idea. Play your own game, that was the mantra. You set your team out the way you liked and that was how you played – no managers changed their team to accommodate the opposition. Nobody mirrored formations. These days, if the England manager is caught out tactically he gets slaughtered; but, even a few years before the Premier League, if the same man came in and said the other team were using wing-backs so he would probably go with a back three, too, and flood midfield, he would have been called a coward. What are we worrying about them for? We're England – let them worry about us!

I must admit, I find the point of Prozone baffling at times. Yes, you've got it – but so has the team you are playing. So while you're watching them, they're watching you, and while you're changing to deal with them, they're doing the same. We all go along with it, but where's the edge? I can call up statistics on every opponent we'll face on Saturday. How far they've run, how many touches they've had, who eats what for breakfast. But I know my opposite number will be doing the same with my players. So we're back to square one.

The arrival of Arsène Wenger in 1996 certainly heralded a change in English football. He was very successful very quickly, and suddenly all the talk was about his revolutionary new training methods. He only trains for an hour … does everything on the stopwatch … the players are wearing heart monitors at training … he gives them supplements … There is always some new idea that is meant to hold the secret. There will be another one along soon, you watch.

What certainly altered was the way you tried to build team spirit. The old methods were very simple – bonding sessions, getting the lads to go out for a drink or have a day at the races. Everybody laughs, falls about, gets into a few scrapes. A typical jolly boys' outing. The foreign players didn't want to know about that. I can remember during my time at Tottenham Hotspur I took the lads to the Cheltenham races. I thought we'd have some fun, relax together, come back a bit tighter as a unit – you would have thought I'd took them on a prison visit. We got on a coach at the training ground, a lovely coach with nice food available, and we had booked a hospitality box along the home straight. We weren't in with the crowd, we had a great view, a lovely lunch overlooking the course – and the moment we arrived I knew I had made a mistake. About eight of them were looking at their watches after half an hour. What are we doing here? Why have you brought us here? Roman Pavlyuchenko never moved out of his seat all day. Just sat there, waiting for the time to get on the coach and go home. All of the atmosphere of Cheltenham, all of the spectacle, he wasn't interested. I thought it was a failure of imagination, to be frank. To have so little fascination with the world around you that you don't even want to come to the balcony, peer over and see what all the cheering is about. I know he is from a different culture, but if you went to Russia and the locals took you to a carnival day – which is basically what Cheltenham is – surely you would be interested, surely it would be a tale you would want to take back home? Not Roman. Wouldn't watch a race, wouldn't have a bet, just not interested in joining in.

I never went anywhere greatly exotic as a player, but I did spend some time in Seattle. One day a year, the people at the club would take us all out salmon fishing in Puget Sound on a giant barge. I remember Geoff Hurst knocking me up at 5am in the apartments where we lived. It was freezing cold, so we all wrapped up warm, but when the sun came up it was glorious. I'd never been sea fishing in my life – but that was the fun. We caught giant salmon, all of us, but they would only allow you to bring three home. That night, though, we were all cooking the catch and the whole apartment area smelled of barbecued fish. It was something I had never done, and something I will never forget. I can understand the new standards of professionalism, but they shouldn't prevent you embracing new experiences. In the end, it has been the English footballers that have had to change because at most clubs now they are isolated. It is a different life for them now; they can't go in the Black Lion after a game, as we could, and I'm not sure they could even go out to some of the nicest places without being bothered. Their level of fame is completely alien to anything we experienced. George Best was famous. The rest of us could walk into any pub in London without a fuss being made. And we were East End boys, not West End boys. A night up town was a big occasion for us; usually we would hang around the pubs in the local area. The captain of England would be drinking in the Baker's Arms in Stratford. Yet none of the players in my team of the first Premier League era would be seen dead there. Well, maybe the odd one.

PETER SCHMEICHEL
(MANCHESTER UNITED)

Sir Alex Ferguson called Peter the bargain of the century, and I'm not about to argue with that. He cost £505,000 from Brondby in Denmark in 1991 which, when you consider West Ham paid £565,000 for Phil Parkes in 1979, does make Schmeichel rather cheap. Not that Phil wasn't a good goalkeeper, too, but in an inflationary market Alex did rather well. He hasn't always been that lucky with goalkeepers – anyone remember Massimo Taibi, 'The Blind Venetian'? – but in Schmeichel he found a gem.

He was a rucker, as we might say in East London. He used to ruck people – really have a go at them. He was always on at his defenders, and anyone else that got in his way. On one occasion he even turned on Alex, who had criticised him after United lost a 3–0 lead at Liverpool, and a lesser goalkeeper might have been out of the club. But Alex knew what he had and, once Peter apologised to him and the team, they straightened it all out.

He had a fantastic presence, a great size and physique. He used to wear XXXL shirts apparently – which shows you another way football has changed. The goalkeepers of my day, even the best ones, were not much different in stature to the rest of us. But Schmeichel came to Manchester United at a time when goalkeepers simply had to be big. Chris Turner was Ferguson's first goalkeeper when he arrived in 1986 and he was only 5 ft 10 in – that couldn't happen now. Modern goalkeepers are a different physique, and Schmeichel had a way of coming out and spreading himself that made him look huge.

As well as being a brilliant organiser, he had a very unique style, which stemmed from playing handball. It's not a big sport over here, but it's massive on the continent and, from what I've seen, goalkeepers don't have much chance one on one. If you think how accurately an outfield player can place a ball with his foot, imagine being able to throw it. The only option a goalkeeper has is to make himself as big as possible by spreading all four limbs – it's called the star jump. Peter introduced that into football and it was very effective. He even used it on the line if there was a header from close range. The chances of reacting to an opportunity in that split second are small, so Peter's star jumps enabled him to cover as much of the goal as possible. Typical goalkeeper, really. It is a very singular role, so they are often the most clearly defined individuals within the team group – the ones most likely to conjure something from left-field.

Some of his saves were simply outstanding. There was one in the Champions League against Rapid Vienna in 1996 that Peter regards as his greatest. It is a downward header from close range, and Peter scoops it up and over the bar much like Gordon Banks did against Pelé in 1970. He doesn't have to come as far across the line as Banks did, and it is probably nearer his body to begin with, but it is still an exceptional effort. There is another from John Barnes in his Newcastle United days that is almost as good – a well-positioned header that should have crept in by the post, but somehow Schmeichel got a hand there. I think the fans voted it the save of the decade in the Premier League's first 10 years.

Great goalkeeping must run in the family because his son, Kasper, is very good, too. He came up with Leicester City last season but I don't think it will be long before he is signed by one of the biggest clubs. He was at a lot of different places on loan and then Notts County and Leeds United, but he has really improved in the last year or two and now looks ready to make a real step up.

Manchester United, like his dad? Probably not at the moment, as David De Gea looks to be finally coming into his own at the club, but Alex has never had the easiest time with goalkeepers and until Edwin van der Sar arrived I think he really struggled to find an adequate replacement for Peter. He left Manchester United in 1999 – and talk about going out on a high. He was captain when they won the Champions League final against Bayern Munich to claim the treble.

I think the rest of the Premier League managers were quite glad to see the back of him while he was at Sporting Lisbon. We rarely used to get a shot at him when I was at West Ham, and when we did, he probably saved it. Most of my memories are of being on the receiving end and getting beat up rather than forcing any heroics from Schmeichel. In fact, there's one particular game against United from that era that stands out for me – not because we caused Schmeichel a lot of problems but because our own goalkeeper, Ludek Miklosko, outshone him.

It was 14 May 1995. Blackburn Rovers and Manchester United were battling it out for the title. Blackburn were two points clear going into the final day, but United had a much superior goal difference. If Blackburn dropped points at Anfield and United won, the title would go to Old Trafford. Few thought it would happen because Blackburn were managed by Kenny Dalglish. Liverpool wouldn't want to deny an Anfield hero the prize and let it go to Manchester United, surely? Yet it was one of those days that restores faith in football's honesty. Liverpool won – with a winning goal scored by Jamie – meaning that if Manchester United took three points against my West Ham team, they would be champions.

What a game. Michael Hughes scored for us in the first half, from a cross by Matty Holmes, and then Brian McClair equalised for United after half time. As the news came through that Blackburn were not winning, United absolutely battered us, but we hung on. I think Ludek must have made about 20 saves in as many minutes – he had the game of his life. Alex seemed to throw on every forward that he had at the club. By the end of the game he was playing Andy Cole, McClair, Mark Hughes and Paul Scholes, with Lee Sharpe bombing on and his centre-halves in the mix for every set play. And then he got the hump because with two minutes to go I brought on Simon Webster as an extra defender. He was going bananas on the touchline, as if we were doing something tricky. He was the same when Billy Bonds was in charge and West Ham beat Manchester United, having already been relegated. He called the effort the players showed that day 'obscene' – because they hadn't played like that before all season. I don't know what else he expected opposing players to do. Roll over and let United win the title? Did Liverpool do that for Blackburn? I thought it was a fantastic day for football: a real gutsy performance from my lads, a master class from our goalkeeper, and Liverpool probably going against the wishes of their own fans to beat Blackburn and almost cost Kenny the title.

As it was, because we drew with United, Blackburn still won the league even though they lost the match. And Alex quickly calmed down. Within a minute or so he was in my office asking if I knew what had won the big race at Lingfield – but still moaning about my extra defender.

GARY NEVILLE
(MANCHESTER UNITED)

Gary Neville said he expected to be asked to leave Manchester United's academy each year of his young life from the age of 11 onwards. He would turn up 45 minutes early for training every day and practise furiously in an attempt to survive in the same company as the teenage Paul Scholes and Nicky Butt, local lads who were regarded as the cream of the crop. Then the batch from outside Manchester arrived: David Beckham, Keith Gillespie and Robbie Savage. Neville redoubled his efforts to keep pace. He feared that any week could be his last, ending with a tap on the shoulder and the polite order not to return. Yet Neville played over 600 games and was a quite exceptional full-back for his country. Don't be fooled by the negativity and cynicism often directed at him, and his brother Phil. Nobody plays that number of games for the biggest club in the country without deserving it. The partnership Gary Neville established with his friend David Beckham on the right is also among the most devastating this country has produced.

Gary was a class act, good on the ball, and deserves an enormous amount of credit for the way he worked with Beckham. He had a great understanding of his role in that partnership: when he needed to overlap or come inside, when he needed to play Beckham back in, or when he should be available to receive it. You wouldn't look at Gary and say he was particularly big or physically imposing, and although no slouch he didn't have blistering pace either. Yet, every week, he was a 7 out of 10 man – very steady, never rattled, knew what he was doing, knew when to play or when to make a pragmatic defensive decision. These were great Manchester United teams, yet there was never a thought of replacing Gary. He made the right decision 99 per cent of the time and was always smooth, never rash or erratic. He ended up as Ferguson's captain as well, succeeding Roy Keane, so that says a lot about his strength of character. You can't be a flapper and lead Manchester United.

So much of the play in the modern game comes from the full-backs. I don't think you can get away with not having a good technical footballer there any more, and Gary is a classic example. He was a much better passer than he got credit for, and I always felt there was a real sense of enjoyment in his partnership with Beckham. They had grown up together, had come through the ranks at United, liked each other a lot, and it showed.

Gary got into the England team very young. He had only played 27 matches for Manchester United when he was picked for the squad for the Umbro Cup held the year before the 1996 European Championships. People think international friendlies are a waste of time, but if you look at that competition – games against Japan, Sweden and Brazil – it ended up solving one of England's biggest problems. At that point England's right-backs were Rob Jones of Liverpool, who was very injury prone, and Warren Barton of Wimbledon, who was probably just short of international standard. But after Gary was picked to play against Japan and Brazil, he didn't miss an England game until the semi-final of the European Championships with Germany the following summer. Apparently, when Terry Venables, the England manager, asked Ferguson about Gary Neville, he tried to steer him in the direction of his brother, Phil. A lot of people believed Phil was going to be the better player at the time – but he was younger and had played even fewer games, just three by the end of the 1994–5 season. Venables decided against taking Alex's advice and picked Gary (although Phil was also in the squad by the time of the 1996 tournament) and his hunch was proved right. It wasn't only age that got Gary in Manchester United's starting line-up more frequently than his brother.

Sometimes a player doesn't develop the way you predict. Phil never was quite as good as Gary, as it turned out. Even the greatest managers can make mistakes. It wasn't so long ago that Alex was comparing Phil Jones to Duncan Edwards, which was a very bold statement. It's fair to say he has a way to go yet. Sometimes we're not as clever as we think – and the career Gary Neville mined from his talent, and from the hard work he put in from his beginnings at the academy to his 600th game, surprised us all.

TONY ADAMS
(ARSENAL)

Tony Adams was one of the finest captains there has ever been in this country. He was a great leader, a great organiser, and everything I have heard about him throughout his playing career sets him apart. Jamie said to me that at the 1996 European Championships England almost didn't need a manager. They had a great one in Terry Venables, but Tony was such an influence that he as good as ran the dressing-room.

As a manager I think what you look for in a captain is someone you can talk to, that you can involve in important matters such as team selection. Your captain is close to this group – so what does he think? You will have the final say, but you value his input. Beyond that you want somebody who can go out and organise the players and make decisions for you in the heat of the moment. You can't keep shouting from the touchline all day. Often you can't make yourself heard, so the captain has to be someone that you trust to carry out your wishes out on the football field. And strong characters like that are getting harder and harder to find now. There are a lot more quiet footballers, not as many real personalities as there used to be. If you can find a good one, you are very lucky.

George Graham said there were occasions at Arsenal when the bullets were flying and he would look out there, see Tony Adams in the thick of it, and think, 'Thank God he's my captain.' Most managers will know what he means. I would imagine Brendan Rodgers says that about Steven Gerrard, and José Mourinho about John Terry. Teams that are going well usually have an inspirational skipper, whether it is Bobby Moore, leading by example, or Tony Adams, who was more of an 'up and at 'em' type. Tony had presence and took responsibility – and I noticed that from the moment I saw him.

He would have been about 16, playing for Arsenal in a youth team game. I don't think I have ever seen any player of his age prepared to be the boss in that way. He was ordering everybody about – 'Fucking get it out, squeeze up, push in, tuck in here, play it there.' People talk about Tony as if he was under George Graham's control, but at his age that level of leadership comes from within. He was the sort of player that you didn't need to tell twice. Obviously he had been coached on how a defence should be organised, but there was nobody passing on instructions from the sidelines. This was his team and he was taking care of it. He knew what was expected and he had the will and confidence to carry it out.

I remember a couple of years ago a friend of mine went to an Arsenal game and saw Kieran Gibbs, their young left-back, coming forward to join an attack. The ball was being switched left to right, as happens with Arsenal, but now Gibbs was involved in the pattern of play. With that, Bacary Sagna, the right-back, went on an overlap but Gibbs continued following the ball. It ended up with Arsenal's two full-backs standing on the same wing, up by the opposition penalty area. Madness. My friend saw Lee Dixon, the great Arsenal full-back, after the game and asked him what Graham would have said had that roving wantonness occurred during his time as manager. 'George wouldn't have had to say anything,' Dixon replied. 'Tony Adams would have threatened to knock me out as I was making the diagonal run across the pitch. I would have heard this voice: "Come here – where do you think you're going?" Tony worked even harder than George at keeping us organised. He would almost bully you in the changing-room before the game.'

Tony was a complete defender. If you were up against him there wasn't much that you could tell your forwards about how to get around him. He wasn't short of any particular quality and I never saw him get a chasing, even though he wasn't the fastest. It was simply a fantastic back four, with Steve Bould as his partner, and later Martin Keown. The two full-backs were amazing as well. Nigel Winterburn came to West Ham later in his career and was as good as anybody I have ever seen at closing players down. He wouldn't just do it the conventional way; he got after people, like he was going to assault them, really. Stuart Pearce was the same. Lots of the very modern full-backs, they stand five yards off. Nigel was on you, like Dixon. David Ginola says Dixon was like a pitbull when they played against each other. I think Arsène Wenger was very lucky to take over that back four with David Seaman in goal. George had organised them so well, the machine almost ran itself. I'd say that could probably also be said of Roberto Martínez at Everton after David Moyes left.

Yet Tony was the pick of it. He was so committed, so brave with his headers – absolutely fearless. It sounds as if he lived that way off the field at the time, too, judging by some of the stories Paul Merson tells. A lot of the Arsenal players from that era talk about the Tuesday Club. Wednesday was always a day off, so Tony used to lead these huge sessions on the Tuesday, involving players like Dixon, Winterburn, Merson, Ray Parlour and Perry Groves. When Paul talks about some of the stuff that went on it was amazing they could play so well, year on year. Apparently, everyone had sobered up by Thursday morning training, though, so George Graham didn't mind. It all changed when Arsène Wenger took over – and Tony changed, too. He announced he was an alcoholic in 1996 and, from there, was a different person. It's funny – when Paul Merson admitted his alcoholism in 1994, Tony says he was sceptical. He said he was going around telling people, 'There's no way he's an alcoholic – I drink more than he does.' He reckons it took him another two years to work out that was the problem. It is amazing a player like Tony could live life as he did and still play well, week in, week out in the Premier League.

I ended up adding Tony to my staff when I was at Portsmouth because I had heard so many good reports about his leadership qualities. I liked Tony, but he was on a different path by then. He has done brilliantly in confronting his demons, but it has brought out the quieter, more introverted side of his character. He wouldn't come away with us on a Friday night, and wouldn't travel with the team, because he didn't want the temptation of having dinner and being with the staff when they were getting on the wine. I had a lot of respect for him over that. He's had his problems and he's come through.

SOL CAMPBELL
(ARSENAL)

I first saw Sol at Tottenham Hotspur, playing in the youth team. He was another kid who had come from that fantastic East End production line, Senrab FC. I can't think of a goalkeeper they have produced, but you could make up one hell of an outfield team from ex-Senrab players. How's this? Ugo Ehiogu, John Terry, Ledley King, Sol Campbell, Ashley Cole, Ray Wilkins, Lee Bowyer, Vince Hilaire, Jermain Defoe, Bobby Zamora. There's plenty of others, too, like Muzzy Izzet, David Kerslake and Paul Konchesky – there's not been another boys club in the South of England like it.

When I watched Sol he was a 16-year-old striker. He converted to centre-half later. He was already becoming the player we remember from his professional days – lightning fast, strong, imposing physique, just a monster of an athlete really. He was heading them into the goal as powerfully as he was heading them away from it later in his career, a real handful. If he had persevered I'm sure he could have made it as a goalscorer, too. I suppose what attracted Tottenham to him as a defender was that he was so hard to break down. We had a lively striker at West Ham in John Hartson, but you always knew your man had to be at his best if he was up against Sol Campbell. He moved from Tottenham to Arsenal, and having better players around him just brought that strength out even more. He was part of a team that won the double and another that went a season unbeaten, and you've got to say a record like that stems from the defence. Sol made a good team into a great team under Arsène Wenger and I think those were his peak years.

After he left Arsenal in July 2006 I took him to Portsmouth. It was an incredible deal, really. He told the club he wanted a new challenge and they agreed to cancel what was left on his contract – about two years. I think the feeling was mutual – he wanted out and they wanted him out, but it was remarkable because he was walking away from a deal worth in excess of £10 million. He was on massive money and took a £3 million-a-year pay cut to join us, about half of what he was earning at Arsenal. I arranged a meeting and I couldn't believe it came off, particularly once I knew the figures involved. It wasn't even as if he took a rest – he left Arsenal and a month later came to join us. It was really strange and I wasn't sure quite what to expect – but he was as good as gold. Arsenal had a state-of-the-art training ground and were moving to the Emirates Stadium; we had Third Division facilities and a stadium that was falling to bits. But he never complained. Well, only once. Then I reminded him of where Senrab used to play, on Wanstead Flats. I told him I knew where he'd come from – where I'd come from, where so many of us had come from, in fact. And he never said another word after that. I partnered him with Sylvain Distin and they were as hard as nails as a duo. Distin was fast and powerful as well – we made it hard for anybody to break us down.

I made Sol my captain, too, and I know there's been some controversy recently around this issue. Sol said he should have been England captain, and that he didn't get the job because he was black. He's entitled to his opinion but I don't agree. I don't think Sol was overlooked because he was black – maybe the England managers had more options than I did at Portsmouth. I liked Sol, I thought he was a good lad – but he was a far bigger fish at Portsmouth than he would have been at international level. He'd been there and done it all and players looked up to him. With England there were a lot of players that had Sol's CV and commanded the same respect, and there were many who had his quality and presence on the pitch. I was surprised that

Sol felt the way he did because I could not imagine any England manager ignoring his captaincy claims because he was black – all the years I have been in football I haven't heard of anyone doing that. The manager picks the captain, not the Football Association, and managers go with the best man, always. Are we to believe that Kevin Keegan and Sven-Göran Eriksson are racists? I don't think so. It never enters your mind whether a player is black or white when you make those selections.

I think it is more likely that the managers thought Sol was a quiet lad, which he is. He has a presence, an aura about him, and you only had to look at him and you wouldn't want to mess with him. He was a real big, strong, powerful guy – but he wasn't about to shout and scream. He would organise, but he was never as vocal about it as Tony Adams, for instance. With Sol, I think it depends on the team. He could captain Portsmouth and did a fine job – and he did captain England on occasions. But generally I would say there were people in the England team who were more vocal, more in tune with the manager and perhaps more forthcoming within the group. Thinking of the team I had at Tottenham – Sol would be captain. At Arsenal last season – Sol would be captain. Yet he wouldn't necessarily be captain at Liverpool in front of Steven Gerrard, or Manchester City ahead of Vincent Kompany, or Chelsea before John Terry. He'd certainly be captain of Portsmouth now, though – in fact, if he fancied it, he might even be able to play up front again.

Looking back, I had a lot of experienced players in that team – a lot of potential captains. Lassana Diarra certainly wanted the job, and guys like Distin, Patrik Berger, Glen Johnson, Hermann Hreidarsson and David James were all contenders, but Sol had the edge. Glenn Hoddle always said that your captain should be your best player. If he is leading out the team in Italy, say, he is the guy the fans see first and he needs to be impressive. They should be a little worried by him, a little daunted, they should be fearing having to overcome him in the match – and, for us, Sol had a little of that. He wasn't a match-winner like Hoddle's England captain, Alan Shearer, but I imagine people might have looked and wondered how they were going to get round him.

There were some fine central defenders around in that era, too – not least Colin Hendry at Blackburn Rovers and Steve Bruce and Gary Pallister at Manchester United. Bruce was a great competitor. I had been telling everyone about him at Gillingham before he went to Norwich City, but he made a strange first impression. He wasn't a great mover, he wasn't fast – he was a bit of a funny shape. I can see why people turned him down. Yet he ended up a wonderful player for United – and he's still going strong as a coach with Hull City. I made Tony Pulis and Steve the managers of the year last season. Even if he hadn't reached the FA Cup final with Hull he would have been in with a shout for it. Looking at that team, I thought he would do well to keep them up. I bumped into him on holiday before the season began, told him that, and he agreed.

I hear Sol is doing his coaching badges now. I'd like to see him get into it. I had a lot of time for Sol when he was with me, and maybe coaching will afford him the respect and the acknowledgement he thinks he should have been given as captain of England.

STUART PEARCE
(NOTTINGHAM FOREST)

I think if you asked any right-sided player for his least favourite opponent, Stuart's name would be top of the list. He had the lot – powerful, strong, aggressive, but skilful when he needed to be. I tried to take him to West Ham when he left Nottingham Forest in 1997, but my chairman, Terry Brown, said no way. 'He's too old,' he told me. 'He's finished.' He was 35, but that didn't stop Kenny Dalglish signing him at Newcastle, where he played 34 matches in his first season, including games in the Champions League against Barcelona and Dynamo Kiev. Newcastle reached the FA Cup final, losing to Arsenal, and Stuart would have been involved considerably more the following season too, had he found favour with new coach Ruud Gullit. So when he was finished at Newcastle, I persuaded Terry Brown to change his mind and signed him at the second time of asking. By then Stuart was 37, but despite his age he was fantastic for us and ended up playing 50 games over two seasons. In 2001, he was named Hammer of the Year.

Stuart was one of those players that made me wish I had worked with him in his prime. He was such a ferocious competitor – ferocious runs, ferocious ability to boot people up in the air, just an intimidating presence on that flank. I worked with Julian Dicks at West Ham, too, who was probably the only left-back in Stuart's league at the time. If anything, Julian might have had a fraction more technical ability. He could have played for England but he didn't have Stuart's control. Stuart had a way of directing his energy, while with Julian it often turned nasty, which was unhelpful. He got sent off in one of his early performances for England's under-21 team, and when it looked as if he was under consideration again, he got banned for three matches for stamping on John Spencer of Chelsea – but not before he had been sent off for the eighth time in his career for a foul on Ian Wright of Arsenal. Stuart was a hard man, too – but in the end more reliable. I'm not saying he was an angel – he got sent off five times in his career, too – but for the most part he was hard and fair. Occasionally, hard and not fair – but I don't know a defender who isn't.

Someone once asked me, as a winger who played on the right, how I would handle coming up against Stuart Pearce. I told them I'd change wings. I don't know how you would handle him, really, because he was on a search-and-destroy mission from the start. The first time the ball came to you, he was going to smash you, run all over you, chip you into the stand and then take the ball, run forward and shoot. Then he'd get back just as fast as he got up. He was a dream left-back, really, exactly what any manager would want from a player in that position. I can't remember him ever getting a roasting or being turned inside out.

He was also a player you could trust. On the odd occasion, he would ask me if he could stay home, because he still lived in the Midlands and he found driving to London every day a chore. He always promised to do some fitness work over the park – and I know for a fact that when he made that promise, he kept it. Even on Christmas Day, so his wife said. He always trained Christmas Day, even during his non-league career, and one year I let him have 25 December at home. And off he went, training over the park as promised. He said he wouldn't be able to look me in the eye if he had said he'd gone and it was a lie.

He was such a team man, too. There is a great story about Stuart getting headbutted by Basile Boli of France in the European Championship. It opened a big cut on his chin, but the referee didn't see it. Stuart knew it was Boli, but instead of having it out with him, he went straight over to the little winger he had been marking and blamed him – because he knew this lad would be absolutely terrified of retribution and wouldn't be able to focus. Sure enough, he spent the next 20 minutes protesting his innocence and went completely off his game.

Nobody ever ran rings around Stuart. The new way is to play a winger on the wrong flank – a right-footer on the left, left-footer on the right – and I've seen players like Arjen Robben causing havoc that way. I think Stuart would have handled it. There was a lot more intelligence to his game than many realised.

He worked in warehouses as an electrician, and I think that kind of experience may help in producing a stable character. It is what I would call an old-school upbringing. You appreciated being a footballer; you loved it. Stuart said he never used to dream of playing professional football because when you are in some big shed in Stonebridge it doesn't feel like it is something that will ever happen. I think there was a lot to be said for the old way. Even the lads who were on the books at football clubs had their feet on the ground. You cleaned the boots, you got the kit ready, and come Friday you went back in the afternoon and polished the brass at Upton Park. Nobody does that any more. You mustn't clean the boots, you mustn't clean the ground. Suddenly they are all 17, driving big cars, and have agents claiming they're as good as Gareth Bale. Yet if you do come across boys who haven't had all that, they tend to be the ones that appreciate it the most. Ian Wright was like that, and Alan Devonshire who was a fork-lift truck driver. It happens less and less now. Can you imagine a player from Southall going straight into West Ham's first team these days?

It was Bobby Gould who spotted Stuart playing for Wealdstone, and Bobby who probably gave him the lesson that defined his career. When they were at Coventry City together, before a game with Tottenham, Bobby took their striker Terry Gibson to one side and, in front of Stuart, asked him, 'Who do you prefer going up against in the Tottenham team, Terry? Graham Roberts or Paul Miller?' Terry said he preferred playing against Miller. 'Why?' Bobby asked. 'Because Graham Roberts kicks me all over the place,' Terry replied. Bobby looked at his new signing, the former electrician from Wealdstone. 'There you are, son,' he said. I don't think Stuart ever forgot that.

MATT LE TISSIER
(SOUTHAMPTON)

Matt Le Tissier's 10 greatest goals would stand alongside those from any of the greatest goalscorers in the world – Lionel Messi, Cristiano Ronaldo, even Diego Maradona or Pelé. Le Tissier at his scoring peak would not look out of place. As for the Premier League, if you collected the 20 best goals over its 22 years, he would be responsible for a quarter, at least. Off the top of my head, there is the chip over Peter Schmeichel against Manchester United in 1996, the incredible long-range shot against Blackburn Rovers in 1994, the ball that bends from the middle to the top corner against Coventry City, the run against Newcastle United that begins with him back-heeling the ball from behind and over his head on the run, before he beats one player, lobs the centre-half, meets it on the other side and slots its past Mike Hooper – and, in the same game, the winning goal that he takes on his thigh and volleys in from 25 yards, as cool as you like. I'm sure there are plenty more that I've missed and would be contenders. He had such ability with the ball that he used to shoot from corners.

The goal against Blackburn is possibly his greatest. Tim Flowers, Blackburn's goalkeeper, had a Union Jack towel that he used to hang from the stanchion at the top of the goal. Le Tissier and Flowers were old friends from Southampton and before the game Matt kept teasing Tim, saying he was going to hit that towel with a shot. When the chance arose he did not disappoint. He picked up the ball inside the Blackburn half, broke forward and struck a right-foot shot from a good 30 yards. At first it appeared to be floating, almost like a chip, but then it just gathered pace and by the time it crossed the line it was going like a rocket – bang, against the stanchion and Tim's towel. There are not many players who could do that, and I think Le Tissier would have been famous worldwide had he not been content to stay with Southampton throughout his entire career. He had offers – Terry Venables wanted him at Tottenham Hotspur, and Matthew Harding, the late Chelsea director, used to say it was his life's ambition to bring him to Stamford Bridge. Yet Matt was happy where he was. His last goal for the club was the last goal ever scored at The Dell on 19 May 2001. Matt didn't start that day, but came on as a substitute and says he felt that goal was his destiny. It was a beauty, too – a pinpoint shot on the turn to win a game against Arsenal. A perfect Le Tissier moment.

He was a one-man band there for a lot of the time, like Sir Tom Finney had been at Preston North End, and because he came from Guernsey and wanted to stay close to home, I think some people had him down as a bit of a country bumpkin. Why is he stuck down there? Why isn't he playing for Manchester United? Yet anyone who knows Matt will tell you he is far from dumb. He was just happy to be at a club he had known since he was 16, happy to be 30 minutes away from his family in the Channel Islands. I think he would have been brilliant at a club like Arsenal, but just because he didn't make that jump doesn't mean he's not smart. He was just one of those great natural footballers from a real football family – all of his brothers played and are still involved in running teams on Guernsey – and he got his buzz from the game itself and his contribution to it, not from constantly pursuing wealth and prizes. He once said that later in life, when all the ex-players are reminiscing at the bar, there may be some that will be able to say they won more trophies but there won't be too many who can say they were better footballers. Matt says that is good enough for him, and more power to him for that.

I can say with confidence that Matt is a natural because I've seen him play other sports. There isn't any effort in it at all – as he played football, that's how he is at golf, for instance. We're both members at Remedy Oak in Dorset and the last hole there is a 365-yard par four with a dogleg right. Everybody drives down to the fairway – not too far as there's a devilish bunker if you're too long – and then hits across water to the green. Not Matt. He takes a short cut, up and over the trees, over the water and on to the green for one. They're massive, those trees, but it doesn't bother Matt. He hits the ball an absolute mile and with near enough the same accuracy that he strikes a football. No wonder he's a five handicap. Another day a Bournemouth XI played a Southampton XI in a charity cricket match. Matt walked in and started flipping balls for sixes. There was no effort in it at all. Clip – six. Flip – six. His hand-eye co-ordination was as good as anything I had seen. He's a very natural all-round sportsman.

Like the maverick players from the 1970s, there should have been more caps for England. He only won eight and it was a shame the way that soured his relationship with one of his heroes, Glenn Hoddle. Glenn was Matt's idol growing up and they had many similarities as players – but I think Matt feels Glenn made him a scapegoat for the defeat by Italy in 1996 and their relationship deteriorated after that. Having heard his after-dinner speeches, I think it is fair to say that this episode still rankles with Matt. He should definitely have had more opportunities at international level – and it seems strange that Venables tried to get him for Tottenham, but rejected him for England.

Terry played him in the game against the Republic of Ireland that was abandoned in 1995, and he didn't start him again after that. He must have felt he had seen enough in those 20-or-so minutes. Glenn later gave him a surprise start against Italy, but lost faith very quickly and didn't pick him in his extended World Cup squad of 30 in 1998, despite a hat-trick for the B team. It was a shame that throughout his career Matt was regarded as a left-field selection, even though we all knew what he could do.

Something Sir Alex Ferguson said sticks in my mind. He said he wouldn't put Le Tissier in his own team – but he was never happy to see him lining up against Manchester United for Southampton. That sums up the contrasts. Venables, I'm told, thought Matt's best position was in the centre of forward midfield, but he wasn't mobile enough to play there at the highest level as he would simply be picked up by any man marker.

Venables thought that if he named Le Tissier, a thinking coach would simply put a man on him. Fine, if Le Tissier was willing to drag that man about left and right, creating space for others to run into, but if he remained static the game would simply become 10 against 10, with England losing a playmaker and the opposition a crude destroyer – which wasn't a fair exchange. I can understand that but, surely, there was a way of accommodating him, a way of setting the team up to highlight what Matt could do, rather than his weaknesses. He could score goals, he could take free-kicks, corners, penalties. There was always an end product to him – and out of nowhere he would turn a game. You could ask what happens if we don't get a free-kick or penalty, but Matt usually had a way of involving himself in a game. He was very confident in his own ability. He certainly didn't stay at Southampton because he was shy.

I know he liked Alan Ball, who took over from Ian Branfoot as Southampton manager in 1994. Branfoot didn't appear to trust Le Tissier's talent and often left him out, but Alan made it clear he thought Matt was Southampton's best player and he would build the team around him. He scored six goals in Alan's first four games, and eight in the last six of the season to keep Southampton up. He chipped in like that year on year, with the vital goals to avoid relegation. Like Preston and Finney, Southampton were relegated relatively soon after Le Tissier retired. I think Alan gave him the love he needed. He would tell him how great he was – and wouldn't be slow in telling the others to get the ball to him, either. Matt would have responded to that, I'm sure – it shouldn't have been so hard to work out how to handle him.

He's a player I would have loved to have in my teams because at any time you could be struggling, or even outclassed, and he could turn the game in your favour. At West Ham I had one like him in Paolo Di Canio, and he always made you think you had a chance. We could be playing Arsenal and they might be stronger and better than us, but Paolo would do something and the game would change in that one moment. Matt could pick it up from 25 yards and – pow. Make as if to shoot, drag it past in the other direction and chip it over the goalkeeper's head. He made The Dell an intimidating place to visit. It was never the same once they moved to St Mary's – but that was partly because Le Tissier was missing. You knew you didn't have him around to hurt you, either. They have had some real aggressive teams down there, but with Matt it was aggression of a different kind. It was a rundown stadium, and the crowd were on top of you, but Matt gave it a different edge – a feeling of the unknown. You could be playing your best football of the season but that wouldn't matter if he got the ball in the right spot. It didn't even have to be the right spot, really – goals came out of nowhere. And that is a daunting thought for an opposition coach.

I can remember the day Manchester United were getting such a beating at The Dell that they changed the strip at half-time. They were wearing grey, and the players said they couldn't find each other in the crowd. That's when you know it's got to you. The greatest manager in the world on the touchline and he had no other answers beyond blaming the kit. A player like Le Tissier can send you loopy.

Of course, by picking Le Tissier in this team I'm leaving out David Beckham. I know some people will think I've gone mad. But David was a fantastic player in a fantastic team, whereas Matt was performing heroics that built a football club. Without him, Southampton couldn't have stayed in the top division for so long, and without that they would not have been able to build their new stadium and its fabulous academy. He was paid a £2,000 bonus per goal after 1997, but in reality those goals were worth millions when you consider the way they moved that club forward. Think how many of Southampton's young academy players have now been told about Le Tissier by their dads or mums. For me, that loyalty to a small club at a time when it simply wasn't done sets him apart.

David was a brilliant technical player, a great crosser of the ball and scorer of phenomenal goals and free-kicks. In the end, though, I decided that what Le Tissier meant to Southampton was extra special. You talk to the fans down there and they haven't got as many idols as Manchester United, but what they have got is Le Tissier – Le God, as they called him. So this is one for the small clubs and the men who keep them going. I realise I'm probably blowing any chance I've got of managing Beckham's new club in Miami. Maybe Matt will put in a word for me at Guernsey FC instead.

ROY KEANE
(MANCHESTER UNITED)

Our scout in Ireland told me about Roy Keane's start in football. He said Keane was the only kid in their national schoolboy team that didn't have a club – the other 15 had all got fixed up. He called Barry Lloyd at Brighton and Hove Albion, who were struggling for young players, and recommended Keane. Barry wouldn't go with that alone, but he said he would come over and watch Ireland's youth game the following Tuesday. So the scout went to see the schools manager and explained the situation – that this was Roy's big break and he could become an apprentice at Brighton if they liked the look of him. 'He's been in every squad, but he hasn't played a minute of any game,' he said. 'Can you make sure he is involved on Tuesday?' The coach said no. 'We're not here to showcase kids, we are here to win football matches,' he said. Keane never played and Brighton didn't take him – they probably don't realise the poor turn that youth manager did their club to this day. Keane ended up working as a hospital porter and playing part time for Cobh Ramblers. That was where he was spotted by Nottingham Forest scout Noel McCabe in an FAI Youth Cup match against Belvedere, from Dublin.

My friend Alan Hill, Brian Clough's assistant manager, told me what happened next. They invited three Irish kids over for trial and they couldn't train because of the snow – so the trial was rearranged, but this time only one lad, Roy Keane, could make it. They took him on a trip to a tournament with the youth team and he wasn't bad – even Brian liked him – so they signed him. The following season, after a pre-season tour, Clough wasn't happy with the make-up of the squad. On the day they came back there was a reserve fixture in the evening. Clough had been sitting in his office having a few whiskies. 'Is the Irish fellow playing tonight?' he suddenly asked. 'Come on, let's go and watch.' So Brian and Alan jumped in the car and drove to Mansfield Town. Alan went to find out the starting line-up from Archie Gemmill, the reserve coach, while Brian took a seat at the back of the stand. He wasn't happy with the news. 'He's not starting,' Alan told him. 'Who's playing instead?' Clough demanded to know. 'Archie's boy, Scot,' Alan told him. 'That fucking little Scots bastard,' Clough exclaimed. At half time, he told Alan to go to the dressing-room and tell Gemmill to put Keane on. Alan duly did as he was told. They came out for the second half, but no change had been made. Keane was still in his tracksuit on the bench. 'Fucking hell,' said Clough. 'I'm not having this.' And he climbed over the rows of empty wooden seats, over the perimeter fence and marched straight on to the pitch. 'Referee, referee, stop the game,' he insisted. The play was halted 'Right,' said Clough. 'Gemmill: off. Irishman: on.' And he stood there waiting while Keane got his gear on and only when the substitution had been made did he take his place again in the stand. That was the beginning of Keane's career at Nottingham Forest. He started him in the second game of that season, 1990–91, away at Liverpool and he never looked back.

And do you know why it took so long for Roy Keane to get his break? He was a bit timid. Unbelievable isn't it? But those were the words of our Irish scout, and he knew him inside out. He was a right-winger at the time, and they thought he was a bit soft. It is amazing how people change. Brian Tiler, my best pal who died in a car crash in Italy in 1990, came across Norman Hunter playing with Rotherham Schoolboys and said the same about him. 'A timid little left-winger' was how he described Norman. He ended up the fiercest centre-half in the country. 'Norman bites yer legs' as he was known.

As for Keane, he was another player who just had a marvellous presence – another type like Graeme Souness, really, with a bit of the devil in him. I think even his own team-mates were in awe of him – or maybe just intimidated by his intensity. He was the driving force behind that great Manchester United team, the treble winners, and I think it is a real shame the way it ended between him and Sir Alex Ferguson at Manchester United. When he'd been been such a great captain and won so much, it is a pity that relationship could not be patched up and there was no place for Keane at Old Trafford. I know that he went too far in his criticism of team-mates by the end, but I wonder if that could have been reined in earlier. It seems such a waste to have a man of that stature outside the club. Would Manchester United have come seventh last season if Keane had been around to pull the players up? He would have been after them as he always was – in the peak years when there were no short-cuts at United and those messages were passed from Ferguson, through Keane.

There is a story of him laying into Mark Bosnich, the goalkeeper, for turning up late on his first day of training. Bosnich said he got lost. Keane's point was that on his own first day at the club, he got up early, hired a taxi and followed it to the training ground in his car to ensure he arrived on time. He had these incredible professional standards and expected the same of everybody. It's great to have a player like that in your team. Every manager wants a Tony Adams, John Terry or Roy Keane really – we all want someone who will have a go, fighting the manager's battles and those of the team, too. I imagine the treatment meted out to Ryan Giggs and David Beckham by the opposition might have been a lot harsher if they didn't think they would be answering to Keane.

I know he had a reputation for being high maintenance but I never found him that way. He was as good as gold as a manager and if you asked him about players you always got excellent, straight opinions. I've appeared on television with him, too, and he was absolutely different class. There are too many stories for him not to have a bit of an edge, and he can obviously lose it, but every time I've been with him I have absolutely loved his company. John McDermott is the academy manager at Tottenham and he says the same. John takes a lot of the Pro Licence courses for the Football Association and told me of all the players he has taught, Roy Keane had the most presence when he was coaching. I know he's been with Sunderland and Ipswich Town and it hasn't always worked out for him, but John thought he was excellent.

PATRICK VIEIRA
(ARSENAL)

It is impossible to write about Roy Keane without mentioning that other great warrior-midfielder from the start of the Premier League era, Patrick Vieira. Gareth Southgate tells a story that links the two, even in retirement. Keane hadn't long started his career as a pundit with ITV and they were covering a Manchester City match away in Europe. ITV have this set-up where the experts stand around a raised table pitch-side before and after the game and at half time, but on this occasion the presenter told Roy there was a special guest coming to see them – someone he might remember from his playing days. With that, Gareth could see Patrick Vieira walking towards them, in his new role as Manchester City ambassador. Roy could see him too, and Gareth says the change in his demeanour was terrifying. His mood darkened, his eyes narrowed, he stiffened and his grip on the table was almost white knuckle. The presenter was now wittering on, oblivious to the fact that at the very sight of Patrick, nearly 10 years after they had last played each other, Roy had gone into battle mode. Gareth said it was like being transported back into that tunnel at Highbury in 2005. Anything could have happened from there. The others around the table were looking at Roy's face and beginning to take a step back. His eyes had just glazed over. Patrick was completely unsuspecting, approaching the table with a big smile ready to reminisce. It looked as if it could backfire horribly, except the first words out of Patrick's mouth were so complimentary towards Roy it just diffused the situation. He was asked about big nights in Europe and he said none of them were the same as playing against him, pointing at Keane. They were the best nights of his life because Roy was such a fabulous competitor. Keane couldn't be anything other than pleasant after that; the glare disappeared, the muscles relaxed and the other guests breathed a small sigh of relief. Business as usual – but it shows you how much it means to the very top players. Even all those years later.

Quite how Vieira has ended up on the staff of Manchester City – he has moved on to running their Elite Development

Squad now – I do not know. Shouldn't he be at Arsenal? I can't understand why when you have such a leader on the pitch, you don't follow that through and get them leading your backroom staff, too. At Bournemouth I got my captain Tony Pulis on board as a coach for that reason, and had I stayed at Tottenham I would definitely have found a role for Ledley King. Patrick was a fantastic signing for Arsenal and I find it a little bizarre to see him now in a Manchester City blazer representing a club he only played for 46 times.

Vieira was the ultimate box-to-box footballer. He was a lean giant of a man, 6 ft 4 in tall, and the power behind Arsenal's Invincibles. He is still a legend at the club – but what people don't know is that he almost signed for me at Tottenham. It was before the 2009–10 season, my first full campaign at White Hart Lane, and he was not being picked by José Mourinho at Inter Milan. I thought it was an incredible decision to want to come to us when he'd been such a hero at Arsenal. I met him at his house in Hampstead and he had no fear about what people would think or what reception he would get. He had enough confidence in his ability to just brush it away.

I remember talking to Daniel Levy, our chairman, about him. He said the crowd would be hostile. I knew that – but if he had enough bottle to want to put on our white shirt after all that had gone before, I thought it said something about the man. I can imagine what it would have been like for him at Tottenham previously. Our fans would have been slaughtering him because he was captain of Arsenal, and he would have been winding them up because Arsenal would have been, almost certainly, winning. If he had the nerve to put it all to one side and come to us, it shows what character he had. I was expecting him to run a mile, to be honest. Not a bit of it. In the end, his circumstances changed and he decided to stay in Italy, but he was definitely up for the move that summer. When we spoke, Patrick was convinced that Inter wanted to get rid of him – and then José suddenly named him in his squad. When Patrick rang to tell me he sounded completely surprised. It was a shame because by the time he did become available – the following January – our needs had changed and Manchester City snapped him up.

Patrick is the player Arsenal have never really replaced. He could run with the ball in that long, loping style, but he was powerful, too, and aggressive – he could take care of himself, even against the toughest opponent. I think every major club would like to have a Patrick Vieira now – certainly Arsenal could do with one. Arsène Wenger doesn't really discover players like that any more. In recent years, Arsenal signings have been well-established stars like Olivier Giroud, Mesut Ozil or Lukas Podolski. People forget how original his ideas were when he first arrived. Nobody had heard of Vieira or Emmanuel Petit – these French names seemed like a big gamble, but proved very successful. Vieira and Petit were great signings, and great additions to the English league – two six-foot midfield players absolutely dominating the centre of the park. They operated like pistons pumping, one forward, the other back, never caught out, always in the right place. It isn't as easy to pull off as it looks – think how hard we tried to get Steven Gerrard and Frank Lampard working together like that for England. Vieira and Petit were a special partnership, really, as valuable as any pair of strikers or central defenders. They were dangerous at set plays, strong going forward, fearless defensively; they could both head the ball and were impressive technically. Everyone talks about Arsenal's passing, but at goal-kicks they were on that second ball faster than anybody. They walked over teams, really, just trampled over them in the middle of the park.

It is ironic that so many associate Arsène with the beautiful game, yet his Arsenal teams did as much as anybody to introduce real physical power into the modern Premier League. Teams got bigger to compete with Arsenal because they were so strong. To go a season unbeaten, as they did in 2003–4, is a quite incredible achievement. They were up there with any of the great post-war teams, I think – the Busby Babes, Tottenham's double-winners, Revie's Leeds United, the great Liverpool teams, Manchester United under Sir Alex Ferguson – they deserve to be mentioned with any of them. Players like Vieira or Thierry Henry would have got into any team in the world.

I would say Tottenham's first double-winning team was the best – until Leeds came along, because Revie had them so finely balanced. I think the game that would decide it, though, would be Arsenal's Invincibles against the Manchester United treble-winning team of 1999. They were only five years apart, but the teams never really met. Remarkably, eight of the regular starting XI from the Invincibles were not even in Arsenal's first team when Manchester United won the treble (Vieira and Dennis Bergkamp were the only regulars, while Freddie Ljungberg played 14 games) and by the time Arsenal went through the season unbeaten only four regulars from United's treble season (Keane, Gary Neville, Paul Scholes and Ryan Giggs) plus Phil Neville (who had a lesser role behind Denis Irwin in 1999) remained. It would be a fascinating match-up if they could meet. Who would win? My money would be on the treble-winners. Just.

RYAN GIGGS
(MANCHESTER UNITED)

Here we go again with the story of another unsung hero from the world of talent-spotting. Harold Wood was a local newsagent in Manchester who used to work part-time as a steward at Manchester United's training ground. He was the man who first told Manchester United scouts that there was a young lad training with Manchester City who was regarded as exceptional. His name was Ryan Wilson and he was the son of Welsh rugby-league player Danny Wilson, who was at that time playing second receiver for Swinton. The young Wilson, Wood said, was a Manchester United fan and would prefer to play for the Reds. Nobody followed up on his advice, so he repeated it, this time to Alex Ferguson. He immediately dispatched Joe Brown, who had briefly been manager of Burnley after a playing career mostly spent at Bournemouth, to check this out. Brown offered a positive report and a trial was quickly arranged. On first sight, Alex needed no further encouragement. 'If we can't make that one a player we might as well give up,' he is believed to have told Brian Kidd. Giggs (he used his mother's surname) certainly was exceptional as he fast-tracked his way through United's academy.

What a player. Will we see his like again? Probably not. Retiring only last summer after 24 seasons in the Premier League with Manchester United, Giggs stands out as *the* footballer of the Premier League era. He burst on to the scene as a flying teenage winger, and left it as a cultured central midfield player, trusted to run the team as caretaker coach after David Moyes was sacked. Right to the end he maintained his ability and intelligence and was capable of turning in great performances. He was just a natural athlete. He kept himself fit and found ways of extending his career beyond any reasonable expectation. He looked after himself for longer than most players are prepared to, really. In the end, they get bored with the demands of a fitness regime, but he never did. There wasn't an ounce of fat on him, even at the very end. I think everybody knew when he was 17 that he was going to be special – but nobody could have imagined how special. Sir Alex once said that 20 years on the wing for Manchester United would never be done again – and he went on another four years beyond that.

I remember Paul Merson telling me how all those years ago George Graham used to sit him down when they were together at Arsenal and order him to watch videos of Ryan Giggs. George has now been away from Arsenal for 19 years, Paul Merson went into management 10 years ago – and Giggs was still going strong until the summer, so he may have been on to something. George loved the way Ryan tracked back and wanted that level of commitment from Paul. Good luck with that, by the way.

Ryan just had an athlete's physique. He could run all day. The only other player I've seen like that was Billy Bonds. He was all bone really, a real tin ribs. He never blew up in the summer, never put weight on year to year, and that was Giggs too. I remember when he took his shirt off after scoring that wonder goal against Arsenal in the FA Cup semi-final replay in 1999 – there was nothing of him, really. He was muscular, yes, but you'd think a powerful full-back would be able to bash him up. They couldn't. I think every Englishman wishes he could have played for us because we had a real problem on the left throughout the 1990s, but his family is all Welsh. He played for England Schoolboys, but the moment it came to senior football he could only represent Wales.

It could have solved so many issues had he been able to play for England because we ruined a succession of players out on that left flank: Paul Scholes retired because he kept getting stuck out there; Joe Cole made a decent fist of it for a while; they even tried my lad Jamie out there in one game. It's a scary position if it is not yours by right because it is so hard to get in the game. Ryan was born there; he had pace, he could cross, come inside or go outside. Alex has had any number of players on the right side for United – but until recently it has only been Giggs on the left. He helped build a modern club and defines a style of play. I can remember Peter Schmeichel talking about the famous goal against Arsenal. He said that, seeing it, United felt invincible. And with Giggs in full flow they were, on their day.

DENNIS BERGKAMP
(ARSENAL)

Thierry Henry said he was a dream of a striker, and he was certainly the best number 10 of the Premier League era. He linked up, scored great goals, made the final pass, but was always clever, clever, clever. He always had his head up, so he saw the game in a way others do not. It was as if he played with telepathy, but really it was about vision. Every young player should be made to study Dennis Bergkamp, the way his head was always on the swivel, taking it all in, so that when the ball came it would go out again so quickly, and with such precision. He didn't watch the ball, he watched the play, so he was a step ahead of the rest. It was like seeing a ballroom dancer in motion, he was so smooth, so classy; there really was no one like him.

I think the number 10 role is one of the great losses in the modern game, so thank heavens the Dutch, in particular, still produce them. I had Rafael van der Vaart at Tottenham, and I think Ravel Morrison has the wit to play the position, too, if he is willing to channel his energy, but the bottom line is you have to score goals from there or make telling final passes, otherwise it turns into an ego-trip. I think the reason the role has increasingly faded from the game is that there were too many players who were simply not effective in it. It is no good the number 10 dropping deep and looking pretty – you've got to be up there, weighing in, otherwise your striker is utterly isolated and the position is wasted. It is about intelligence, and Bergkamp had a football IQ at genius level. The way he would take up positions between the centre-halves or in between midfield and defence, and pull teams apart with his movement, was extraordinary to watch. When you see 10 played well it's a great position because there are the gaps to exploit if you think about the game. It is not like being the centre-forward, up there with two hairy-arsed central defenders sticking the boot in. You drop into little pockets, play between the lines – but you need to be smart.

One of the great flaws in English football over the past decades is that we don't produce enough artistry. We miss out on the Bergkamp type of player. Even now, with a lot of the promise around the England team, there isn't a great number 10 coming through. Raheem Sterling can play through the middle, but is more of a winger, and Ross Barkley is clever enough for it, but we need to see if he makes the role his own. Wayne Rooney has not been allowed to play there, even though it is probably his best position – there have always been coaches wanting to shunt him into a wide forward role or play him as an out-and-out striker. Matt Le Tissier was probably the nearest we've had to it recently and, like Bergkamp, he scored great goals from that position. Matt was one for the long range, though, whereas Dennis was more intricate. He scored wonderful goals, but they would be full of lovely one-twos, chips and flicks. Exquisite. His play always seemed very delicate – there was nothing nasty in the way he performed, and no big shows of strength.

Dennis could hit them – as Bolton Wanderers and Southampton among others will testify – but replaying his greatest moments in my head it is the stunning close control in the penalty area that I recall. Drag-backs, flicks and audacious keep-ups that found the net against Leicester City, Tottenham Hotspur and Newcastle United, or perfectly executed chips against Derby County, Sheffield United and Bayer Leverkusen. Trying to work out how to play against Dennis was always a puzzle. What you needed was a deep holder in midfield and maybe a cluster of three eating up his space, because if you sent the centre-half out to deal with him Arsenal were going to rip you to shreds. You had to keep them squeezed up and you certainly didn't want the back four dropping off – because if he found space and there was a nice hole for him, he was going to kill you. Arsenal were so difficult to work out, in their prime. The forwards would all disappear, Henry to the left, Bergkamp upfield, Robert Pirès and Freddie Ljungberg to wide midfield, and your centre-halves would be standing there with no one to mark when, suddenly, there was a stampede and they were all breaking at you from every angle. Fans get frustrated if you play one up sometimes, but if you have the right players it can be so effective. West Ham United played 4–6–0 at Tottenham last year, and ended up winning 3–0. I remember being at Portsmouth in a match with Reading. We had one fit striker, Benjani, who hadn't scored in about five years. Actually, that's not true. He'd scored one goal the previous season against Wigan Athletic in April. We were hoping he might nick another one against Reading and we could get away with it. He finished up getting a hat-trick and we scored seven. The final score was 7–4. I'd told everyone beforehand that we were setting out to be hard to beat because of circumstances and it could be a dour game. Scored seven, let four in. It was like playground football. The highest scoring game in the history of the Premier League.

There is a statue of Bergkamp at the Emirates Stadium now, and so there should be. Players like him won't come around too often, and Mesut Ozil, all £42 million of him, can only dream of filling Bergkamp's shoes at present. Chelsea should put up a statue to Gianfranco Zola, too. He was another genius little number 10, who changed the dynamic of his club. He was hugely important to the development of Chelsea, and if it wasn't for Bergkamp he would walk into this team.

ALAN SHEARER
(BLACKBURN ROVERS)

Alan wasn't a clever player like, say, Thierry Henry, but he was a proper English striker. As an opponent you knew you were in for an afternoon's work if Shearer was in the team. He came to prominence at the time the Premier League began and I remember the first game he played for Blackburn Rovers, away to Crystal Palace. He had signed from Southampton for £3.6 million that summer, which was the British transfer record, and everyone thought Kenny Dalglish had taken a bit of a gamble at that price. He scored twice at Selhurst Park in his first game, two absolute stunners from long range, and then got the winner at home to Arsenal three days later. He just looked an old-fashioned centre-forward, but with a cherry on top because he could score goals from anywhere. A player like Gary Lineker was expert from close range, and Matt Le Tissier was a danger from long range – but Alan scored from all over. He got the little sniffer's goals and the ones that got the stadium on its feet. And he was relentless. He scored 11 hat-tricks in the Premier League because once he got two there was no way he wasn't hunting down that third. He could be selfish – yet his partnership with Chris Sutton at Blackburn was one of the best the Premier League has seen.

They had such a great understanding. There is one goal that is just a succession of one-twos between the pair of them, working their way from the centre circle to the penalty box. Sutton made great channel runs and took defenders away, and Shearer came charging into that space. He didn't have electric pace, but he was fast and once he got in front of the target he rarely missed. Neil Ruddock, who was an ex-team-mate of his at Southampton, used to have a standing bet with him. He would give Shearer £10 a goal, but Alan had to pay £20 every time he played a match and did not score. Neil thought this was such a good deal, but he always ended up out of pocket. Shearer was a goal machine – he got his headers in, he picked up the bits and pieces, and he had an incredibly powerful shot. I think his career represents the passing of an era in the English game, too, because he won the league with Blackburn Rovers, which may be the last time a club from outside the elite achieves such a feat, and then he chose his hometown club, Newcastle United, over Manchester United. He wanted to go back there when he was still at his peak, rather than as a favour at the end of his career. We won't see that too often, either. People think he must regret not signing for United, but I'm told he doesn't. He did everything that he wanted with his career, and I admire that.

Jack Walker was a wonderful man for Blackburn and the team he allowed Dalglish to build is underrated. To do that, from scratch, at a club with no pedigree is very difficult, particularly when you have a club with the clout of Manchester United as your main rival. People talk about Blackburn at that time as being like Manchester City now, but the sums involved are tiny by comparison. They were still getting beaten in terms of salary and transfer fees by clubs like Liverpool, whereas nobody could outbid City in a straight fight for a player now.

Alan's time as England's striker also coincided with a real upsurge in standards for our game. Terry Venables decided very early on that he was going to be his number nine at the European Championships in 1996, despite competition from Robbie Fowler, Les Ferdinand and Andy Cole. Then Alan went on a terrible run with England – he didn't score for 12 games. Venables wanted to rest him more often to give the others a chance, but he knew that if he did that when Alan hadn't scored, it would be perceived as him being dropped – and the negative headlines might harm his confidence. So Venables kept him in. The moment he scored he was due to be out – but Shearer went 21 months, a 12-game run, without finding the net prior to Euro 96. I think it shows Alan's fantastic strength of character that he never lost faith – and that Venables didn't lose faith in him – and it paid off because he began scoring the moment the serious business started. He ended up top goalscorer of the championship with five – and made UEFA's team of the tournament.

For a striker who was supposedly selfish, there was another great partnership, forged with Teddy Sheringham for England. Teddy was a smart number 10, the perfect foil for a conventional striker like Alan. He could lead the line or drop out of the front two; he wasn't quick but he caused you constant problems. I can remember going to Old Trafford as West Ham manager, and Manchester United smashed us to pieces. Teddy came short, Andy Cole made runs in behind him – our centre-halves didn't know what to do. You had to really think about the way you controlled Teddy back then, or he would murder you, and I think England's 4–1 win over Holland in the Euro 96 tournament is the best I have seen our team play in the modern era. I know we won 5–1 in Munich under Sven-Göran Eriksson, which is an incredible result, but the Germans were having a sticky patch at the time. Getting a point in Italy to qualify for the 1998 World Cup under Glenn Hoddle was also impressive because nobody really fancied us in the Olympic Stadium in Rome. Yet, as positive as the result was, the game was still drawn. Fabio Capello's wins over Croatia were also impressive – but the Croatians aren't really a force in world football. To beat Holland 4–1, and to play them off the park as we did that year, is the stand-out result in this time for me. Venables should have been England's manager for years after that. He was doing a great job, and you've got to wonder how the Football Association managed to blow that one

– it says everything about the running of English football, really. That was a genuinely good, balanced team – and to see them slaughtering Holland shows what can be achieved with proper coaching and direction. We knew what we were about at that tournament – we had a way of playing that brought the best out of our players. It certainly got the best out of Shearer – he was outstanding that summer.

He had to be, really, because if he had flopped a lot of questions would have been asked about Fowler being overlooked. In any other era Fowler would have won a lot more caps for England, but he was unfortunate to come along at the same time as Shearer, the way that Ray Clemence was unlucky to be fighting against Gordon Banks and then Peter Shilton.

It was after the tournament that Alan signed for Newcastle, and it is a pity he couldn't replicate the revolution at Blackburn in his hometown. It was written in Alan's contract that he had to wear number nine, and I think that shows there was a romantic element to the move. He wanted to follow in the tradition of Newcastle's greats – Hughie Gallacher, Jackie Milburn and Malcolm Macdonald. Some people think it flopped, because he didn't win a trophy, but I can't agree. In his first season with Newcastle he was top goalscorer in the Premier League for the third year in succession, and players are still chasing his record of 260 goals in the Premier League. That's good enough for me.

PREMIER LEAGUE I: THE TEAM

PETER SCHMEICHEL

Manchester United

GARY NEVILLE

Manchester United

TONY ADAMS

Arsenal

SOL CAMPBELL

Arsenal

STUART PEARCE

Nottingham Forest

MATT LE TISSIER

Southampton

ROY KEANE

Manchester United

PATRICK VIEIRA

Arsenal

RYAN GIGGS

Manchester United

DENNIS BERGKAMP

Arsenal

ALAN SHEARER

Blackburn Rovers

CHAPTER SIX

. . . .

PREMIER LEAGUE II

I sometimes get asked whether, if I'd had my career in modern times as a Premier League footballer, I would still have gone into management, as I did at Bournemouth in 1983. The answer has to be no. I didn't have a bad career. I played seven seasons in the first team at West Ham United, made close to 200 appearances, played for an ambitious lower league club, and played in the United States earning reasonable money. These days that would have been enough. A lot of modern players talk about wanting to get into coaching, but when the reality presents itself, it's not the job they thought it would be. Take Frank Lampard. Now he's finished at Chelsea, would he really want to take a job at, say, Gillingham, the way I worked at Bournemouth? He might have earned three times as much in one week as the Gillingham manager would in one year. The financial imperative that players of my generation faced simply will not be a part of Frank's life.

Let's face it, if you've been earning £200,000 a week, are you going to take a job for £80,000 a year that involves going out every night watching inferior games and inferior players on the off chance of finding a gem? The chairman is driving you mad because he wants success just the same, whether it is League Two or not, and you're commuting to a rotten training ground in the middle of winter, with players who aren't in the same class as the lads you've played with all your career. Mark Lawrenson left Oxford United because he got tired of giving ordinary footballers the same training ground lesson day after day – in Mark's Liverpool team nobody needed telling twice – and believe me the standard hasn't got better. If you have been brought up around world-class players it is going to be very difficult, and I greatly admire anyone from the modern generation who fancies putting themselves through that.

It's different if a top player is going to walk in and manage Chelsea. But in years gone by that didn't happen. Kenny Dalglish's appointment as Liverpool manager came as a huge surprise. Everyone else took the same, less glamorous route – with your coaching apprenticeship starting low down the leagues as soon as you had finished playing. We all did it. Even Bobby Moore, England's World Cup-winning captain. He ended up at Southend United, while Sir Bobby Charlton got a job at Preston North End. It made no difference then that you were a great player. Kenny's path was the exception. As for the rest of us, was it for the best? I think so. Kenny was a natural and had an outstanding backroom staff at Liverpool who filled in the gaps in his education. Mere mortals have a lot to learn: the basics of working with players, finding a way to win and how to rough it away from the five-star lifestyle. For the great players now, the top players, it is going to be hard for them to just walk in and do a job, without serving that lower league apprenticeship. They are missing so much by not learning the ropes the old way because there is still so much to understand. Also, if you are successful, that grounding will make you appreciate those moments more. I can't see too many of today's successful professionals wanting to do it, if they don't need to.

I look at the make-up of the television panels these days, and there are some of our brightest minds and best players sitting in the studio, guys that could really have made a difference. But they don't need the money, so do they want the hassle? I even ask myself that question from time to time. In the end, I think all of our young British coaches will end up being ex-players from the lower divisions. If you look at League One and League Two now – even the Championship to some extent – the overwhelming majority of managers are former players who did not have particularly successful careers. There is the odd exception – Nigel Clough at Sheffield United, James Beattie at Accrington Stanley – but I don't see guys like Sol Campbell rushing to take a post in the lower divisions.

It's hard work down there. To do the job at Southend properly you've got to be out every night of the week, looking for talent, as I was at Bournemouth. You've got to become a regular at non-league grounds and get used to not seeing your family in midweek. You've got to like travel – but not of the exotic kind. As a lower league manager you spend a lot of time on motorways at midnight in the rain – you embark on a lot of fruitless missions, devote time you will never get back to watching a player on the merest whisper of recommendation. The modern millionaires won't do that. I had no retirement money when I came out of the game – I had no idea what to do with my life. The only option for me was to have a go at being a coach. If you've spent your career at Tranmere Rovers, that won't have changed. Different if you had 10 seasons at Chelsea in the Roman Abramovich years. Those lads won't get out of bed for what the manager of Exeter City gets paid.

Take Ryan Giggs. It was never even considered that he might follow the Bobby Charlton route and end up at Preston. If he was entering coaching it was going to be at Manchester United, or nothing. If Stockport County had phoned him up I think it would have been the shortest conversation of all time. Steve Bruce has been around some smaller clubs, and was he even considered for the Manchester United job? No, because a few times in his career, it hasn't worked out. Yet that would be true of Louis van Gaal, too, if he had spent his managerial life at the likes of Sheffield United, Huddersfield Town – or even Hull City. Van Gaal couldn't have done a better job with Hull than Bruce did last year. Yet has that made a ripple at Old Trafford?

So Giggs has not taken that risk – why would he test himself against a guy like Steve Evans at Rotherham United? Evans will never get a Premier League job, but his record as a lower division manager is outstanding. He gets in a lot of trouble over his comments to referees and officials, but he has won promotion with Crawley Town and Rotherham in two of the last three seasons. Would Giggs know what he was doing in a lower division, up against him? Evans knows where to look for the players, he's obviously out grafting all the time, and he knows how to put a League Two or League One team together. Giggs wouldn't have a clue by comparison. These guys are specialists in their own way, just like the lads Bobby Moore and I came up against during our brief time at non-league Oxford City. They would be part-time coaches working in the meat market by day, but they were familiar with every player in that league. What was the captain of England going to know about the Isthmian League? Brian Clough wasn't a non-league expert either, but he knew that I was during my time at Bournemouth – so when he read that I was about to sign a player from Runcorn called Ian Woan, he did a bit of research and hijacked the deal. Would Giggs, or any Premier League player, know who is the sharpest boss for that market now, who has a good track record of taking lads from outside the league? Would he know who to follow, which of the guys have a clue? Would he even know what gets a team out of League Two?

I've been around plenty of Premier League dressing-rooms and I don't hear too many players talk about watching matches lower down. I don't see John Terry going over to take in a game at Leyton Orient. The modern players are as likely to want to be media men or agents as run a team. I don't blame them. A player like Jamie Carragher, who was used to being involved in the big European nights with Liverpool, will still yearn for that taste of the Nou Camp or the San Siro. He can't get out on the pitch any more, but at least he can be around the big game, in the stadium, soaking up the atmosphere, seeing other ex-players, adversaries and friends that are in the same position now. If he's the manager of Leyton Orient he'll be playing the same night as the Champions League, and on a coach back from Milton Keynes someone will tell him Liverpool have just beaten Barcelona 2–1. He's out of it – and dealing with players who aren't a patch on the ones he used to play alongside. I still watch lower league football, but my wife Sandra is in better condition than some of the players I see there now. They're a different shape to the guys in the Champions League. Cristiano Ronaldo takes his shirt off and he looks like Mr Universe. He lives differently. If you are used to those professional standards it would be too frustrating to start in League Two and work your way through.

But how many of this generation of English footballers will be able to find a job higher up? That is the big question now. Foreign players, foreign coaches, foreign owners. It is not just the continental influence on the pitch that has come to define the second decade of the Premier League, but the influence of foreign chairmen. There is barely an elite club that is in the hands of a local businessman or diehard wealthy fan these days – Bill Kenwright is the exception at Everton, but even he would sell if he received the right offer, I'm sure – and this has changed the culture of the English game forever. Despite all our best efforts to encourage homegrown talent I can only see the opportunities for English coaches and players getting fewer – there seems to be a lack of trust in our own football people, which started at the top when the Football Association appointed Sven-Göran Eriksson as England manager, and later Fabio Capello.

At club level the foreign owners come in and, obviously, they only know big names. So it's big names they want – they are not interested in delving into the Championship to give somebody a chance. There are only two ways an upcoming young English manager gets a job in the Premier League these days: he gets promoted, like Sean Dyche at Burnley or Nigel Pearson at Leicester City, or he takes over a club that looks doomed, as Tony Pulis did at Crystal Palace, and somehow stays up. And it is not just the top clubs that have foreign owners. Even Bournemouth and Derby County are owned abroad these days.

So the whole dynamic around English football has altered. I know that during one of their rows, Roy Keane accused Sir Alex Ferguson of having changed. And I know Alex's response. 'Of course I've changed,' he told him. 'How could I have survived this long if I hadn't changed?' He's right, of course. We've all had to change to deal with the demands of modern football. It's not just that players have agents – it's that those agents sometimes have a better line of communication to the chairman than the manager. And it's not just that the players know who the chairman is – it is that they are on first-name terms and think nothing of putting in a call if they are unhappy with anything from team selection to training.

I've got a great relationship with Queens Park Rangers's owner Tony Fernandes – and I'm too old to be a creep, so believe me, I mean it – but not every manager is as lucky. The chairman talks to current players, he talks to ex-players, he talks to agents, to a ring of yes-men – and then he comes away thinking he knows more than the manager. Sometimes a foreign coach gets the benefit of the doubt, but British managers are increasingly coming under particularly harsh scrutiny. Did Steve Clarke really deserve the sack at West Bromwich Albion? Was Pepe Mel truly the better man?

Then there's Chelsea. Unless Lampard or Terry gets the job, do you really see Roman Abramovich appointing an Englishman or even a British manager? He's had enough chances in 11 years now and hasn't done so yet. Brendan Rodgers? Maybe – but would he leave Liverpool for Stamford Bridge? Either way, it's hardly a big list – just one name. I don't see anybody on the horizon, either, and that is worrying. Even if you look at the England team, who is the next manager after Roy Hodgson? Who jumps out at you? Gary Neville? He's never even managed a club. He's not done his apprenticeship, even on the coaching staff at Manchester United. Gareth Southgate is in charge at under-21 level, but I think he should go off and do well in club football before he gets that chance.

When you manage it's a different ball game. It's fine being a coach, you can be friends with everybody. Take a bit of training in the morning, have a laugh with the boys; you're not picking the team, everything's lovely. Then try it the other way – leaving them out, letting them go, even playing them in a position they don't like. Suddenly, they hate you, their wives hate you, their mates hate you. And the England job is the most demanding of all. The pressure of the country is on you, the press are on you. Fail and there's no escape.

I think it was a blow for British managers that David Moyes did not do better at Manchester United, although I always thought whoever got that job would find it hard succeeding Sir Alex Ferguson. I didn't think it would go as badly as it did, mind you, but it was still a setback for the managers here. It will be different for van Gaal. They can see the team needs rebuilding now, and are doing so with some urgency.

I was desperate to see Liverpool win the league last season, just for the fillip it would give the domestic game, with so many English players and a British coach – but increasingly the team with the biggest wage bill wins the league. That's the modern game, sadly. It used to be about having the best players, or the best manager – now it's often down to the best or richest owner. You can buy a successful team. Take over Leicester tomorrow and, if the owners have the money and want to spend it on world-class players, you are going to be up there challenging. Roberto Mancini, Manuel Pellegrini, Yaya Touré, Sergio Agüero – they've all played a part. But the bottom line is that Manchester City have come from where they were because of Sheikh Mansour.

Keep throwing the money at it and, eventually, you'll be all right. Yet will this new breed of owner give English coaches a chance? No, I don't think they will. Here's my final team of the decade.

PETR CECH
(CHELSEA)

Not long ago I had a call from my old friend Harry Gregg, the great Manchester United goalkeeper of the Busby Babes era and beyond. I always look forward to speaking to Harry; he talks so much sense about the game. We were just chatting away and the subject of goalkeepers came up. 'Harry,' he said, 'where have they all gone? Where have the British keepers gone? What's happened?' And he's right – there is such a shortage at the top level these days, particularly in England. Joe Hart has come through, but compared to the days when we had Peter Shilton and Ray Clemence fighting it out with Joe Corrigan and Phil Parkes, what has gone wrong? I like Hart, but I think he would have a serious challenge on his hands if any of those lads were about today. Yet, beneath him, there is nothing. My goalkeeper at Queens Park Rangers, Rob Green, was as good as any of the lads that went to the World Cup to understudy Hart, and I think it is a real pity that England managers seem to ignore the Championship division completely these days. It means that any player with international ambitions has to leave if his club is relegated from the Premier League. That is another of the big changes in the game. If you look at the players in the early chapters of the book, even some of the greatest among them spent time outside the top division. Nowadays that would be career suicide. You play in the top league, and for a top club, or you are nowhere. Even a career outside the Champions League is not enough for a lot of them.

Harry Gregg was right, though. There is a shortage of great goalkeepers across the board. I don't want to damn Petr Cech with faint praise here, because he has had a marvellous career with Chelsea and has definitely been the pick of the bunch in the modern Premier League era, but I can't help viewing him as the best of a pretty ordinary lot. Is he better than Gordon Banks? No. Pat Jennings? No. Peter Shilton? No. Peter Schmeichel? No. Is he better than some of the second best goalkeepers from previous decades like Ray Clemence or David Seaman? No. If I'm honest I haven't always been Cech's biggest fan. I can think of great saves he has made – and he is a strong, imposing presence in the penalty area – but there have also been times when I've been disappointed in him and I can see why Chelsea have been so anxious to develop the young Belgian goalkeeper Thibaut Courtois.

Maybe in a few years' time we will look back on Hart's career and place him on a par with some of England's greats from previous campaigns, but he is not there now. I thought Manuel Pellegrini handled him very well when he left him out of Manchester City's team for a while last season. A degree of over-confidence had crept into his game, and that short spell on the bench seemed to bring him down to earth.

I just don't think you see as many great goalkeepers as you used to. Some of the best ones from previous years were behind ordinary defences, too, whereas Cech has benefited from having some outstanding protection at Chelsea. I think he did well to recover from the serious head injury he sustained against

Reading in 2006 – he was brave in the way he came rushing out that day, and I haven't noticed any change in him after he recovered. Then again, Harry Gregg was pulling people out of a plane that was about to blow up in Munich, so I suppose with goalkeepers a casual disregard for danger goes with the territory.

It is amazing that goalkeeper has become a problem position, really, because there has never been more coaching and instruction available for them than there is now. Every team has at least one specialist goalkeeper coach, and usually more, yet when you think back to the heyday of Banks and Shilton there was no such thing. Goalkeepers arrived in the morning and went off and practised kicking balls at one another down the field. Then the manager would call them over to go in goal while the rest of us worked on our shooting – and that was it. They didn't get separate coaching. They didn't go off with a specialist for detailed work. Goalkeeping coaches are a new thing. Banks would have done no more than face daily shooting drills – yet Hart will get all the training in the world. So where have the English goalkeepers gone? I don't understand it.

I suppose the influence of foreign goalkeepers will have played a part. A young English midfield player isn't as vulnerable to being shut out of the team because he has a variety of options. There might be a foreign player blocking his way on the right, but he could be used on the left or in central midfield. The same for all outfielders, really. But if Arsenal have a foreign goalkeeper, there is no way through. It is a unique position and if that place is filled there is just nowhere to go. I think it will become an increasing problem for the England manager in the future. An injury to Hart, and then what? There isn't much out there.

PABLO ZABALETA
(MANCHESTER CITY)

Zabaleta came in from Espanyol in 2008 and when I first saw him I wasn't sure. He looked full of energy but I was dubious about his discipline. He seemed like one of those players who is all over the place and very committed, but lacks direction and focus. I've changed my mind since, obviously. He's a real leader, another of the type you can mark down for 7 out of 10 as a minimum, even before the game starts. He's up and down, he's committed, and you never really see him get slaughtered by any winger. I know Micah Richards has had a lot of injuries recently, but when he first came into the game he was tipped for big things – he was in Steve McClaren's England team after just 28 appearances, for instance, and was the youngest defender to play for England, beating Rio Ferdinand's record – so to keep him out of the Manchester City team, as Zabaleta has done, is a big achievement. There is no longer even a debate about the best right-back at the club, and that is testament to Zabaleta's consistency and determination.

Speaking as a manager, he just looks the proper sort. He's tenacious and he knows his job. I think right-back has been a difficult position for England since Gary Neville came to the end of his career and, much as I like Glen Johnson, I think Zabaleta would get into our team right now. Glen is outstanding going forward, but so is Zabaleta. His crossing, in particular, is very accurate and I think he has more to his defensive game than Glen. He reminds me a little of Stuart Pearce, one of those guys that runs backwards almost as quickly as he runs forward. He is capable of getting into great attacking positions, but always seems to be able to recover with enough time not to get caught out. He's quite an English style of right-back really – he's tough and aggressive, not a nutter, but he can put it about. All of our best full-backs would fit that description.

I know he has captained Manchester City on occasions, and I think the fall-out they had with Carlos Tevez would have been a big proving ground for him. The players of one nationality tend to stick together at clubs and, if you lose one, the chances are his mates will follow. I imagine City might have expected the issues with Tevez and Roberto Mancini to spread to the other Argentinians within the club, but Zabaleta didn't get dragged into it, and as a result it didn't then influence Sergio Agüero. That was the leader in him coming through; he kept his head down and carried on doing his job. I bet there was a fair amount of pressure to take sides with Tevez but it shows you how professional he is that he didn't let the club down. He's 29 now, and I think it was a good move when City went for Bacary Sagna in the summer to take some of the strain off him. Even so, he looks as if he has got a few years left in him yet. He is the type of player that survives managerial upheaval, too – because we all want a Pablo Zabaleta in our team.

JOHN TERRY
(CHELSEA)

The modern Tony Adams – I can't pay him a higher compliment than that. John Terry embodies the same qualities I saw in Tony Adams all those years ago. He has the same organisational skills, he's a leader on the pitch and a player who would run through a brick wall. Simply a fantastic centre-half. After Queens Park

Rangers were promoted last season, I remember saying that if we could take Terry from Chelsea I would feel very confident, just with that one signing alone, that we would stay up. He is that influential. He's one of those players that change a club. He gets people at it, he's a talker, he takes charge of the dressing-room. I know that off the pitch he has had his problems, like Tony – but I think managers are prepared to overlook that because he is a real voice within the team. I could imagine him in a Rangers shirt heading balls out of our box and making everybody else defend properly. No one would shirk with John around.

You don't get talkers these days, you don't get organisers. I don't know why, but it is so hard to find a player that is prepared to speak his mind, that uses his mouth the way great leaders from past generations did. I'm thinking of some of the characters I've written about in this book – Bobby Collins, Danny Blanchflower, Dave Mackay and Bobby Murdoch. Those players, those days, are gone. You won't find them like that any more; they're not coming through in the same way. Maybe it is the coaching. A friend of mine who rides horses in event meetings said that accidents are on the increase because the animals are now so highly trained they respond completely to rider instruction and no longer trust their own instincts. In times past, if a horse was approaching a fence at the wrong angle because the rider had made a misjudgement, it would simply stop and refuse. It knew it couldn't make the jump, so it didn't jump. Now, the horses have been so highly trained they override their natural common sense, jump, fall and everyone gets hurt. Maybe it is the same with footballers. They get told what to do, so they don't think for themselves – and now they don't know how to tell others, either. Everyone is waiting to receive information; they all exist in their own little worlds. They don't talk to each other off the pitch or on the coach. Everyone's sits there with headphones, looking at an iPad or playing a computer game. Is it any wonder modern players lack communication skills?

So Terry is a throw-back in the way he bosses a team. I've got a lot of time for John, even though I know his career has not been without controversy. I just think we only hear one side of a story sometimes. I saw a documentary on television earlier this year in which John spent time with this little kid who was seriously ill, and he looked a genuine guy to me. People will say he was acting up for the cameras, but looking at the way he was affected by this poor boy's problems, I don't agree. He gave up his time, came in before the game, after the game – he really looked like he cared. I already liked him as a player, but when I saw that he went up in my estimation.

To see what an influence he can be you only have to look at what he did for Gary Cahill at Chelsea. His partner became an international defender just by being around John. Nothing else changed in Gary's approach other than he was suddenly alongside Terry. He taught him the game. Some people may think John is a dubious role model, but I would have no hesitation in saying to any of the young academy defenders at QPR: go and watch Chelsea tonight, go and watch Terry, study him all game. If they pay attention they will learn more in that 90 minutes than in a month of training sessions. It's still the best way – watch Terry, see what he does, how he organises people, how he pulls them in, keeps it tight. To play alongside him must have been a fantastic education for Cahill, and I think he's even come out of himself more now; you can see that he talks more. He's a different defender because of Terry.

Maybe he won't ever be as influential as John, but that vocal confidence is either in you or it isn't. I could never coach a player to be a talker. If someone isn't happy communicating, no amount of encouragement from me will change that. John is a natural, like Tony Adams. Standing with Frank Lampard senior watching the teenage Tony Adams run a youth team game like no kid we had ever seen is a memory that will stay with me for all time. It was so unusual, almost unreal. I know his dad ran his boys' team in Dagenham, but even so. He might have been able to tell his son how to defend, but he couldn't have taught him to be such a forceful personality. That comes from within.

I also think John is a much better passer than he is given credit for. Adams only proved himself in this area once he was with England and Terry Venables encouraged him to play. George Graham, at Arsenal, was never too keen on the centre-half bringing the ball out from the back, but it was an integral part of Venables's plan at the 1996 European Championship; he encouraged Tony and it worked. I'm sure he found it quite liberating after years of being told to play in a more conservative style. John on the other hand was always good with the ball, and showed it. Jamie Carragher said he thought John was actually a better passer than Rio Ferdinand.

Rio was great with the ball at his feet, running with it, working it out of defence, while John was a fantastic long passer. He's a very clean striker of the ball.

It is so important to have good distribution from the back. Not long ago my son Jamie was with Roberto Martínez, the Everton manager, and he was talking about his time at Wigan Athletic. He told Jamie about Emmerson Boyce, who Martínez inherited when he went there in 2009. We played Wigan in the play-off final and Boyce is a good passer now, but Martínez said when he first met him, he just didn't want the ball. He wouldn't accept it or show for it because successive managers hadn't trusted him in possession and had told him just to kick it. They even told his team-mates not to pass to him. Roberto said he spent hours with him every day, working on getting the ball, passing the ball, becoming comfortable on the ball. He'll never be Franz Beckenbauer, or even John Terry, but it just shows how you can improve people, given time. It happens too often in the English game that the centre-half is just there to boot the ball up the pitch. It makes me even more of a John Terry fan. If Chelsea ever lose faith in John, I'd take him like a shot.

RIO FERDINAND
(MANCHESTER UNITED)

A tough one this, choosing between two great centre-halves at Manchester United. I loved Nemanja Vidić – he was just such a great competitor. I don't think it was United's decision to let him go to Inter Milan at the end of last season and, although he was approaching the end of his career, I still think he will be a big loss. He was the backbone of the team, and I knew he would be a player the first time I set eyes on him alongside Dejan Stefanović. I went to watch Serbia play to have a look at Stefanović when I was Portsmouth manager – Vidić caught my eye that night, too, but he was very young and we were looking for someone with more experience, and cheaper. He went to Spartak Moscow soon after that and then on to Manchester United, and he was everything you wanted in a centre-half – strong, good in the air and a real tough character.

Yet there is no way I can leave Rio Ferdinand out of this team because I tipped him at 16 to be the greatest centre-half in Europe and I think, for a time, that is exactly what he was. Vidi´c was a tank, but Rio was a Rolls-Royce. You could see it from day one. He had pace, absolutely electric pace, and was so comfortable on the ball. He could have played in midfield, without a doubt. In fact, I used him there against Wimbledon one night when he was about 18 and he ran Vinnie Jones ragged. He was drifting by him, drifting by all of them actually, running half the length of the pitch with the ball, laying it off. He had that natural, long-legged running stride, and once he hit it he was gone.

I think it is one of the consistent failures in our game that we haven't realised the potential in some of the players we have at centre-half. We tend to go for the hero types, the ones who head it clear and hoof it out, who just defend and nothing more. Yet the game has changed now. Everything starts from the back. The full-backs push on and centre-halves split and those players must be able to play because you can't get going if your centre-halves can't pass. If you see a goalkeeper booting it downfield all game these days it means only one thing: the centre-halves can't play. All of Rio's teams could build from the back because he was such a smooth footballer. He used to roll it into Paul Scholes in midfield and away Manchester United would go. Rio was fantastic, and United's best times of late always seemed to coincide with his good spells. I never doubted for one second that he would go on to become a top player and achieve so much in the game. From the day he walked into West Ham we knew he was special. Nothing he has done since has surprised me.

Now it's come full circle and I'm lucky enough to have Rio at QPR showing he's a class act, with that touch and that leading of the game, still there after all these years.

ASHLEY COLE
(CHELSEA)

I think there have been a few times when English football could claim to have the best left-back in the world – and Ashley Cole is the most recent player to hold that unofficial title. Fantastic energy, fantastic ability, just up and down, run after run after run after run. Even the greatest in the game, like Cristiano Ronaldo, couldn't get the better of him. I was amazed when Chelsea let him go last summer. What a free transfer he was: Manchester United, Real Madrid, Barcelona, they should all have been in for him. As far as his non-selection for England at the World Cup in Brazil goes, that was less of a surprise. I thought Leighton Baines had come to the fore, certainly in Roy Hodgson's mind, and he also had the opportunity to take Luke Shaw, who is young but is going to be a top player. I could see his reasoning on that, more than I could understand Chelsea's decision.

Ashley is a Stepney boy, like me, but he didn't play for the famous local club, Senrab, like John Terry and Ledley King. He was with Puma, their big rivals, who also played on Wanstead Flats. He was a striker and came to Arsenal's attention because he scored 100 goals in one season. When I saw him he was in the Arsenal youth team playing wide left midfield in a cup final against West Ham; our lads won but he certainly looked a player. He had the low centre of gravity that a lot of naturally quick players have and he worked really hard. I know he has had a playboy image at times in his career, but you don't have Ashley's stamina and physique without really putting it in on the training pitch. Whatever distractions he might have had, it never really affected his performance. He was always consistent, always a match for the best players. His attacking energy was perhaps the best of any player I have seen. I would imagine his weekly Prozone statistics would have been incredible in terms of the ground he covered. All of the greatest full-backs are players who want to run, but I think Ashley took it to a new level. He was relentless. Towards the end of the game you are still looking at your full-backs to make those runs, particularly if you are chasing the game, but by then even the best ones are sometimes too knackered. They don't want to attack because that means chasing back twice as hard if the move breaks down. Yet Ashley would go, time and again. He was a machine. After Chelsea's first game with Atlético Madrid in the Champions League last season, the statistics showed that Chelsea's two most forward players over the 90 minutes were the full-backs, Cole and César Azpilicueta, who played on the right. Azpilicueta is 24; Cole is 33. I think it shows he still has his appetite for the game – and his fitness.

I've always said football has two disciplinary codes – one for players who can play, and another for the rest. Ashley is proof of that. The episode with the air rifle at Chelsea in 2011 – when he brought the gun to the training ground and accidentally shot a 21-year-old student, there for work experience – is evidence of that. I imagine a lot of people would have been sacked by their employers for that – and a lot of footballers, too. Yet Chelsea let it ride, with an apology and a disciplinary hearing. If that was a player they wanted out he would have been gone the next morning. But Ashley survived. That's when you know they rate you.

Is Cole the best left-back England have had? I'd say yes, though it's difficult. Kenny Sansom and Stuart Pearce would both have claims, and for a while I thought Stuart was right up there, even with Paolo Maldini. Yet Cole at his peak was close to faultless – he was cleverer than Stuart on the ball, as powerful and strong as Sansom, and he had the attacking instincts of a left-winger. He was the top man, for me.

CRISTIANO RONALDO
(MANCHESTER UNITED)

Sandra and I were at the Hotel Pitrizza in Sardinia last year and Cristiano Ronaldo was there with his family. I made sure not to sit too near to him on the beach, obviously, but what a lovely man. He must have had 20 of them out there with him, including his girlfriend, who looked like Miss World, and his little mum, a widow, who was always in black from head to toe. They looked typical working-class Portuguese, but every day they made their way back from the most exclusive shops in the town of Porto Cervo absolutely laden with gear. They had so many bags hanging off them they could hardly walk – Gucci, Prada, the best designer labels in the world – and he was paying for it all, obviously. They stayed two weeks in one of Europe's finest hotels and he looked after everything. A lot of footballers treat their families like that. It's a side that people don't see, and he just looked really happy to be back with them all again. He had quite a few little cousins or nephews out there and you could spot them a mile off because they were tiny Cristiano clones. Same hair, same cheeky grin – it was really nice to see. Each day he would stop and have a chat with us. He seemed really down to earth, for all his wealth, success and fame.

In the Messi versus Ronaldo debate I've always just about been in Lionel Messi's camp – until the last year. Not because I met Ronaldo and he was a genuine bloke, but because he has stepped up to a new level in that time, and I very much supported the vote that won him the prize as the World Footballer of the Year. I like the way Messi and Ronaldo are constantly inspiring each other, driving one another on.

Jamie Carragher wrote an article in which he made a great point, saying it helps that they genuinely don't seem to like one another. That adds to the rivalry, in the way it did for Alain Prost and Ayrton Senna, or even Don Revie and Brian Clough. If Messi and Ronaldo were great mates it wouldn't have that edge – and what makes their duel so compelling is that they seem genuinely concerned about out-doing one another. If Messi scores two goals on Saturday, Ronaldo wants to get three on Sunday – and don't tell me Ronaldo wasn't inspired by the desire to break Messi's record when he went in search of the greatest number of Champions League goals scored in one season. He did it, too. I just hope that at the end of their careers they realise that they were both fantastic for each other and make up.

An extraordinary thing about Ronaldo is that he has almost invented a new way of kicking a football. I know there are innovations in sport all the time, but to find a fresh way of doing something so utterly basic is, to me, quite astonishing. The way he makes the ball dip and then rise when he hits a free-kick has got players trying to imitate it in training like the old Rivelino stepover. After Ronaldo did it, Gareth Bale worked and worked until he could do it, too – but Ronaldo was the first. I suppose it was like watching Jonny Wilkinson take those penalty kicks and conversions in rugby union for the first time. One minute, he had a unique style and then suddenly everyone was trying to copy him.

Messi's trademark is that lovely little dink over the goalkeeper – the way, when he is through one on one, he just lifts it up and over as the goalkeeper goes to ground. He reminds me of the best kid in the school playground. The other boys are trying to kick lumps out of him, but they can't get near him because he's 10 times better. I saw a game when I thought Atlético Madrid were going to kill him, but he kept skipping around them, time and again. I also love the way he is prepared to stop in the middle of a game, and think about what he is going to do next. Then it is always an intelligent move, a dart into a gap, an angle that nobody has considered. He makes space just by standing still. He's not running in there where all the bodies are, he comes out of the crowd and works out a better route. Very few are brave enough to do that, and fewer still have the intelligence to make it work. They think if they stop they will just lose momentum – yet Messi never does. We are privileged to see this duel, really, because I cannot recall a time in the game when two players of such wonderful ability went head to head like this. Pelé and Diego Maradona were not contemporaries, and the peak years of Johann Cruyff bridged the gap between the two of them. Yet when you think Ronaldo scored 17 goals in the 2012–13 Champions League campaign to break Messi's joint record of 14 set in 2011–12, it shows you what a magnificent contest this is.

Ronaldo is an amazing footballer. He can do the lot – his dribbling is sensational, his shots are unstoppable and he heads the ball with the bravery and power of an old-fashioned centre-half up for a corner. He scores a quite ridiculous amount of goals, particularly when one considers that those 17 in the Champions League haven't been scored in routs against the champions of Luxembourg, as they were in the old days. He has an incredible physique for such a nimble player. He's 6 ft 1 in and, as I've said, when he takes his shirt off he looks like Mr Universe.

He has scored so many great goals but one of his headers stands out, the first goal in a Champions League tie for Manchester United against Roma. The cross comes in from Paul Scholes and Ronaldo isn't even in the picture when the ball leaves Scholes's boot – he arrives at full speed, off a quite astonishing spring and the ball goes in like a rocket from a good 14 yards out. In mid-air Ronaldo gets clipped by a defender and goes down heavily, but his injury could have been far worse. If one of the Roma players had also gone in with his head he could have got his teeth knocked out or his face smashed in, but he had no thought for that – only for the goal. He has got a lot more substance to his game than people think.

When Ronaldo first came to England, some people were saying he was a show pony, all tricks and flicks, and he would never make it in our game. I thought they were mad. He wasn't dancing around the ball. He was using incredible skill to move past people in a way we didn't often see in England. You knew that sooner or later those shots were going to start crashing in the top corner and he was going to be unstoppable. And that is exactly what happened. I think Manchester United's 3–0 win over Millwall in the 2004 FA Cup final changed a lot of perceptions of him because he was absolutely mesmerising that day – but I always thought he was the real deal.

STEVEN GERRARD
(LIVERPOOL)

Roy of the Rovers. It's surprising to me how often people have used this tag as a criticism of Steven Gerrard and his all-action playing style. He wants to be everywhere ... he deserts his position ... he can't play in the middle because he'll leave a gap. What nonsense. Roy Race was a comic book hero and Steven Gerrard is a real-life one. He's been the driving force behind Liverpool for more than a decade now and I think all true football fans were disappointed when last season he could not realise his dream of leading them to a first title of the Premier League era.

I saw him when he first broke into the Liverpool team in 1998 and I had no doubt then that we were seeing the beginning of a truly great player. Why? Well, he played like Roy of the Rovers! It was as if he was taking the game on, one against 11. He covered every blade of grass, he drove the team on despite being the youngest there, he made great passes, he wasn't scared to shoot – he looked a real player. You could see he was going to end up their captain. When I was Portsmouth manager we tried to man mark him with a player called Richard Hughes. Richard was a big, strong lad – a very dogged type who had done that kind of job for us before. He couldn't get near him. Gerrard just ran all over him, and us, and by the time he was taken off with 16 minutes to go they were winning 3–0. It was the full repertoire – box to box, shooting from 30 yards, he did everything bar score. Now he has changed his role and is playing as more of a holding midfielder, but at his peak he could play anywhere. I've seen him play right-back in an emergency, and I know England managers who have considered using him as a right wing-back because he is so versatile.

To be fair, my son Jamie was even quicker on to Steven's quality than I was. I can remember him calling me after Liverpool training one day to say that they brought a 16-year-old over to play with the first team and he was absolutely outstanding. When Jamie struggled with injury in the 1998–9 season it was Steven who took his place in the team. He just got on with it, as he always does. I know Steven says that, looking back, he was very nervous in his earliest games but he has always been hyper-critical of his own game. If he was below par in those days it was only by his own, impossibly high, standards. I've always found Steven very honest and knowledgeable about football. I think it is one of the positives about the top players of his generation that they are all good lads, and proper football people. If I wanted an opinion about a player at Liverpool I knew I could pick up the phone to Steven or Jamie Carragher, ask a straight question and get a straight answer. They wouldn't put you wrong. Even a player they liked as a lad, if they thought he was struggling with injury or his heart wasn't in it any more, they would tell the truth.

So, Roy of the Rovers? Even if he was, what is wrong with that? He is a more disciplined presence now because he has no choice, but in the days when he could be in his own box one moment and over by the opposition corner flag the next, why not? I've heard that managers like Rafael Benítez thought he lacked discipline, but Benítez also won two major trophies at Liverpool – the 2005 Champions League and the 2006 FA Cup – that he wouldn't have got anywhere near without Steven, so I'm pretty sure he did more good than harm. I think that if he was one of the two in midfield, it was up to the coach to make sure a dedicated holding midfielder covered for him. I would never have tried to take that energy away from Gerrard because the goals he scored and the games he dominated poured that same energy back into the team.

So no place in my team for Frank Lampard. I know – I'm not going to win any uncle of the year awards, am I? I picked Frank at West Ham and was accused of nepotism every week, so at least here I've avoided that charge, but the fact is my faith in Frank has been borne out 100 per cent. Frank has had the fantastic career I predicted many years ago and, even now, I don't think people realise the lengths he went to in order to become a professional footballer. He remains the most dedicated professional I have ever come across, overcoming weaknesses in his game and even a period during his teenage years when he became so obsessed with getting his weight down that his late mum, Pat, feared he had become anorexic. He was like a bag of bones and we had to get help for him. Luckily he pulled through and became one of the greatest players in this modern Premier League era. I think Frank has the edge on Steven for his goals, but Steve is a better all-round player – by a whisker. A better passer, perhaps; defensively so strong and aggressive. I wish I had room for them both – but there is no way I am leaving this next lad out.

PAUL SCHOLES
(MANCHESTER UNITED)

You'd try to tie Paul Scholes down when you played against Manchester United but it was impossible. You just couldn't balance your team up to get anywhere near him. I tried having someone sit on him, but he always found a way to get space. As for his passing, he had eyes in the back of his head, and his instinct for goal was exceptional. One of the highlights for me was the two he scored for England in Scotland in the 1999 European Championship play-off – goals that show his stunning reading of the game and his ability to define matches, even with his head. The first goal is a cross from Sol Campbell that Scholes meets on the run, jumping up and taking it on his chest to go past Colin Hendry and tuck it past Neil Sullivan. The next is a header from a David Beckham free-kick, ghosting in between taller men the way Martin Peters once did. He is only about 5 ft 7 in, but he took those goals like a man a head taller.

He saw everything on the football field – where his team-mates were, where you were as you tried to stop him. That's why Manchester United did all their best work through him. He'd come deep, pick it up, run off the back of you, get in the box. He was a master, and yet at the same time a completely unassuming guy. Speak to Brazilians about England's players of the last 20 years, and Scholes is the one they rave about. They saw him as one of their own, and Socrates said he would have got into any Brazilian team. The boy with the red hair and the red shirt, he called him. I saw an interview with Xavi in which he too said Scholes was his favourite player. 'He was my role model,' he said, 'the best central midfielder I've seen in the last fifteen or twenty years. He's spectacular, he has it all: the last pass, the goals, he's strong, he doesn't lose the ball, he has vision. If he'd been Spanish he might have been rated more highly. Players love him, too.' Pep Guardiola said Scholes was the best midfielder of his generation, and Thierry Henry said he was the Premier League's finest player. That's some line-up of fans.

He won plenty with Manchester United, but can you imagine him in Xavi's Barcelona side? Sir Alex Ferguson said he was the one player that he never got an offer for – because it was well known all over Europe that he would not consider leaving Old Trafford. Even so, we can dream. Scholes was playing tiki-taka football when nobody in England knew what it was. He was another of those players, like Denis Law or Bobby Moore, who at the age of 15 probably looked as if he wouldn't make it. Too small, you would think – can't run, dumpy little ginger nut – but then the ball would come to him and he would dazzle you.

Out of all that great Manchester United team I'd put Scholes right at the top. Roy Keane would be the driving force, and Ryan Giggs had the greatest career, but Scholes was the best footballer, for me. He played in the middle, and that's where you've really got to know your stuff to survive in the modern game. When the ball arrived, he knew everything, he already had the information and he never gave it away. If he had 90 touches in a game there would be 89 successful passes – and one diabolical foul, of course. I never bought that one, the idea that Paul Scholes couldn't tackle. Oh, really? So he can play the greatest passes you'll see, score the most beautiful goals, but a skill as basic as tackling eludes him? Do me a favour. He knew exactly what he was doing with every one of those fouls. He knew when to break the game up and when to get an opponent back, too. And he didn't care what people thought, either – which seems to be his attitude when it comes to giving his opinion now he has retired from the game.

I was out with Paddy Power just before the World Cup – yes, he does exist, his father David was one of the co-founders of the business – and he said, 'Harry, you'll never guess who we've signed up as a columnist. It's so left-field. It's a guy that nobody has ever heard speak.' I guessed straight away: Paul Scholes. If no one has heard him talk, people will be interested in what he has to say – that was their logic, and they were proved right. Paul was an excellent World Cup columnist – outspoken, forthright in his opinions about England and invariably right. He called it just as he used to play it – he saw all the angles, eyes in the back of his head.

GARETH BALE
(TOTTENHAM HOTSPUR)

I'm so pleased with the way Gareth's first season in Madrid has gone. I'll admit: I was worried for him. I thought he might shrink into the shadows a bit around a big personality like Cristiano Ronaldo, but those two goals – against Barcelona in the Copa del Rey and Atlético Madrid in the Champions League final – have made him. They've proved what a fantastic talent he is, and now that the Real Madrid public believes in him, he could go on to be an all-time great, even at a club of that size. He's like Ronaldo mark II – he's a supreme physical specimen, he can dribble, he can shoot, he takes great dead balls and, as they now know, he scores headers, too. Fantastic stamina – he can run all day. Tottenham Hotspur thought they had done good business, but losing a talent like that was always going to take a toll.

The moment I saw it I knew the goal against Barcelona would be the making of him. It was just a wonderful moment of athleticism. The Barcelona defender, Marc Bartra, tries to knock him off the pitch but he just runs around him – and from there his pace over 80 yards is electric. His ability to run long distances without slowing reminds me of Ronaldo. Some wingers drop off as they get near the penalty area, but Gareth almost seemed to get stronger. The power is so impressive, but then the finish is so subtle. He may end up the best winger in the world – but Gareth could have stayed at left-back and been the best at that, too. Wherever he had played he was destined for greatness. There is one particular game I remember, against Benfica in a pre-season friendly in 2010, that has to rank among the best individual performances I've seen. He made a goal for Peter Crouch, which was disallowed, and in the end he scored the only goal of the game – but what I most clearly recall is the number of forward runs he made from left-back. The length of the field, it seemed, something like 40 times. It was one of the games that persuaded me to move him to left wing.

Yet Gareth could play anywhere in forward midfield. I switched him to the right and I played him through the middle. The crowd didn't like it. 'Gareth Bale, he plays on the left,' they used to sing because all they wanted him to do was go flying up that wing, whereas I could see the advantages of him on the right coming inside and having a shot, or playing off the striker as he did against Norwich City one night. He ran amok. Plays on the left? He plays where he wants to play – that's how it should be. That's what the great ones do: Messi, Ronaldo, Suárez, Bale – let them have their freedom.

I'm so happy that he looks to be enjoying his football in Spain. Having an English coach at Real, Paul Clements, will definitely have helped, and Carlo Ancelotti has always struck me as a lovely guy. I think Paul said he knew Gareth was good but he didn't realise how good, and I think a lot of people who haven't worked with Gareth won't have appreciated that yet either. They will see him as a flying machine, but he's so much more. He wins game after game for you, and I don't think even Tottenham were fully aware of that when they took Real Madrid's money. Buying half a team for £100 million having sold one player sounds a good deal, but you can't replace him as a match-winner. Looking at Madrid in the Champions League final, there were two ex-Tottenham men, Bale and Luka Modrić, who were worth all of Tottenham's subsequent signings put together. Tottenham have nobody capable of influencing the game like that pair.

The next two years could be very big for Gareth. The increased numbers of qualifiers for the 2016 European Championships in France have given Wales a better chance of getting there, and although they have a tough group with Belgium and Bosnia-Herzegovina in there, with even the third-placed team going into a play-off they will never get a better chance. Wales have got a few decent players at the moment – Aaron Ramsey of Arsenal, Ashley Williams, his former team-mate Neil Taylor at Swansea City, and I know Crystal Palace think very highly of their young midfield player Jonathan Williams, too. It would be another huge achievement if Gareth could inspire those lads to their first major tournament since 1958.

THIERRY HENRY
(ARSENAL)

The first time I saw Thierry Henry he was playing on the left wing for France's under-21 team against Norway. I was on a scouting mission to look at John Carew, who had been recommended to me, and while Henry looked as if he had plenty of skill, it wasn't immediately obvious that he was going to become one of the Premier League's great goalscorers. Norway won and it was Carew who looked the best bet, creating havoc in the French defence. He went on to have a good career with, among others, Valencia and Roma – but he couldn't dream of scoring the exquisite goals that Henry conjured up. It shows how even the greatest players mature with age.

What a signing Henry was for Arsenal. On his day, he was one of the few strikers that were simply unplayable. He could rip you to pieces and there really was nothing you could do. He was that modern phenomenon – the highly skilful player who was also a good size and a physical handful. Didier Drogba is an even greater example of that. He had a delightful touch, but before using it would give you an absolute battering. Henry wasn't quite as combative as Drogba – but he still presented a physical challenge to any opponent. On their best days, the Arsenal of Henry and Dennis Bergkamp asked more questions of you than any other team in recent memory. Bergkamp dropping in, Henry going beyond and making runs – what hope did defenders have, apart from prayer? We had a good back line at Portsmouth in particular but, even so, it was very difficult. What do you do? If you drop off, Henry picks it up deep, turns and runs at you. If you get tight, he'll turn and run in behind you – and he had astonishing pace. He found these pockets of space all over the pitch and the moment your move broke down Arsenal counter-attacked at demon speed.

What makes Henry and Bergkamp's success all the more surprising is that, basically, these two players destroying Premier League defences were both on the rebound from failed careers in Italy. Bergkamp couldn't cut it at Inter Milan and Henry was a flop at Juventus, where he was used mostly wide. They were bold signings by Arsenal, really, because they could easily have come here low on confidence and disappeared again. Bergkamp did have a slow start, initially; but Henry, definitely, fitted in straight away. Wherever he has been since, Arsenal has always felt most like his home to me. The crowd fell in love with him instantly, and as he lifted the club his confidence grew. They just fitted – and he fitted with Bergkamp, too. They were magnificent together. Henry was so smooth, I sometimes used to go to Highbury just to see him – and managers don't tend to get involved like that. If I didn't have scouting on and I was near London, I'd watch him almost like an Arsenal fan again, for the sheer fun of it. If Arsenal were in trouble there was sometimes a moment when you could see him switch on – as if he had decided, 'Right, I've got to do something about this.' And then he'd go out and win the game on his own.

Wayne Rooney? It was a tough call leaving him out – but I think Henry was consistently a better player. There were never any real problems with Thierry, whereas Wayne has been high maintenance at times and that has led to him losing his way and his form occasionally. For me, Henry has the edge.

LUIS SUÁREZ
(LIVERPOOL)

Despite all that has happened in his career since, one of the biggest regrets of my life in management is not taking Luis Suárez to Tottenham Hotspur when we had the chance. We were looking for a striker and he was one of the players recommended to us. I asked around and Ruud Gullit, in particular, fancied him for his life. 'You've got to take him, Harry,' he said. 'He's fantastic.' Yet all of our scouts' reports said that at Ajax he played wide off a striker, whereas we were looking for a proper front man. We had lots of support players – Gareth Bale, Aaron Lennon, Rafael van der Vaart – but no forward target. Every time another report came in saying Suárez didn't play through the middle I became less certain. I think the last man to go and see him was Tim Sherwood. The reports were all positive but Tim, like everyone else, wasn't convinced that he could operate in a defined central role. There were doubts about his character, too, and even in Holland not everybody was convinced he was worth taking a chance on for the money, which was £15 million. And then, just when I was on the verge of taking the plunge, the price went up. Ajax must have had Liverpool in at that point and knew they had a market. In the end he was sold for £22.8 million. We wouldn't have paid that.

It didn't take long for me to realise what I had missed. Can he play through the middle? Absolutely. He can play anywhere he likes – and he never stops. He's a perpetual motion machine in the style of that other Liverpool great, Ian Rush. I put it down to that will to win that the greatest players have. He works and works because he so hates losing. He's a pest, a defender's nightmare. Never gives you a minute's peace. He's got all the ability in the world. When he has the ball he runs at you, and when he gets near to an opponent, the tricks start. He'll nutmeg you, or play it off your legs, or hands. He improvises all the time like the great street footballers, showing the opponent the ball and then nipping it past him. He is another like Paolo Di Canio: when he is in the team you have always got a chance because he can suddenly conjure a goal from thin air.

His work-rate is such an important quality because, when the best player in the team is putting himself about like that, the rest of them cannot stop either. Team-mates take their lead from him and you can't stand and watch while the best player in the team runs around like a lunatic. Last season he inspired Daniel Sturridge doing the same, putting a real shift in, leading by example. Steven Gerrard is similar in that he sets an example to the rest of the team. Suárez and Gerrard were arguably Liverpool's two best players in that season – and the hardest working, too. You can tell there was a bond between the pair, and I'm told Suárez was a very popular guy in the dressing-room. They could see that he always wanted the best for the team and it's not just about him.

He reminded me a little of Wayne Rooney, too. The way he runs, it looks as if he just loves playing football – and Rooney also has that quality. Rooney reminds me of the first kid out into the playground at lunchtime – the one who couldn't wait to get through the classroom door and start playing. Suárez is the same. Brendan Rodgers, the Liverpool manager, says that's the way he trained like that every day, and I'd say until this last outrage he was not far off being considered for World Footballer of the Year. Cristiano Ronaldo was the top man last season, obviously – it was a pity he was injured in the World Cup – but with Suárez in the Champions League this season, it was his crown to win. If he scored at the rate he did in the Premier League, anything was possible. Now he has ruined that chance.

I always had a feeling he could leave Liverpool after the World Cup, but I believed it would be his form in the competition, not another controversy, that would secure his move to Spain. Having appeared to make great personal improvements, the circumstances around his departure came as such a shock. I'm not going to pretend I understand biting an opponent even once – but to have done it on three occasions? That is beyond belief. When Suárez bit Giorgio Chiellini, at first, I wasn't sure what I had seen. England were playing Costa Rica at the same time as Uruguay's game against Italy, but we had already been knocked out after two matches by that time, and our game was dull and meaningless. I kept flicking over to see how we were getting on through a sense of loyalty really, but if I am being honest the match I wanted to see was Uruguay and Italy – because both teams were playing for their lives to get through to the second round.

I saw Suárez put his head towards Chiellini and my instinct was that he had tried to head-butt him. 'Funny sort of head-butt – in the shoulder,' I thought. 'What was the point of that?' As the replays were shown it became clear it was a bite. Another bite! It didn't make sense. Is he mad? How does he think he will get away with this stuff? It isn't like the old days. When I played, someone could throw a right-hander and nobody – apart from the bloke on the receiving end – would know. Even the players were clueless about half the stuff that went on. These days there are television cameras everywhere, at every game. The bigger the match, the more footage there will be. The level that Suárez plays at, he is always going to be found out. He must have a screw loose.

I've been a manager a long time now. We all know players can do irrational things. Tackles that are beyond the pale, handball, spitting, diving, saying despicable things in the heat of a moment. I don't condone it, but I understand that it happens. And thankfully, the worst behaviour is usually a first, and last, offence. Make it clear in no uncertain terms that spitting at another player is unacceptable and it never happens again. I really don't know where a manager goes with a player like Suárez who insists on reoffending. Liverpool must have been at the end of their tether dealing with the fall-out. They must have felt they had already done so much.

His behaviour seemed to have improved, too. Given the choice between having a shot and biting someone he now seemed to prefer having the shot. Professionals are always seeking an edge, but sometimes they look for it in the wrong places and that is what Suárez tended to do. And then he regressed. What I cannot work out is what he thinks he gains from this behaviour. I don't agree with diving, but I can see why players do it. We all know games that have been won, goals that have been scored, because a player has dived in the penalty area and fooled the referee. It's wrong – but I do see the benefit. But biting? Can anyone tell me a goal that was scored by a brilliant piece of biting? Why would any player do that?

If Suárez at last channels that energy into a more positive enthusiasm he can be as big an asset at Barcelona as he was at Liverpool. His partnership with Lionel Messi is one we will all want to watch. Without a doubt, he is an impact player, and as good as drove Liverpool into the Champions League last season. Brendan has done a great job at Anfield but I'm sure he will admit that to walk in and have a player of Suárez's calibre at the peak of his game was the biggest bonus. My fear for the club now is that Suárez will be like Gareth Bale was for Tottenham Hotspur last season – and prove impossible to replace. Liverpool threw a huge amount of money at rebuilding, but what Suárez brought was unique and over a season we may increasingly realise that. I would certainly place him up there with the true Liverpool greats, like Rush, Kenny Dalglish and Kevin Keegan, for all his faults. He may not have their same qualities as a person, but as a player he sits beside any in the modern era, and he will leave a big hole in our game.

I know there are a lot of players in this last team who have been accused of diving throughout their careers – Ronaldo, Bale and Suárez in particular – but I'm not about to get on my high horse about it here. Frankly, there are a lot of managers who worry more about diving than they do about a player going over the top and trying to break someone's leg – my old friend Tony Pulis is on a permanent campaign about diving, but when one of his players gets away with it, this doesn't seem to be such an issue. Look, it happens – and frankly I feel sorry for the referee. It's the hardest decision in the world to call, in my experience. I've refereed games in training where I've given a penalty and all the players have started laughing. 'What's wrong?' 'He didn't touch him, boss.' 'Are you sure? He looked like he did to me.' I've seen incidents on television 20 times over and even then still can't make my mind up. Sometimes momentum carries a player over and he gets the blame. And even some of the most blatant dives look like fouls in real time. There was a horrendous dive by James McClean of Wigan Athletic against us in the play-off finals last year – a real rotten one because he was trying to get our goalkeeper, Rob Green, sent off as well as win a penalty. In slow motion it looked really poor. In real time? I thought it was a penalty and Rob was a goner. I don't know how the referees do it sometimes.

And I'll be on the touchline again this season, trying to work out how to stop some of the other names I've mentioned in this book. The last time Suárez came to Loftus Road he destroyed us – we were beaten by four and it could have been double that. So I'd be lying if I said I was looking forward to seeing him again.

You want to know the truth? When it was announced that he was banned, the first thing I checked was whether any Rangers matches against Liverpool were included and when I found out one was, I had a big smile. Now he's gone, I'll miss his input to English football, but not the task of trying to stop him. When any manager says he is looking forward to the challenge of pitting his wits against the greatest players, he's kidding you. Do you think any of us wants to have to deal with George Best or Tom Finney or Matt Le Tissier or Luis Suárez? Sir Alex Ferguson had the best defenders in the league, but by his own admission he was never happy when he saw Le Tissier's name on the team-sheet. He would much rather have played Southampton without him. I wasn't wishing for serious harm to befall Suárez but that ban suited me just fine. And if Brendan Rodgers wants to rest Steven Gerrard for a big Champions League game the next time we play, he can be my guest. I've loved every second of watching these guys; trying to beat them is another matter. You need to be lucky – and good. I'll keep trying, and hoping we can be a bit of both.

PREMIER LEAGUE II: THE TEAM

PETR CECH
Chelsea

PABLO ZABALETA
Manchester City

JOHN TERRY
Chelsea

RIO FERDINAND
Manchester United

ASHLEY COLE
Chelsea

CRISTIANO RONALDO
Manchester United

STEVEN GERRARD
Liverpool

PAUL SCHOLES
Manchester United

GARETH BALE
Tottenham Hotspur

THIERRY HENRY
Arsenal

LUIS SUÁREZ
Liverpool

PICTURE CREDITS